Network
SECURITY

Network SECURITY

Steven L. Shaffer
SSDS Inc.
Inglewood, Colorado

Alan R. Simon
Jackson, New Jersey

AP PROFESSIONAL
A Division of Harcourt Brace & Company

Boston   San Diego   New York
London   Sydney   Tokyo   Toronto

AP PROFESSIONAL
955 Massachusetts Avenue, Cambridge, MA 02139

An Imprint of ACADEMIC PRESS, INC.
A Division of HARCOURT BRACE & COMPANY

United Kingdom Edition published by
ACADEMIC PRESS LIMITED
24–28 Oval Road, London NW1 7DX

ISBN 0-12-638010-4

Printed in the United States of America
93 94 95 96 97 98 EB 9 8 7 6 5 4 3 2 1

336615

This book is the direct result of the generous time given to me and substantial sacrifice by my lovely wife, Joan, my daughter, Jordan, and my son, Dylan.
—Steven L. Shaffer

For Ann, my parents, and my brother.
—Alan R. Simon

Preface

This book is an attempt to bring network security out of the closet. As with many technical disciplines, network security has been the domain of the "network security expert." As a result, a separate language filled with acronymns and unique jargon has developed. There have been a number of very good technical reference books written that effectively address fundamental security mechanisms such as encryption, trusted computing bases (TCBs), auditing, access control, and the like. There have also been a number of security books written about security utilities and secure operating systems.

The specific purpose of this book is to provide those individuals who are responsible for network security in their organization with a practical approach to network security. This book will appeal to system and system security administrators, both in the government and commercial sectors. Many corporate MIS departments have recently seen an upsurge in network security awareness and visibility. In some cases, larger corporations have created an MIS security position and allocated substantial budgets to support overall system and network security programs.

Many corporations are in the process of transitioning their closed and proprietary information processing infrastructure to open, standards-based, integrated enterprises. For the transitioning organization, the ability to maintain and extend security is of paramount importance. Federal, state, and local governments are increasing the importance of network security. This book will also appeal to the average network security practitioner who is interested in understanding practical security approaches and implementation techniques for networks. In addition, several colleges are offering graduate courses in network security as part of an MS degree in MIS or computer science, and the material in this book will be of value to students and faculty members.

Acknowledgments

Pete Wiedemann (Chief Engineer at SSDS, Inc.) provided invaluable insight in the areas of trusted distributed processing and covert channels.

Contents

1

Principles of Distributed Computing and Networks

1.1 INTRODUCTION

In *The Papers of James Madison* in the U.S. Library of Congress, there is a letter written from Thomas Jefferson to James Madison on August 2, 1787. In the letter, Jefferson includes a curious mix of words and numbers that at first glance appears to be meaningless. The third and fourth presidents of the United States were, in fact, exchanging writing using coded communications due to the sensitive nature of its content. In the case of this particular letter, the discussion was of the "king and queen" (presumably of England), the "king's passion for drink" (which was encoded as "the 1647' 678.914. for 411.454"), and similar statements. In the body of the message, Jefferson tells Madison, "I cannot write these things in a public dispatch because they would get into a newspaper and come back here." (My, how things haven't changed much in over 200 years!) In that last sentence expressing his concern, even the word "newspaper" was encoded as "1039.7.207."[1]

It's important to understand that the subject matter of this book—network security—actually can be more broadly defined as "security of communications" and in fact dates back thousands of years. The above example is simply one of thousands, perhaps millions, of encoded communications that have been passed through the ages.

Encoding, or encryption, is simply one of the most highly visible aspects of communications security that has been formalized into security for computer networks, but, as we will see, the discipline encompasses much more.

The need for network security, and measures in that area, roughly parallels the evolution of computing from centralized, mainframe-based to distributed. Initially, most network security strategies were based around physical security measures such as the isolation of terminals and other access devices, guarded access to computer rooms, and similar steps. A large portion of those strategies revolved around personnel requirements, such as issuing security clearances, providing adequate security-oriented training, and so on.

As interception of messages became a major problem (as it had always been even for noncomputer-based communications), encryption began to play an important role. In addition to front-end communications processors, many computers passed their communications streams through encryption and decryption devices. Accompanying hardware-oriented solutions were software security mechanisms, typically hosted on mainframe computers. All access to computer systems and any application and maintenance of security mechanisms were totally under the back room control of the data processing department, which had the effect of centralizing the security function.

As distributed processing—based around workstations and PCs on the desktops and departmental midrange systems—became widely adapted, each system needed its own hardware and software security measures, and two problems surfaced:

- each different system type had its own security requirements and solutions, and all were not compatible, and

- most of the security measures remained under the control of the centralized MIS data center, which resulted in problems similar to those experienced in the early days of the distribution of computing resources in general: slow communications, overplanning for simple functions like deploying a PC, and so on. In fact, most early deployments of desktop resources were blissfully absent of any security procedures, especially dealing with remote system access.

As mission-critical applications (not just the departmental mailing lists) became rehosted onto decentralized, distributed resources, the centralized communications security mechanisms, which had been for terminal-to-host or interhost access, needed to be redeployed to take into account the use of workstations and PCs as terminal emulators.

Network technology that virtually front-ends devices to provide access to a shared bus or a network became popular. Examples included terminal servers both for terminals and for workstations and PCs. Gateways were provided for hosts to access the network. The vast majority of these networks were composed of broadband CATV technology. These cable plants were bulky and very expensive to maintain. Ethernet networking technology took root very quickly and immediately dominated the market. Devices like workstations and PCs could now be connected directly to an Ethernet network through a network interface card (NIC), which enables 10Mbps broadcast data transfer (digital). The internetwork connection devices—bridges, routers, and gateways—became widely used to provide security mechanisms, as we'll see. *The bottom line is: as systems became distributed, so did the security protections of the system.*

In this first chapter, we'll discuss the background and reasons for which network security (and, therefore, this book) exists: distributed computing resources, as widely deployed in most of today's organizations.

1.2 THE NETWORK COMPUTING REVOLUTION

To understand fully the scope and importance of network security, let's first discuss briefly the snowballing trend towards network-based information systems. Networking and distributed processing technology are expanding exponentially, creating systems of systems that are complex, heterogeneous, and highly dynamic. One hundred Mbps local area network (LAN) technology is readily available and gigabit (one billion bits per second) speeds continue to be demonstrated and are becoming less and less expensive. We are seeing advanced research into terabit (one trillion bits per second) networking. The computer industry and related technology areas are experiencing approximately a 100 percent increase in performance every 12 to 18 months and there are few impediments in sight to hinder future progress. Witness the discussions within the past year about high-speed "information highways."

There are, however, certain critical areas that may not stop the advancement of technology, but, if not adequately addressed, could very possibly cause the usefulness and utility of our high-performance networks of tomorrow to erode rapidly. Network security is one of these critical areas. The risk is that network technology stagnation will ultimately occur without a focused agenda that addresses network security as an enabling and facilitating technology. This risk applies to federal, state, and local governments, as well as the commercial sector and encompasses virtually all facets of our daily lives.

As we progress through the nineties, the networking revolution is sure to continue, and it is time to consider a more balanced and practical approach to network security. Approaches used to protect centralized monolithic systems of the past must be enhanced and improved to support secure networking technology. In fact, a fresh and different view of security must be ascribed to if security is to be effective and useful in networks. This book describes important security technologies and approaches that are necessary to achieve effective network security in the face of budget reductions, rightsizing of corporations and information systems, increased efficiency, aggressive migration strategies to open systems and standards, and rapidly advancing distributed information technologies.

1.3 FOCUS AND OBJECTIVE

The focus of this book is to provide practical and useful information on the very complex and diverse subject of network security. The need for network security is explored as well as a detailed description of the challenges that will surely be encountered when implementing and managing a network security program. A comprehensive approach is defined for network security, beginning with senior management awareness and commitment and extending through the implementation of security countermeasures into the subsequent management of the overall network security program. Advanced network security technologies are explored and discussed.

The need for network security has never been more apparent. Classified government information, international corporate trade secrets, personal and private information, and financial data are all freely communicated across the United States and internationally. This information is subject to exploitation. A global economy has increased the need to protect sensitive business, research and development, and overall business strategy and marketing information. Network technology has greatly facilitated the dissemination of information, and the value of this information continues to climb.

Attempting to secure a network is a very tough problem and one that requires a tremendous amount of technical understanding, political savvy, and patience. The most common stumbling block when attempting to secure a network is the perceived paradox that exists between networks and the role of security in networks. While LANs and LAN internetworks are designed to provide global access and extensive resource sharing, the security discipline is commonly viewed not as a facilitating service, but rather as something that attempts to restrict and mediate users' actions and the information and services they access. A primary network design and implementation goal is to foster cooperation among computing elements and ease of access to information processing resources. Security normally implies limited cooperation, confinement of users, processes, and data, reductions in communications, and limitations placed on access to network resources. The technical frustration that results from attempts to satisfy both the need for security and the benefits of networking are caused, to a large extent, by this perceived fundamental paradox between networking and security. This perception must be overcome before substantial strides can be made in effectively securing networks.

Even given today's tremendous challenges, success stories for effective network security programs exist. The practical utilization of inherent security attributes is a very cost effective and easy way to approach a large portion of network security vulnerabilities. Common sense and practical ways of working within the organization, defining common security goals and objectives, defining a network security policy, and providing continuity and continuance of security management all provide many of the fundamental keys to success. Implementing network security in open systems, once thought to be mutually exclusive concepts, is proving to be a myth fostered by the common human reaction to change (i.e., ignore it or shoot it down). A total shift in the way network security is approached is occurring. The shift represents the recognition that security must be a supporting service that facilitates and promotes authorized communications, rather than a hindrance and a self-serving end in itself. Advances in technology are focused on providing effective accountability and real-time monitoring of events versus the standard use of access controls, locks, and barriers.

1.4   SECURE DISTRIBUTED PROCESSING

The following discussion is provided as an introduction to security in distributed processing and networks. It provides a structure and an assessment of ways to determine the attributes of distributed processing, all of which have a direct impact on one's ability to secure effectively a network computing environment.

Any meaningful discussion of security as applied to distributed systems is necessarily premised upon the existence of a common notion or understanding between the author and reader regarding the concept of distributed processing. This section will illustrate popularly held notions on that subject, pointing out the need for a common framework for discussion. Such a framework is then suggested and used throughout the remainder of the book to explore security issues related to distributed processing and networks.

Many Existing Views of Distributed Processing

Like many other terms commonly used in the computer industry, such as "integrated," "user friendly," "enterprise computing," and "network," the term "distributed" has many different meanings (Figure 1.1). It is the intention of this book to discuss the practical security aspects of as many of the commonly held interpretations of the terms "distributed" and "networked" as practical. The following interpretations of the terms are by no means intended to constitute a complete list. They are intended to cover most of the popularly used interpretations. The purpose of their citation is not to

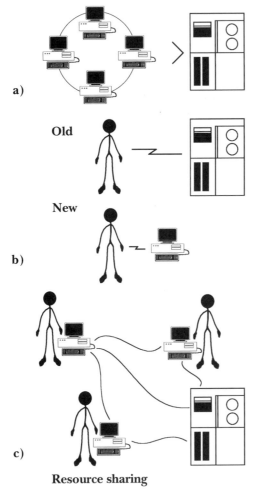

Figure 1.1 Views of distributed processing

provide a definition but rather to show the difficulty of arriving at a single definition that is widely accepted. They are presented in no particular order of preference or importance.

- Putting computer resources where the people are.

- An organizational structure for data processing with centralized capability, processing at least part of an application in a decentralized way.

- The philosophy of physically dividing up an organization's computing resources so that they are geographically and organizationally as close to the application as possible.

- Three criteria by which to define distributed processing: First, the system should possess two or more geographically separated processors; second, the processors should be linked; third, the processors should serve a single organizational entity.

- Replacement of a large centralized DP facility with separate small computers that are not necessarily connected by telecommunications. Their selection and use are entirely the responsibility of local management.

- A distributed processing system is one in which applications programs and/or data reside in separate interlinked processing nodes and are designed in an integrated and tightly controlled fashion.

It appears from these and other definitions that there is considerable divergence in the definitions. It is difficult to determine the characteristics that must be present to call a system distributed, and thus the ability to characterize a system as a network or as a specific type of network with distributed processing attributes implies additional challenges for the security practitioner.

Notions of a Distributed System

There are three widely held notions that drive the evolution of distributed processing. The earliest notion of distributed processing is that several (often smaller) processors together can perform better than a single larger processor. Although it is the earliest notion, much interest and work occupies this area today, especially in so-called fifth generation supercomputers, currently more of interest in Japan than in the United States (but the level of interest in the United States is growing, particularly in the area of MPP— massively parallel processing). Such multiple processors each have a shorter software path length and can operate simultaneously, thereby processing the whole job faster than one more powerful processor could. A group of smaller processors are also frequently less expensive than a single larger processor of equivalent processing capacity. Coupling among such multiple processors can range from close to loose. They may perform the same task as a group (parallel processing), or each processor may separately process a different task or a discrete portion of a larger task (multiprocessing). Typically, such multiple processors are being migrated from the same complex to the same room, cabinet, board, and, recently, the same integrated circuit.

The second currently held notion is that distributed processing moves processing power and data closer to the user or problem. Physical proximity of processing resources to the user or problem means local control, fast response, less reliance on remote resources and communications, and better isolation from communications malfunctions.

The third notion, most prevalent today, is the use of local and long distance communications facilities to allow the user access to data and, to a lesser degree, processing facilities and other resources that were inaccessible before. This is commonly called resource sharing. The user normally has a microcomputer or is connected to a minicomputer or mainframe. The application on the local machine is usually a terminal emulation program rather than a partition of a distributed application, such as a database management system. The user's local computer, by emulating an input/output device, can access applications on many other remote computers. Database applications that can be accessed include real estate, medical, legal, financial, and scientific data. Users can join several office automation environments, including calendaring, scheduling, and mail functions in remote systems. They access discussion forums and bulletin boards and can be contributing members of electronically bonded communities. Users also interchange data files through direct or indirect file transfers. Such users are frequently referred to as networked users. Another popular application of this notion is the use of virtual services such as virtual disks (file servers) and virtual printers (print servers).

These three notions are not mutually incompatible and are often used together in the same system. They often cause confusion for those attempting to approach distributed processing in an organized fashion, such as in addressing the impact of physical distance upon the design. In the first notion, distances to other processors may become very large, from meters to millions of meters, requiring the support of a complex, indirect, and robust communications infrastructure at relatively low data rates (typically 1,200 to 64,000 bps). Each of these processors frequently runs under its own independent operating system (called loosely coupled). In the second view, interprocessor distances are typically very short, from millimeters to meters, and interprocessor communication is very fast (typically 1Mbps to 1Gbps), direct, and reliable. Clusters of such processors typically run under a single operating system (called tightly coupled). Under these circumstances, making broad generalizations on the impact of physical distance upon the design becomes difficult.

The following is a list of characteristics, some of which are present in most networks and distributed processing systems. Not all, nor even most, are required to allow the system to be called distributed, but a system lacking all of these characteristics is unlikely to be described by any expert as distributed. To the extent that more of these characteristics are present in a system, that system is more distributed, and, conversely, the fewer of these characteristics that are present, the less distributed the system is.

- The design of the system shows an overt attempt to move processing or data resources or both closer to the user.

- Processors are linked to each other by communications channels. Such channels include, but are not limited to, a bus, an I/O channel, a local network, and a nationwide or international network. The channel need not be electronic. Output of one processor being transferred through nonelectronic means (physical movement of disk, tape, paper) and input into the next processor still constitutes a channel. Nonelectronic channels are sometimes called "air gaps."

- Processors are geographically separate. Such separation can range from less than millimeters to many kilometers.

- Processors process applications essentially independently. This does not preclude that the applications are cooperative, or that a single application be executed on several processors. Direct or indirect cooperation of applications on essentially independent processors is one of the more important hallmarks of distributed processing and may be one of its essential characteristics.

- Data are geographically distributed. Such separation can range from less than millimeters to many kilometers. In minimally distributed systems, users may need to be aware of the locations of data using offline or online (system provided) references and requesting the system to make explicit connections from a processor to the required data. In well-distributed systems, the application (usually a DBMS) is aware, or can easily become aware, of the current data residency configuration of the entire system, or at least of enough of the system to allow it to find all its currently needed data without user intervention. The most distributed systems use a single design for data throughout the system.

- From the user perspective, a system is more distributed if an aggregation of geographically separate processors and data appears as a single system. The user's actions are then the same whether the processing is done only on the local processor, only on a remote processor, or on a combination of processors, each of which may be located anywhere.

- An architecture is present (by intent or de facto) that defines conventions (protocols) and standards used by hardware and software to exchange information between or among the distributed nodes. The International Standards Organization (ISO) has provided a structure and framework for the hierarchical, layered classification of communications protocols, which ranges from conventions used at the physical and electrical layer (which is the lowest layer), through link, network, transport, session, and presentation layers, to the application layer (which is at the highest level). Above the application layer reside the applications themselves. Although other protocol models exist, most support the notion of hierarchical layering, lower layers providing service(s) to higher layers, and peer exchanges between nodes, at the same layer. A system is considered more distributed if it can exchange information meaningfully at higher layers in the ISO structure, and especially if it can exchange information meaningfully at all layers, including application to application. The system is less distributed if it can only communicate at lower layers. An example of the former would be a query program in one node being able to access and query meaningfully and update the data files produced by a DBMS in another node. An example of the latter would be a node that can properly receive Ethernet packets (layers 1 and 2), but cannot use this mechanism to receive files because it lacks a standard file transfer convention to interpret and control the content of the packets.

- A system is distributed to the extent that control over its processing is performed under a unified purpose. The ideal distributed system would physically distribute its processing and data while coordinating all processing as part of a single, larger activity under a unified system-wide hardware/software operating system. The ideal distributed system has a single "mind."

An ideal distributed system, then, can be summed up as one with a unified purpose, integrated design, and independent execution, especially when processing capability and data are located closer (in distance, responsiveness, or cost) to the users (information sources).

1.5   DISTRIBUTED SYSTEMS ELEMENTS STRUCTURE FOR THIS BOOK

To address the security issues related to distributed processing in an orderly manner, it is necessary to create a structure that delineates the elements of computing systems that are distributable. *Without structure, it would be difficult to relate specific security issues to specific aspects of distributed computing, because discussions and issues tend to be homogenized into an amorphous quagmire.*

The structure used in this book consists of a three-dimensional matrix whose three axes are *elements, distribution,* and *control objectives.* Elements are those things in a computing system that can be distributed. Distribution allows qualitative measurement of the degree of "distributedness" of an element and, ultimately, of a system. Together, elements and distribution allow a qualitative measurement of what facets of the system are being distributed and to what degree. Control objectives address the security impact of an element migrating from a non- or less-distributed implementation to a more or highly distributed implementation. The terms element, distribution, and control objective will be discussed in detail in the corresponding sections below.

The majority of distributed systems can be individually characterized by plotting the degree of distribution for each element. More than a single point may be required in any element for accurate characterization. For example, a distribution of users frequently encountered has a large number of users clustered at headquarters and a more scattered user population in the branch offices. Characterization would then require two points on the user element scale. Such multiple plotting may be needed for other elements as well.

Security considerations then become the third axis in the structure, behind the two-dimensional matrix consisting of elements and distribution. At any unique point in the three-dimensional matrix, issues and guidance for one particular environment should be located. For all but a few distributed systems, multiple points in the matrix will characterize its environment. This simply means that several guidelines need be followed for that system.

Elements of Distribution

Elements of distribution are those aspects of computing that are typically thought of as being distributable. These include, but are not limited to, users, processing, data, control, and connectivity (Figure 1.2).

- Users
- Processing
- Data
- Control
- Connectivity

Figure 1.2 Elements of distribution

Distributed Users

In this book, the term "user" is broadly interpreted. It is any entity that introduces data into the system, consumes data from the system, or causes system actions or activities desired by that entity. The user may be a human. The user may also be another system. Input may come from a keyboard, sensors of a weapon system, sensors on an assembly line, and the like. Output may be consumed by a screen, printer, fire control portion of a weapons system, an industrial robot cell, and others. Both input and output may be control data (requests of instructions). Control data may come from such sources as a keyboard, a process control computer, a pilot's voice recognition system, and similar sources.

In the second and third notions of distributed processing outlined above, systems became distributed in the first place because of a desire to decouple geographically users from centralized computing facilities. One could postulate an exception, where users are clustered in one place, needing to use data or processing resources at several remote locations. But the fact that these needed resources are remote instead of local indicates that they are probably used by other users at each of those or other locations, thereby again producing an environment of distributed users.

The degree of user clustering can vary widely with differing system topologies. The most prevalent topology in business and government is still the central office or campus containing the bulk of computing resources and the largest machines and a number of field or remote offices with smaller machines. User clustering is intense at the main office and small to moderate at the field offices. In service environments, a central computing complex serves widely distributed individual users or small clusters of users. Travel agency reservation systems, real estate listing systems, university systems, and public access databases are examples of this kind of user distribution. Increasing in popularity are topologies in which small systems exchange information among themselves—where each system either has a single user or a few users. Microcomputer and minicomputer networks in government and industry are examples. Most data sharing is done through file transfers with other systems in the same building or campus, although some file transfers also occur across intercity or interstate distances. Traffic volume is roughly inversely proportional to distance.

Distributed Communications

It seems intuitively obvious that the degree of communications distribution should be essentially equal to the degree of user distribution, since, for most systems, each user must have connectivity of some kind. But, for communications, the concept of distribution is less related to physical distance and more related to the degree of independence that the communications environment has from applications, topology, physical infrastructure, and centralized facilities. This may be one way of distinguishing the older, physically extended centralized communications from today's notion of distributed communications.

Physically extended, centralized communications are typically star-shaped topologies or tree structures, both of which converge on the central computing complex. The oldest topology used dedicated links connected directly between the central complex and each remote device. These remote devices often had local peripherals such as printers or card readers that shared the link with the primary remote devices, but data could not be sent directly from one remote peripheral to another without flowing through the central complex. All devices in a given system were built by the same vendor or were functionally identical clones. Some experts still consider this arrangement to constitute a distributed system, but find it more and more difficult to reconcile with today's notion of distributed computing.

The next step toward distributed communications was to use a more flexible and cost-effective infrastructure. Data concentrators and multiplexers were introduced to decrease the number of physically separate links and better use the aggregate bandwidth. Intelligent communications processors, so-called "front ends," provided more communications independence while relieving the host processors at the central site from the low- and mid-level communications chores. Control units were moved out to remote sites, allowing local low-level interaction and control such as device polling, further reducing required link bandwidth. The communications architecture (the set of communications protocols used) was highly proprietary to vendors, with examples such as Systems Network Architecture (SNA) from IBM and DECnet from Digital Equipment Corporation.

The next level of distribution unfettered the remote sites from dedicated links. Diverse switching and routing using part-time and dial-up links made connectivity more flexible because it allowed a choice of transmission facilities; more robust because it allowed for cost-effective alternate paths; and less costly because links could be dissolved when not needed. This process reaches its zenith when any communications device can use any transmission system, whether public or private. To connect computing devices to intelligent communications facilities provided by various vendors, standards for interfaces and expectable services were established. As vendors began to conform to the communications standards and became compatible with standardized communications services, they also became de facto compatible with each other. Vendor heterogeneous systems became increasingly possible and were implemented. Industrywide long distance standards such as X.25 and X.21 as well as short distance standards such as Ethernet and IEEE 802.3 began to appear. Attempts to standardize the structure of the service layers provided by these protocols resulted in the International Standards Organization Open Systems Interconnection (ISO OSI) model. Protocols initially intended for long distances were also applied to local networks. The preeminent examples are the TCP and IP protocols, which were originally intended for communications across the Department of Defense's ARPANET (now included in DDN) but are now also commonly found in many LANs. These further isolated the computing devices from knowledge of the communications infrastructure by providing virtual circuits, which acted like real links but could be implemented at their lower levels with virtually any workable distribution system. Real networks, instead of proprietary data distribution systems, now emerged.

Fully distributed communications systems are highly stratified and any layer of communications services can be provided by heterogeneous devices from different manufacturers using industrywide standards. These devices can be connected to a wide array of communications service providers' networks. Each layer can be processed by separate intelligent entities. The services that each lower layer provides to each higher layer are fully defined. Interfaces are similarly defined. The communications rules or protocols by which layers communicate with the same layer in another node (peer communications) are well established. At the top of the layered architecture, the applications layer has a defined interface to which all applications desiring communications services must adhere.

Distributed Processes

As expected, the distribution of processes is highly dependent upon which notion of distribution is applied. Where cooperation is a factor, lack of standards is noticeable. No ISO-like industrywide layered processing or peer processing standards have been established.

In notion one, the degree of distribution is dependent primarily upon number and cooperation. Interprocessor communications conventions (interprocessor protocols) are provided, usually at low levels, and are invariably of proprietary design. Maximized distribution is provided when the largest number of processors process tasks in the most cooperative and efficient manner.

In notion two, the degree of distribution depends upon proximity and cooperation. The actual or perceived closeness of processing in terms of power and responsiveness is the principal measure of distribution. The degree to which these processors can and do cooperate in slicing up tasks based on individual, specialized, or combined capabilities is the secondary measure of distribution.

In notion three, the degree of distribution is dependent primarily on proximity (usually virtual proximity) and number. Number addresses the "reach" that the user has in accessing processing resources. Proximity measures the availability and usefulness of the processing facilities in solving a local problem or answering a local need. Not much work has been done on cooperation under this notion between the local processing entity and the remote computing and data resources. Typically, terminal emulation, sometimes supported by relatively nonintelligent (cannot handle many host or communications contingencies) keyboard scripts, comprises all processing at the user site. An area of somewhat better developed cooperation is the background processes involved in virtual print and virtual disk services.

Distributed Data

Data distribution usually takes one of two forms, depending on whether notion two or three of distributed systems is in effect. In notion two, data accessed by the user is stored as close to the user as possible. In notion three, data is typically not stored near the user.

In notion two, data residency decisions must be made. Modern communications systems are frequently hierarchically arranged. Small LANs interconnect workstations and officewide or departmental resources. These are interconnected directly or via a common backbone medium to form campus or complex-wide LANs. Different LANs are interconnected via a packet data network or other carrier to form large interstate or international so-called "internets." Location of the data in this hierarchy depends on many factors, some of which are frequency of access, to what degree data at one location is shared by other locations, response time required for data, and data currency requirements. To meet data currency needs, data often need to be duplicated at several locations. This creates data consistency concerns. Updating and locking conventions become very complex. Security issues related to these concerns will be addressed below. Notion two data requirements are often met through the use of a single scheme and database that are distributed into the participating processing and storage nodes, with a high degree of cooperation among nodes. Proximity and cooperation therefore become the major metrics for degree of distribution for this notion of the data element.

In notion three, data is distributed by types rather than user proximity. This simplifies the problems since all data of one type or of one organization can be aggregated in one physical location. Data currency and consistency problems are essentially nonexistent and data locking is manageable. Security issues will entail primarily accountability issues, especially trusted paths. The most relevant distribution components to determine the degree of distribution are cooperation and number. Cooperation concentrates on availability of the data and the ability of the user terminal to produce the correct terminal emulation and data transfer protocols. Where virtual disks and virtual print services are used, degree of distribution is determined by the extent to which these virtual devices simulate the real devices in capacity, application independence, response time, and control.

Unlike the communications element, the data element has seen less standardization. There are no widely accepted industry standards for generation of queries (SQL is a start in the relational world, but much of the computing world's data still exist outside of relational databases), schemas, data residency, data consistency, locking mechanisms, and control conventions. Some work has been done on a model for layered, cooperative interaction among heterogeneous databases, but full-functioned frameworks that serve this area are still some years away.

Distributed Control

The computing resources of a centralized computer are usually orchestrated through the actions of a control program called the operating system. As the other elements of computing are distributed, the span of control of operating systems in the individual nodes usually is not expanded in proportion. Notion one is the exception in that a single operating system typically oversees all of the closely coupled processors, or each processor has a portion of the operating system and all portions collectively form a very localized distributed operating system. In view two, only centrally dominated, hierarchical systems have anything approaching a unified operating system. These invariably use proprietary rather than industry standards. View three is especially devoid of cooperating controls. Network resource and control management is very primitive, especially in multivendor environments. Recently, substantial advancement has been achieved in network management, such as simple network management protocol (SNMP) and X.500, and the ability to proactively monitor events and networking conditions, such as knowledge-based applications and relational database management systems (RDBMS) engines. Nevertheless, the notion of systems management and control, where all elements of a network computing environment can be managed and controlled, is far from reality.

Measurement of distribution of control is determined by number of nodes and especially by the degree of cooperation among control functions in various nodes. Again, there is a standardization vacuum. There are no generally accepted industry standardized protocols or conventions by which health and status monitoring information is interchanged, or by which control information is distributed throughout the entire network to include control information and mechanisms internal to the nodes. There is no ISO-like hierarchical model of layered control with cooperating peer entities and no standardized protocols to convey control information.

Ideal control of distributed systems is usually thought of as distributed status monitoring and reporting, distributed execution and enforcement of control actions, and centralized control from one, several, or potentially any node(s). The degree to which a system approaches this ideal is the degree of distributedness for the control element.

Distributed Security

This element, actually a subelement of distributed control, is cited here to underscore the notion that security can be distributed as much as any of the other elements above. Before security distribution can be undertaken, one needs to deal with the security issues that arise from the distribution of the other elements of computing.

1.6   DISTRIBUTION

Before addressing those elements of a system that are typically distributable, this section provides the dimensions of measurement that can be used as a qualitative or relative metric for each element of distribution. One can think of each distribution as a factor in establishing the "distributedness" of a system such that the aggregate value of all three distribution components represents the qualitative measure of the degree to which an element is distributed. For example, for the element of processing, say that there are many nodes far apart that cooperate so completely that together all the processes are seen by the user as a single, seamless process. The processing element is then considered highly distributed.

Proximity

Proximity is the approximate inverse of distance, where distance is the actual or user-perceived distance to processing or data resources. This is the most obvious distribution component of a distributed system. The distribution of proximity also can be applied to the control and communications elements. In determining the degree of distribution, proximity between the user and essential processing and data should be maximized. From the perspective of security, distance between any two elements and between instances of each element is of concern and is addressed in the section on security issues. Proximity applies mainly to the first view of distributed processing and is not very significant in the second view.

A distinction should be made between real and virtual proximity. Real proximity deals with physical closeness of computing resources to the user or problem. Virtual proximity can be achieved when the computing resources are physically remote but appear to the user or task as physically close, owing to the high effectiveness of the communications capability. As will be seen, real and virtual proximity can produce markedly different security concerns.

Number of Nodes

A node is simply defined as any location where one or more of the elements is or can be active. The number of such nodes can be used as another measure of the degree to which a system is distributed. Most observers would agree that a system with 100 processing nodes and 20 data nodes is more distributed than a system with 10 processing nodes and only one data node.

Cooperation within and among Elements

The principal measure of the degree to which a system is distributed is the degree of cooperation that exists among nodes, either between elements or within the same element between nodes. The basic concept of distribution breaks the wholeness of a system through physical separation and is exacerbated by decreases in proximity and number of nodes. Cooperation is the ingredient that reconstitutes the wholeness. The ultimate goal seems to be a combined maximizing of logical and physical separation while retaining the cooperation found in a monolithic system. For the element of communications, cooperation can be assessed using a layered communications architectural model such as the ISO model. For the other elements, lack of a hierarchical standard of interaction makes assessment of the degree of cooperation far more subjective.

1.7 SUMMARY

In this chapter, we've discussed some of the principles of distributed computing, primarily to get all of the readers on the same page of the playbook with respect to the background information for our subsequent discussions of network security—particularly with respect to definitions and terms. In the next chapter, we'll take a look at reasons why network security is important.

END NOTES

1. Congress of the United States, Office of Technology Assessments, *Defending Secrets, Sharing Data: New Locks and Keys for Electronic Information*, 1987, 14. The cited reference contains a photographic reproduction of the passage from Jefferson's letter to Madison, as well as the translation of the encoded portions.

2

The Need for
Network Security

2.1 INTRODUCTION

Computer and network security is one of the largest problems in the computer technology industry today. A security survey conducted by the American Bar Association found that 40 percent of the respondents had detected and validated incidents of computer crime within their organizations during the preceding year. For this single survey, it was estimated that the tangible monetary loss was between $145 million and $730 million.[1] These amounts only hint at the real cost of network security crime in the United States. The vast majority of organizations are not aware of computer/network crime in their organizations. Moreover, even if security incidents are discovered, most organizations are reluctant to publicize their existence. Experts have predicted that the real cost of computer/network crime is closer to $15 billion annually.[2]

The value and reliance on information, information assets, and information products are critical to our daily lives and the world we live in. The proof of the pudding relative to the need for network security can also be shown in actual security incidents. It is important to note that a very small percentage of actual security incidents are ever reported. There are a number of key reasons for this reluctance to advertise security breaches. In the government, the approach is to limit severely any disclosure of information regarding security holes or vulnerabilities in systems and also to restrict severely any information associated with actual security penetrations. The logic behind this approach is tied to the belief that to publicize such information would cause potentially substantial damage to other government systems because the bad guys would use the information to penetrate other similar systems. In the commercial marketplace, the rationale behind restricting the distribution of security-related information is a simple case of dollars and the bottom line. For example, banks and other financial institutions are very reluctant to publicize their security problems because they are concerned that customers will lose confidence in their ability to protect their assets and will move their funds and assets to another financial institution or bank. The focus on a closed-lip environment is also driven by legal concerns and potential losses. For example, if a company maintains information on individuals that is protected under the Privacy Act of 1987, it can be liable for any unauthorized disclosure of such information. In the event that such an institution's computer systems are penetrated and information protected under the Privacy Act is disclosed, it would be highly unlikely for the institution to acknowledge publicly the loss of such information. Even with the strong desire to restrict information on security incidents in both government and commercial industry, the fact that computers and networks abound in our daily life precludes a complete restriction of such information. Some recent examples of actual security incidents are described below.

- The Christmas card (December 1987): Newspapers across the country reported that a graphic image of a Christmas card had been developed and communicated across a major computer vendor's worldwide communications network. The popularity of the Christmas card was such that enough copies were produced and communicated as to cripple completely the vendor's ability to transmit effectively electronic mail messages. As a result, its critical information network was unusable for two days.

- The Friday the Thirteenth virus (January 1988): Newspapers reported that a computer virus was discovered in the computer systems at Hebrew University in Jerusalem. The virus had been programmed to be activated on May 13, 1988, with a time bomb set to delete all files on all systems infected. The virus also included instructions to explode every Friday the thirteenth after May 13, 1988. May 13, 1988, was selected because it happened to be the fortieth anniversary of the last day of the existence of the nation of Palestine, as ruled by Great Britain under the Balfour mandate. The virus was programmed to infect any vulnerable file whose file name's second qualifier was "COM" or "EXE," operating on DOS systems. The virus increased the size of each infected file by approximately 1,800 bytes. The first time any infected program operated on a DOS system, the virus infected the DOS "execute program" utility. From that point forward, the virus infected any vulnerable program on the computer system.

- The Internet worm (November 1988): A Cornell University computer science major infected the Internet with a malicious worm program.[3] The Internet worm first appeared at Cornell University just after 5:00 P.M., Wednesday, November 2. The worm program exploited flaws in utility programs in systems using Berkeley Software Distribution (BSD)–derived versions of UNIX. The flaws in utility programs enabled the worm program to penetrate those machines and actually copy itself, thereby infecting the machines with a copy of the worm program. The worm program propagated in three ways: through a trap door, through an inherent system software deficiency, and through remote execution under a user account whose password had been compromised. The program spread throughout the Internet very quickly. The code contained no logic or time bombs to eradicate data of file. Rather, the damage caused by the worm was tied directly to the amount of processing caused by its comprehensive and aggressive propagation, which ultimately overwhelmed the processing capacity of each system it successfully entered. Eventually, the worm program infected thousands of computer systems and impeded normal Internet connectivity, performance, and activities for several days.

- The BRAIN virus: The BRAIN virus got its name from the fact that it indicates a copyright of "BRAIN" in the label of every diskette that it infects. This virus was designed to infect DOS computer systems. The virus was also termed the "Pakistani virus" because the names of two Pakistani brothers were found in the virus code. The virus operates depending upon what already exists on the diskettes that it infects. In most cases, the virus does not cause any substantial damage and basically moves data to a new location. Very limited data/file destruction or denial of service occurrences was experienced with the virus. However, if the diskette's file allocation table contained specific characteristics, then the virus would destroy some data. When an infected diskette is used to boot start a DOS computer system, the virus gains access to the system and subsequently infects other diskettes with the boot records that are used without write protection on the same DOS computer system.

- The Michelangelo virus (March 1992): Mass media hysteria brought the Michelangelo virus into the everyday lives of millions of people worldwide. The media named the virus "Michelangelo" because it was scheduled to be activated on March 6, Michelangelo's 517th birthday. Originally encountered in Europe, the virus was found on 500-plus systems being shipped to computer dealers by one hardware vendor. Vendors inadvertently shipped copies of the virus with their software products. The media created hysteria about the incredible threat of the virus for nearly three months. Media reports described the virus as a worldwide threat and indicated that over 5 million PCs had already been infected. Thousands of PC owners and MIS directors made their first investments in virus protection software. Software Add-Ons, a Bensalem, Pennsylvania, company reported that sales of their antivirus software tripled during the week preceding the March 6 attack date. March 6 was being referred to by the media as the "Doomsday of the PC." The virus was designed to wipe out data on computer systems by automatically reformatting the hard disk and thus erasing all data on the disk. With all the hype and anticipation, users were very relieved when the Michelangelo virus never really happened. There were isolated cases, but nothing like what was being preached in the media across the world. The Canadian ministry did find the virus on 30–40 of its nearly 100 PC microcomputers. At the University of Toronto, only three cases of the virus were discovered among the university's 4,000 computer systems. In fact, it is estimated that less than 3 percent of personal computers were infected worldwide. Probably the most important benefit of the Michelangelo virus was the awareness and knowledge that was spread across the world about the dangers of computer viruses. The average person is much more educated now about what computer viruses are and what damage they can potentially effect.

2.2   INFORMATION SERVICES AND VALUE

Information transfer, coordination, and planning are being accomplished with electrons and photons, versus standard mail service, costly face-to-face meetings, and phone calls. The information that traverses these information systems can be sensitive, proprietary, competition sensitive, and/or classified. Many organizations have specified that all information on these networks be protected. This creates an entirely new perspective for the protection of the data, the standards and policies that must be enforced, and the actual security countermeasures that must be employed.

2.3   CLASSIFIED INFORMATION

The Department of Defense (DoD) and government intelligence agencies have always placed a tremendous emphasis on the protection of information and especially the protection of classified information. Federal government information considered to be sensitive but unclassified is also required by law to be protected from disclosure or malicious modification. In fact, sensitive but unclassified government information cannot be communicated over unprotected media, but rather must first be encrypted or otherwise protected prior to and during the transmission. There are obvious costs associated with these provisions and additional time is required to plan for, manage, and maintain system accreditation. Even the most obvious domains for security such as the DoD, national intelligence, and other federal agencies have seen dramatic challenges and changes lately. No longer are information systems built in isolation and secluded from other similar government organizations. Today, information systems are designed and built to support multiple government organizations. The dollars just aren't available anymore to build numerous systems that all provide similar or identical services. Moreover, the threats to the national security of the United States have taken a new and different form. Not only are we concerned about aggression and communism and other assorted political and military threats, but we must also pay very close attention to a worldwide economy and economic espionage against our national information processing assets.

2.4 PROPRIETARY AND SENSITIVE INFORMATION

Like the governmental sector of our society, the commercial sector is also experiencing massive change in information processing strategies. In the past, it was very common to have all information processing assets kept in the "back room." Only the data processing personnel were allowed to touch and utilize computer systems. The next phase of information processing evolution saw departmentalized processing. Now within organizations, there may be several back rooms that typically follow the commonly defined organizational boundaries of the corporation. Nevertheless, even with the information evolution toward departmentalized processing, there was still a clearly defined group of data processing personnel who were the only personnel allowed to touch and utilize the information processing assets of the corporation. In most cases, end users would write up their application requirements and throw them over the proverbial fence only to find that their requirements could not even be considered for 9–12 months. As a result, the processing department was always viewed as being understaffed, overworked, and not able to respond effectively to end-user requirements. One of the major benefits of keeping all computers and development behind closed doors is that it was relatively simple to provide effective security. Basically, security was provided by locking doors, keeping all processing capability in the hands of the DP staff, and by ensuring that all DP personnel were effectively screened prior to employment.

Today, the processing paradigm has totally changed. There are no longer "back rooms," rather there are open doors and incredible processing power in the hands of the end user. End users are no longer forced to wait for their applications to be developed by someone else. Today, end users can develop their own applications on the systems that sit on the desktop. Tools, rapid technology advancement, and education have provided the necessary impetus for these capabilities to be realized. Moreover, with the advances in networking standards, systems can easily interconnect to one another, enabling the exchange of information and the ability to share information.

2.5   TOTAL DEPENDENCE

Virtually every aspect of our lives is affected by computers, network computing, and communications. As a result, information and the protection of that information are of critical importance. Simple everyday examples such as Automatic Teller Machines (ATMs), the Cable News Network (CNN), airline reservation systems, the entire electronic banking industry, and command and control systems such as those employed in Desert Storm are good examples of our total dependence on information and the facilities and technology used to communicate this information.

A good example of the need for network security is the banking and finance industry. Large financial institutions may transfer electronically in excess of $1 trillion in financial assets annually. These institutions are responsible for the financial assets from the time they accept responsibility for them in their networks until they are deposited at their destination. If the network is down, they pay the interest on the money that is not transferred. For example, for every time their network is down, they can pay in excess of $30 million per day in interest. This is a key example of an industry that is totally dependent on a network computing environment, and any security problem resulting in denial of service, modification, or compromise can have staggering financial impacts.

2.6   ECONOMICS

It is anticipated that by the year 2000, information (and hence knowledge) will account for a larger portion of the U.S. gross national product than manufactured products and other physical commodities. As a result, organizations are being focused to adjust quickly to changes in the marketplace or lose market share or possibly be forced out of business. The fundamental ability to manage change through the implementation and effective management of an information infrastructure will become increasingly important in the face of a world economy.

With the advent of a world economy, it is commonplace for a number of companies across many countries to form a partnership or team to pursue jointly the development of a product or to penetrate a particular market segment. The only way in which such collaboration is possible is through the effective communication of information between the team partners. This information may span continents and numerous countries. Protection of such information is obvious. In addition, a partnership may exist for a particular product, but these same organizations may find themselves competing directly in another business sector. As a result, the ability to share information selectively on a case-by-case basis is the key. Partnering and collaboration agreements between multiple companies normally imply certain networking capabilities. Examples may include electronic mail, file transfer, access to shared network servers, imaging, electronic data interchange (EDI), video teleconferencing, and potential multimedia applications.

2.7 SUMMARY

In this chapter, we've taken a brief look, heavily laden with anecdotal tales, at reasons why security of computer and communications networks is important. A great deal of criminal activity involving computer resources is based on the networking and communications aspects of those resources; it stands to reason, then, that adequate protection of the entry points into computer systems is a major step—arguably *the* key step—in protecting organizations and governments from harmful activities by competitors (in the former case) and enemies (for the latter).

The needs for network security may be classified into two overall categories, as discussed in this chapter:

- Financial and economic
- National security

In many situations, a specific reason falls into one category or the other; some reasons, such as ensuring that a foreign government not be allowed access to sensitive internal treasury data or electronic financial assets transfer capabilities, span both categories.

In the next chapter, we'll shift our discussion slightly from the needs aspect, as discussed in this chapter, to challenges (you might view them as barriers to overcome) of network security.

END NOTES

1. "PC Data Is Vulnerable to Attack," *PC* 4, no. 15 (July 23, 1985): 33–36.

2. Ibid.

3. Eugene H. Spafford, "The Internet Worm Program: An Analysis," *Purdue Technical Report*, CSD-TR-823, November 29, 1988.

3

The Network Security Challenge

3.1 INTRODUCTION

Before we begin to discuss the more technical aspects of network security, beginning with historical and background information in the next chapter, let's take somewhat of a philosophical look at aspects of the discipline. In this chapter, we'll look at the fundamental paradox of network security —balancing the needs for openness and connectivity with the needs for privacy and controls—as well as other challenges in the areas of organizational and operational concerns, standards (or lack thereof), and legal enforcement.

3.2 THE FUNDAMENTAL PARADOX

The most prominent problem when attempting to secure a network is that we are dealing with two totally opposing forces—the need for connectivity and cooperability balanced against the need for adequate levels of control. This fundamental paradox between security and networking creates many challenges. The situation is very often thought to be complicated when the notion of securing a network that relies on open system standards is contemplated.

The common ingredient in today's notion of distributed systems is that of cooperation among computing entities, ease of access to resources, and interdependence. The implementation of distributed processing usually involves increased access and the removal of barriers and obstructions. The elemental notions in security include limited cooperation; confinement of users, processes, and data; reduction of communications; limitation of access to resources; reduction of interdependence; and the establishment of barriers and obstacles. Essentially, distributed systems intend to promote access to information while security intends to restrict access to information. The difficulties encountered in imposition of security upon distributed systems arise from this fundamental paradox between the elemental concepts of security and cooperation.

Tradeoffs

No network that requires the highest degrees of openness, flexibility, easy access, cooperation, and interdependence can be very secure. Likewise, no network that severely restricts openness, flexibility, cooperation, and interdependence can be very productive or efficient. In the respective extremes, a network that is totally secure produces little that is useful, while one that is totally productive is extremely vulnerable to being destroyed or disabled. Between the extremes lies a continuous spectrum of combinations. Since either extreme is not tenable, there must arise a compromise between security and efficiency. For each environment, then, some point on the spectrum is chosen, either intentionally or de facto. Technically, even the spectrum is in reality a composite of many smaller spectra, one for each system facet.

While the paradox between networking and security is very real, it is this perception that has prevented any real progress in network security from becoming a reality. In many instances, network security and network services and productivity are thought of as separate fighters in the ring in total opposition. This notion and perception must be challenged and changed if any real progress in secure networks can be effected. Further, just like what has happened in the past, security and the implementation of effective security countermeasures will be left in the dust when compared to the advance of networking technology, unless security and networking professionals approach the problem in a cooperative manner versus an adversarial one.

Principal Issues

The underlying conflict between cooperative distribution and security produces the issues that are detailed in the remainder of this book. The following highlights the major areas of concern. They range from the more intuitively obvious to more subtle effects, some of which will occur as an outgrowth of the implementation of current security concepts.

1. As encryption at various communications layers is used as a security mechanism, key generation, distribution, storage, updating, and (in general) management will become an increasing problem.

2. Covert channels (discussed in Chapter 9), mostly a nuisance problem in monolithic computing, have become a major source of concern in distributed systems. They may ultimately become a major impediment to secure distributed processing.

3. The lack of security standards prevents meaningful and secure cooperation between security mechanisms located in various nodes of the distributed system. The need is as great for vertical cooperation between protocol layers as it is for horizontal cooperation between peer entities.

4. While it is accepted generally that security must be addressed early in a system's design if it is to be tractable, research and practical experience have shown that the issue of eventual cooperative connectability of one system to other systems also quickly hardens into the design and must be considered early on. If not considered at an early stage, secure interconnection to another system may later be very expensive, produce low performance, or be outright impossible.

5. In distributed systems, the one-to-one mapping of user to process and the vicarious use of the user's privileges by a process rapidly become nebulous, as privilege passing traverses a long chain of processes. The user has less and less direct control of his or her privilege and is increasingly less aware of the processes that represent his or her interests. This problem has become one of the limiting factors of secure networking systems.

6. Similarly, the issue of propagation of risk has intensified. As management and organizational jurisdictions continue to be crisscrossed by distributed systems, absence of a cohesive global security policy and consistent security environment cloud the very meanings of trust and secure interoperability.

7. Privilege passing requires finer granularity of privileges so that very restricted proxy privileges may be passed to and used by surrogate processes. There is a movement within the security community to migrate from level-oriented access controls to capabilities-based access controls. As the granularity becomes finer, the need to grant,

relay, propagate, and revoke privileges in very small increments increases. This sets the stage for the next crisis, which will occur when the capabilities management task reaches unmanageable proportions.

8. Because of communications needed in a distributed network, knowledge of things that go on in the network is easy to obtain by any interested node. Accumulation of such knowledge produces a fertile environment for inferencing compromise. Because communication is deeply embedded in network computing, countermeasures to inferencing may rapidly run up against asymptotic limits of effectiveness.

9. The inferencing and aggregation problems of networks may be solvable only by raising the sensitivity level of the low-level components from which the inferences are made. This creates new components from which higher-level inferences may be made. Driven by the churning of routine processing and communications, this process may escalate until all data float to the highest sensitivity level of the system. While virtually all policy models and access control concepts provide few obstacles to raising the sensitivity level of data or processes, and most provide mechanisms that actively promote level escalation, none provide efficient means to lower the sensitivity levels. This sets up a one-way pumping action, which may eventually defeat the very reason for multilevel systems and mandatory access controls (MAC) (see Chapter 4) in the first place. As wider distribution and increased connectivity increase the reach of the system to data and as level pumping escalates the sensitivity level, most data will float to the system's highest level. The user is then in the dilemma of either granting everyone access to everything to fulfill efficiently his or her mission and accept the vastly broadened compromise exposure or dramatically limiting fulfillment of his or her mission because only a handful of persons have access to the high levels to which all data has floated.

3.3   RECLUSIVE AND TIGHTLY HELD SCIENCE

The secrecy that surrounds computer and network security has prevented a large technical following and understanding. The security profession is to a large extent reclusive, owing to the need to protect methods and means of classified information protection. Generally, penetrations are not reported publicly for fear that such information could be used by an adversary to penetrate other systems. As a result, lessons learned and network exposures are not widely known until it is too late.

3.4 INADEQUATE FUNDING AND MANAGEMENT COMMITMENT

The most disturbing issue facing the security of networks is the lack of quantifiable funding and senior management commitment. In the past few years, there have been numerous investigations and evaluation by the federal government to determine the current vulnerability of our information networks. In nearly every case the answer was the same: "We're in bad shape and highly vulnerable." As a result, directions were passed down requiring data valuation assessments, risk analyses, and security policy and procedure development.

On the surface this sounds really great, but there was very little money, if any, appropriated by Congress to meet these mandates. Moreover, there were very few government organizations that could staff these efforts effectively and apply the necessary time and effort, even if there was money to support the effort. The same lack of funding and management commitment can be seen in the commercial sector. Unless security is fundamental to the way in which a company operates and conducts business, the advent of networking technology will not cause the awareness and management commitment to be heightened.

A good example of this is the banking industry. Since the very beginning of banking, security has played a fundamental role to ensure that money was not stolen. Today, the same is true and the banking industry spends a tremendous amount of money to protect their networks and information systems from penetration. In most cases, the primary reason for the common lack of management commitment is due to a lack of technical knowledge and understanding. In addition, because it is often very difficult to prove that network security cannot bring immediate and quantifiable monetary bottom-line benefit, it may always be plagued by a lack of management commitment and awareness.

3.5 ORGANIZATIONAL OPPOSITION

People dislike change. One of the most common reactions to a newly formed network security group or function within an organization is: "Why? Everything is fine the way it is now." People do not like to have to change the way they work, the way they protect information, and most importantly, the information that they are able to access on a daily basis. Status quo is a major impediment to implementing an effective network security program for any organization. Moreover, even if a network security program exists, to change policies, procedures, or to implement new or enhanced security counter-measures can cause tremendous employee concern.

A false sense of security is also a common organizational impediment to network security progress. If the user community has not been exposed directly to a security crime or major compromise, they will assume that everything is just fine and no one need worry about network security. The problem with this is that most security crimes go undetected. The lack of security awareness, coupled with a false sense of security, is the perfect business climate for the would-be perpetrator.

3.6   OPERATIONAL OPPOSITION AND COSTS

Network security is not free. There are few network security programs that do not require investment in hardware and software security countermea-sures, policy and procedure definition, staffing, and continued manage-ment. All of these activities and products cost money. Again, the difficulty in demonstrating bottom-line immediate benefits from the application of net-work security causes the sell to be very difficult at times. Security mechanisms and countermeasures very often impact overall network performance and productivity.

Security is an overhead function (but obviously an important one). Whether network security is implemented and enforced through the use of encryption algorithms or packet header labeling, the fact is that these pro-cesses add additional functions and overhead to the processing environment.

3.7   TECHNICAL COMPLEXITY AND RAPID CHANGE

In order to secure a network effectively, one must thoroughly understand not only the technical, but also the managerial and political climate in which the network must operate. Security extends into all facets of the network and the organization. Complexity results from the need to understand the inter-workings of many heterogeneous systems and communication components and the security mechanisms that they employ. Finally, effective network security requires an understanding of numerous security standards, manu-als, and guidance documentation.

Most of the large networks today are complex and very heterogeneous. A useful network security implementation will rely on numerous control mechanisms implemented across a spectrum of host platforms, workstations, terminals, and networking devices. Likewise, network security mechanisms are commonly provided through networking protocols, operating systems, network operating systems, routers, bridges, network management software, and applications (i.e., X.400, X.500, EDI, privacy enhanced mail [PEM], word processors, etc.). As a result, the ability to acquire the expertise necessary to understand intimately all networked systems and their security mechanisms is a very tough problem. In addition to the existing environment, networking technology is changing so fast that very few things stay the same for more than 18–24 months. In a networked environment, technology is commonly introduced, tested, and developed. In most instances, the security provided by this advanced technology is the last attribute considered prior to purchasing the device and connecting it to the network.

3.8 A MOVING TARGET

Another common security challenge with the proliferation of networks today is that networks are crossing organizational boundaries that heretofore had never been contemplated. Today's organizations are finding that in order to stay competitive, their various organizational elements and divisions must be able to communicate effectively and expeditiously with one another. These communications are provided and facilitated through the use of networking technology. The problem and challenge arise when one organization desires to maintain its system/network security policy and, at the same time, interconnect its network with its sister division's network.

The first fundamental element of any security policy is to define the system. As a result, a security policy must define a security perimeter and system/network boundary. This can be a major challenge given the interconnection of organizational divisions and the continuance of change common to network computing. Chances are very good that each organizational element or division has a different view of system/network security, resulting in great pain when these disparate organizational security views are interconnected. Another challenge is that in most cases, these organizational elements or divisions possessed their own security department. With the advent of these organizational interconnections, it is often difficult to determine who is in charge and who determines the level of security policy enforcement across the interconnected systems. In most cases, the problems and security issues are worked out after the fact, creating a very vulnerable environment for a period of time.

Network security is often affected directly by individual personalities and individual perceptions concerning the value of security and the threats to the network. As a result, everyone has a different view of what is actually required for effective and useful network security. What information should be protected? How should it be protected? What are the highest network security priorities? These are very common questions that may have numerous different answers based on one's position in an organization, responsibilities, experiences, and perceptions.

The Trusted Network Interpretations (TNI) was developed by the National Computer Security Center (NCSC) of the National Security Agency (NSA). The TNI, a government view of trusted networking environments used to protect sensitive or classified information, deals with this issue by defining two separate environments with guidance provided for each. According to the TNI, the issue is whether or not the system is considered a system of interconnected accredited or certified information systems or whether it is considered a single trusted information system. This has a direct impact on the system boundaries for the Network Trusted Computing Base (NTCB). This problem will continue to plague the federal government as more focus is placed on joint operations and cost-cutting measures, which involve the participation of multiple services, research agencies, and intelligence groups who all need to share information and interoperate using a common security policy. Because of tremendous cost reductions occurring in the DoD and with more surely to come, the challenges associated with interconnecting multiple dissimilar and disparate system and networks as one commonly accessible network is further compounded by the existence of numerous security policies and the application of those policies through products and procedures.

Certification (commercial sector) and *accreditation* (federal government) are the terms commonly used when a network has been analyzed and found to be secure based on a defined security policy and permitted to process information. During the days of centralized computer operations, certification and accreditation was a fairly straightforward process. Today, with the dynamic incremental growth of distributed system architectures, it is difficult to have a high degree of assurance that the system that is certified or accredited today will be the same system, with the same protections, tomorrow. Because certification and accreditation are normally very time consuming and demanding, the real question is how often should certification and accreditation take place, given a dynamic and ever-changing network computing environment.

3.9   THE LACK OF NETWORK SECURITY STANDARDS

Another of the major challenges to achieving a satisfactory level of network security in the past has been the lack of standards. In this section, the causes of this lack of standards in the security arena are covered.

It is best to understand this issue in the larger context of the evolution of computing topologies and architectures. Most readers are aware of the trend—one that gained a great deal of momentum in the late 1980s and the early 1990s—away from centralized, mainframe-based environments towards distributed, heterogeneous architectures for information solutions (Figure 3.1).

When centralized solutions were the norm (regardless of the vendor), security solutions were predominantly of a proprietary nature. Terminal access, data encoding, file and directory access control—all of these areas had security answers that for the most part considered only the hardware and systems software of a given vendor. If third-party companies such as application vendors wanted to function in a given vendor's environment, they were expected to adhere to whatever security specifications were dominant.

The major interoperability trends of the late 1980s and the early 1990s—open systems, enterprise computing, and client/server computing—were complementary efforts to replace the often cost-inefficient centralized solutions with distributed environments consisting of desktop and midrange solutions (and, of course, networking facilities) as viable alternatives to mainframes.

Initially, interoperability was achieved primarily on a case-by-case basis by user organizations or vendors. For example, early attempts to connect PCs to IBM mainframes often consisted of proprietary connectivity solutions and home-grown software protocols for connection establishment and management, data transfer, and other functions.

As PCs and workstations became accepted as viable components of organizational information systems (not just toys for the laboratories or office outposts), the need for standardization in the areas of connectivity and interoperability became apparent. These efforts led directly to the open systems movement, in which hardware and software vendors suddenly found religion in the area of intervendor cooperation in lieu of their own proprietary solutions.

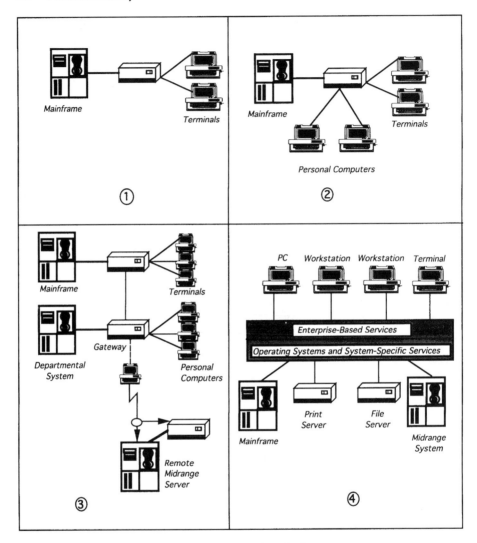

Figure 3.1 Information system architectural evolution

The snowballing trend towards open systems required vendor and user company participation in numerous standardization committees. Company and government representatives struggled to achieve the highest degree of connectivity and interoperability, making their own hardware and software easily accessible to others; in short, peeling back the privacy and security curtains that had been erected over the years. File formats and directory structures were made public; application programming interfaces (APIs) for network access were created and published; and so on.

The Network Security Challenge   39

To achieve as much interoperability as possible without undue complexity, a number of distinct service areas became the focus of standardization efforts. Each service area focused on a single information system functional area, such as:

- User interfaces
- Database management
- Repository management
- Graphics and presentation
- Networking
- System functions (such as queue management, memory management, etc.)

With respect to networking services, the dominant standardization effort has been the ISO OSI Reference Model. The OSI Reference Model was originally proposed in March 1978 (yes, when Jimmy Carter was president) and, 15 years later, is still considered to be an emerging standard. We'll discuss the OSI Reference Model in Chapter 6 as a framework for network security approaches and mechanisms, but for now we'll just say that the architecture of the model—seven layers, ranging from physical to application—causes great complexity in peer layer-to-peer layer (example: between two different transport layers) and interlayer communications.

Okay, enough background information about standards, both in general and with respect to networks and communications. What does this have to do with the lack of network security standards? Quite simply, the complexity involved in creating and implementing standards has often put security on the back burner. For example, the most widely used set of standards for interconnecting heterogeneous environments—the Internet protocols, such as TCP, IP, SMTP, and so on—have traditionally lacked sufficient levels of security. The very nature of focusing on *achieving* connectivity among many different types of systems using a single set of protocols typically meant that preventative measures such as those discussed in this book were left for some other time, another version of some standards document.

This doesn't mean, of course, that standards have been totally absent from the area of networks and communications. The Data Encryption Standard (DES) was first proposed by the U.S. National Bureau of Standards (NBS) in 1977. A series of standards from NBS and other organizations such as the General Services Administration (GSA), the American National Standards Institute (ANSI), ISO, and the American Bankers Association (ABA) appeared in the 1979–1986 time frame (Figure 3.2).[1] Eventually, these stand-

Date	Developer	Standard or Guideline	Principal Target
1977	NBS (NIST)	Data Encryption Standard (DES) (FIPS PUB 46)	U.S. Government
1979	ABA	Management and Use of PINs	Banks
1979	ABA	Protection of PINs in Interchange	Banks
1980	NBS (NIST)	DES Modes of Operation (FIPS PUB 81)	U.S. Government
1980	NBS (NIST)	Key Notarization System (U.S. patent 4,386,233)	U.S. Government
1981	NBS (NIST)	Guidelines for Implementing DES (FIPS PUB 74)	U.S. Government
1981	ANSI X3.92	Data Encryption Algorithm (DEA)	U.S. Industry
1982	GSA	General Security Requirements for Equipment Using DES (FS-1027)	U.S. Government
1983	GSA	Interoperability and Security Requirements of the DES in the Physical Layer of Data Communications (FS-1026)	U.S. Government
1983	ANSI X3.105	Data Link Encryption Standard	U.S. Industry
1983	ANSI X3.106	DEA Modes of Operation	U.S. Industry
1985	NBS (NIST)	Computer Data Authentication (FIPS PUB 113)	U.S. Government
1985	NBS (NIST)	Password Usage Standard (FIPS-112)	U.S. Government
1986	ANSI X9.19	Financial Institution Message Authentication (Retail)	Retail Banks

Figure 3.2 Examples of civilian security standards

ards efforts began to make use of one another's work.[2] As is the case with nearly all standardization efforts, however, differences of opinion often lead to incompatible standards proposals by different organizations within the same functional scope. Of chief concern in the area of network security (and computer security in general) is distinction between military and commercial security requirements. Likewise, many of the standards to date cover only a certain set of security services or are applicable to only a single business area (such as banking).

Therefore, as we have seen, we have had a twofold problem. First, security capabilities were traditionally of a proprietary nature, matching the historically dominant centralized information systems solutions; security solutions were slow to follow the explosion of distributed computing. Second, early network and communications security standardization efforts that were developed in response to this problem often focused on only a small part of the overall security problem.

One of the most frustrating challenges in implementing network security today is the fundamental lack of security standards across the industry. There are a few examples of security standards, but for the most part, security standards do not exist. If a network is composed of IBM MVS mainframes utilizing RACF, pure SNA communications environment with users accessing these systems through cluster controllers with dumb terminals, the need for security standards may not be important. However, if one were to introduce into this same environment Digital VMS minicomputers, UNIX servers and workstations, IBM PCs and networking components including bridges and routers, the need for security standardization is important.

In the networking world, standards have been commonplace and have enabled the rapid interconnection of disparate systems through peer-to-peer processes and protocols. UNIX, POSIX, TCP/IP, and OSI are all examples of standards that have enabled the interconnection of heterogeneous systems. The Internet, the world's largest network, interconnects thousands of systems through the use of a standard set of protocols. This same network, however, has no consistent application of security standards and is commonly penetrated and abused. Instead of standards, the security world has focused on guidance to developers and users. Guidance is wonderful, but, again, interpretation can play havoc with guidance resulting in defined guidance being implemented using numerous different approaches. A prime example of this type of guidance is the Trusted Computer Systems Evaluation Criteria (TCSEC) developed by NCSC of the NSA. This document was developed to provide guidance to vendors developing trusted and secure systems. When this document was published in December 1985, it was revolutionary and provided the first real guidance to vendors developing secure products. The guidance was sound and many products have since been developed using the guidance provided in the TCSEC. However, the systems developed using the TCSEC are not necessarily interoperable because there were never any clearly defined finite security standards associated with the guidance provided.

Some very common examples that illustrate clearly the lack of network security standards include the following:

- Passwords (length, content, protection, rate of change, etc.)
- Information/packet labels (length, content, representation)

- Secure protocols (encryption, labels, OSI layers 2, 3, 4, 6, or 7)
- Auditing (content, events, alarms, actions taken)

The lack of network security standards is further complicated by the inherent need to integrate across a wide spectrum of networking processes to possess an effective and useful network security policy. The problem does not end at the horizontal level (i.e., operating system-to-operating system level or the peer-to-peer protocol integration level); rather, the problem extends to the need for vertical integration as well. For example, in a networked environment, one must be concerned with the preservation of security throughout the entire system. This requires that all processing elements of the network be capable of supporting the overall security policy of the system. Networking components, protocols, network operating systems, host operating systems, file systems, and applications must support the network security policy effectively and in a harmonious manner. This is a very difficult problem given the lack of both horizontal and vertical network security standards.

3.10 LEGAL INADEQUACIES

Still another major challenge to network security falls in the legal realm. There has been a lack of enforceable computer security law, as well as widespread disagreement over the legality or illegality of various actions. In the United Kingdom, for example, the Computer Misuse Act 1990 attempted to place some legal restrictions on what had been a relatively wide open environment for computer-related fraud; prior to passage, hackers who gained access to computer systems were free to read any information and data because theft of information is not a crime in the United Kingdom.[3] The act defines various levels and types of offenses, but still leaves the definition of unauthorized access open to a wide range of interpretations.

Even when laws have been enacted, the legal profession has collectively lacked the technical knowledge necessary to handle fully such cases. Even though computer law became one of the hottest areas in law schools and for attorneys, a great deal of the resources in this area were trained on areas such as patent and copyright protection, especially for the ever-popular subject of software copyrights and look-and-feel issues. Security issues, especially those dealing with network security, are often highly technical and not as easily grasped by most attorneys other than those who have a great deal of expertise in such matters.

Further, even when people have been caught, there has been a disturbing trend until recently of turning the culprits into handsomely compensated consultants, tasked with helping their victims prevent repeat attacks by others, instead of prosecuting the cases. Many companies, embarrassed and mortified by breaches into their networks and computer systems, have focused their salvage and repair efforts not on prosecution but rather on obtaining all of the gory details about how the breaches were accomplished, exchanging immunity for prevention.

Finally, there are those who believe that the tools used to breach network security and potentially wreak havoc, such as viruses and worms (discussed in detail in Chapter 8), are not inherently evil and in fact should be more widely shared (how's this for a slogan: "Viruses don't do computer damage, people do!"). Mark Ludwig, a physicist, authored a book entitled *The Little Black Book of Computer Viruses, Volume I,* in which he attempts to balance the rights of computer professionals and other technically astute people to create and experiment with viruses—under the auspices of governmental abuse of power (in preventing virus use)—against the needs for computer security.[4]

Our feeling on the philosophy of disseminating viral recipes is that many, if not most, programmers lack the general know-how and technical abilities to create viruses on their own. We could take an "all is right with the world" approach and assume that no reader who can learn what he or she lacks in virus creation skills would use the acquired knowledge for criminal purposes, but, hey, call us skeptics, we don't necessarily believe that. Therefore, dissemination of virus creation knowledge will make the challenge of achieving and maintaining network security even more difficult and, therefore, more important.

3.11 SUMMARY

There is one important lesson that you should take away from this chapter's material: Many of the challenges to network security, indeed most of the initial obstacles, have little or nothing to do with technology, but rather with issues such as the law, adoption of standards, balancing ease of access and cooperability with protection, and similar issues.

In the next chapter, we'll begin our in-depth discussion of the technical aspects of network security, focusing on the types of services that are required of such environments.

END NOTES

1. Congress of the United States, Office of Technology Assessment, *Defending Secrets, Sharing Data: New Locks and Keys for Electronic Information*, 1987, 126, table 10.

2. Ibid., 125.

3. David Martin, "Are Hackers Really Criminals? (The UK Computer Misuse Act)," *EXE* (April 1992): 46.

4. Rick Ford, "Balancing Fears, Rights in Wars against Viruses: A Little Black Book Reveals Secrets and Highlights Some Difficult Issues Facing the Computer Industry," *MacWeek* (July 13, 1992). In the same article, David Stang, chairman of the International Computer Security Association, is quoted speaking out against the book, claiming that it lacks antiviral utility definitions and that "defenders of such publications 'have yet to show us an example of a good virus.'"

4

Network Security Services

4.1 INTRODUCTION

Network security services are provided to achieve network security objectives and defined policy. It is important to note that security services cannot be selected and implemented until a comprehensive security policy is defined and documented. ISO published a document in 1989 entitled *Information Processing Systems—Open Systems Interconnection—Basic Reference Model, Part 2: Security Architecture* (ISO/IEC 7498-2) that identifies a specific set of network security services as shown below.[1]

- Continuity of operation services
- Integrity services
- Authentication services
- Access control services
- Confidentiality services
- Nonrepudiation services

(In the above list, continuity of operations has been included as a security service because of its critical importance to the overall success of an operational network.)

In this chapter we'll discuss the various aspects of network security from a service perspective, focusing on the services listed above and their various attributes. First, it is important to put those services in context with respect to the objectives of network security (and, for that matter, computer security in general).

4.2 SECURITY CONTROL OBJECTIVES

The following security control objectives have been extracted from the Trusted Computer System Evaluation Criteria (TCSEC).[2] These control objectives—policy, accountability, and assurance—provide a solid foundation from which network security services can be discussed.

Policy

"Security Policy Control Objective—A statement of intent with regard to control over access to and dissemination of information, to be known as the security policy, must be precisely defined and implemented for each system that is used to process sensitive information. The security policy must accurately reflect the laws, regulations, and general policies from which it is derived."[3]

Subelements associated with the Security Policy Control Objective include:[4]

"Mandatory Security Control Objective—Security policies defined for systems that are used to process classified or other specifically categorized sensitive information must include provisions for the enforcement of mandatory access control rules. That is, they must include a set of rules for controlling access based directly on a comparison of the individual's clearance or authorization for the information and the classification or sensitivity designation of the information being sought, and indirectly on considerations of physical and other environmental factors of control. The mandatory access control rules must accurately reflect the laws, regulations, and general policies from which they were derived.

"Discretionary Security Control Objective—Security policies defined for systems that are used to process classified or other sensitive information must include provisions for the enforcement of discretionary access control rules. That is, they must include a consistent set of rules for controlling and limited access based on identified individuals who have been determined to have a need-to-know for the information.

"Marking Control Objective—Systems that are designed to enforce a mandatory security policy must store and preserve the integrity of classification or other sensitivity labels for all information. Labels exported from the system must be accurate representations of the corresponding internal sensitivity labels being exported."

Accountability

"Accountability Control Objective—Systems that are used to process or handle classified or other sensitive information must assure individual accountability whenever either a mandatory or discretionary security policy is invoked. Furthermore, to assure accountability the capability must exist for an authorized and competent agent to access and evaluate accountability information by a secure means, within a reasonable amount of time, and without undue difficulty."[5]

Assurance

"Assurance Control Objective—Systems that are used to process or handle classified or other sensitive information must be designed to guarantee correct and accurate interpretation of the security policy and must not distort the intent of that policy. Assurance must be provided that correct implementation and operation of the policy exists throughout the system's life cycle."[6]

These three major security control objectives compose the framework under which systems are evaluated. There are variations within the subelements of each of these control objectives based on the evaluation class (i.e., a stand-alone system or a network). In the evaluation of networks, for example, integrity, nonrepudiation, and continuity of service play larger roles in the provisioning of security services.

4.3   CONTINUITY OF OPERATIONS SERVICES

Continuity of operations services is designed to ensure that a network is available to provide the level of service required to accomplish the defined goal/purpose of the network. Very commonly, denial of service is viewed as the most serious threat to networks. One's inability to use the services of a network to accomplish a business function or mission will often outweigh information compromise or unauthorized modification. Continuity of operations is also affected by network design flaws, system/component failures, and peak processing periods caused by unforeseen events.

To detect a denial of service attack, peer connections commonly exchange a set of message blocks to verify that an open and clear path still exists between the two communicating entities. Increasing the frequency of these message block interchanges will reduce the amount of time required to identify a denial of service problem in the network. The obvious concern with this approach is the amount of traffic overhead that may occur as a result of message block interchange to validate clear and open communication paths over a network. Such an approach, if taken to an extreme, could actually cause the network condition that it is trying to reduce.

Network Security Mechanisms— Continuity of Operations

Network security mechanisms and approaches commonly used to support continuity of operations services include:

- Highly reliable and fault-tolerant components
- Redundant components and communications paths
- Alternate routing
- Proactive network management services
- Defined contingency management plans and procedures
- Offsite (redundant) storage and processing facilities

4.4 INTEGRITY SERVICES

As heterogeneous but harmonious processes are used to perform a function, they all must provide the same degree of integrity when the final product is delivered or created. The ability to assess all of the interworkings, communications, control decisions, and processes used to perform a given function will be difficult to ascertain as systems become more distributed and more cooperative.

The issue of *denial of service* will continue to be heated among security professionals. Denial of service, affecting the security of a system (i.e., security label integrity) or threats caused by malicious individuals or processes should be addressed by the security policy. This policy may be implemented by the proper use of reliable protocols, CRCs, or other reliability measures, and the provisioning of adequate physical security countermeasures. Denial of service cannot be isolated into its own corner. All security engineering disciplines must be examined for their applicability toward preventing or lessening denial of service attacks.

Network integrity services provide the protections necessary to protect information from being manipulated or modified in an unauthorized manner. Network integrity services are predominantly focused in two areas: 1) the protection of a single data element or 2) the protection of a data stream, connection, or session composed of more than one data element. To provide network integrity services to protect a single data element a content or integrity check value is normally intimately associated with the data unit and is originated by the sending process. The content or integrity check value can be provided through a number of mechanisms, including the use of a common cyclic redundancy check (CRC) or through the use of point-to-point or end-to-end encryption. The protection of data stream, connection, or session integrity normally is provided through the use of time stamping or sequence numbering.

According to ISO/IEC 7498-2, network integrity is provided in the form of five services.

- Connection integrity with recover service. This provides integrity of information on an N-connection with recovery where recovery processes are attempted.

- Connection integrity without recover service. This provides for the detection of information corruption on an N-connection.

- Selective field connection integrity service. This provides integrity of specific field within information on an N-connection.

- Connectionless integrity service. This provides the integrity of a single connectionless data unit.

- Selective field connectionless integrity. This provides the integrity of selected fields in a single connectionless data unit.

One network security mechanism commonly used to support integrity services is encryption, which protects against unauthorized modification of information. The encryption process provides a protective seal that will be broken and recognized if the information is tampered with or manipulated en route to the destination's decryption process.

4.5 AUTHENTICATION SERVICES

There are two types of authentication services. The first type is referred to as data origin authentication. Data origin authentication enables the sources of data received to be verified to be as claimed. The data origin authentication service cannot provide protections against the duplication or modification of data units. This authentication service is normally provided during the data transfer phase.

The second type of authentication service is referred to as peer-to-peer entity authentication. Peer-to-peer entity authentication provides the ability to verify that a peer entity in an association is the one claimed. This authentication service provides assurance that an entity is not attempting to masquerade or perform an unauthorized replay of some previous association. Peer-to-peer entity authentication is provided during the connection establishment phase or occasionally during the data transfer phase.

Identification and Authentication

User identification and authentication are important security measures in building a secure system. Prior to any information access, resource access, software development, or application usage, each user must be identified and authenticated by the network or network resources being accessed. This process sets the tone for all subsequent actions on the system and is therefore a critical first step in securing the system.

In a distributed environment, authentication must be performed on an ongoing basis, since only one end of the interface is controlled and therefore trusted by the user. If possible, an appropriate identifier should accompany further exchanges. Ideally, this identifier (and the original password exchange) should be unable to be forged. In that way, the authentication function is performed throughout the use of the newly created end-to-end user session.

Distributed Identification and Authentication Services

The ability to rapidly and securely distribute identification and authentication services will become increasingly important. Similarly, as user and process domains increase in scope and capability, the threats posed by spoofing, repudiation, playback, and the inability to track and account for system activity also increase. In this respect, identification and authentication mechanisms must be flexible to support distributivity.

Within a distributed system, a process responsible for supplying another process with a user's identification and authentication information may not need to supply all available ID/AUTH information to the other process. The user may not want all ID/AUTH information known by other processes, subjects, and audit trails that don't require the information for access or permissions. It is conceivable that certain identification and authentication information associated with a user or process could be sensitive or even classified. Given this possibility, there may need to be an interactive process-to-process communications protocol that requests only the required ID/AUTH information necessary to gain access to the system. The sending process would then respond with only the ID/AUTH information requested.

Distributed technology complicates the issues associated with identification and authentication mechanisms and practices. This complexity can be seen through another process-to-process example. Assume that a user of a system requests certain information from a system, and, as part of this request, a process (acting on behalf of the user) carries this user's ID/AUTH credentials with it as it collects, processes, and manipulates the information requested. Once the information is collected and presented to the user, the process uses the user's ID/AUTH information to gain access to information for another malicious user. As systems become more distributed and cooperative, security mechanisms and protection must support this technological progression in parallel.

Cascading Authentication

Cascading authentication is a prevalent issue in distributed systems. The issue stems from the need for a user or process acting on behalf of a user to be able to pass (unmodified and with a high degree of assurance) its authentication information to multiple nodes and processes in a network.

According to K. R. Sollins, in his paper on the topic, the problem is incurred when disparate computer systems are being called upon to cooperate in the absence of complete trust of each other. Furthermore, the systems are utilized in a cascaded fashion, where one invokes a second, which invokes a third, and so on, until the final service is invoked.[7]

For example, a user logs on to a network and subsequently to a host on that network. The host identifies and authenticates the user. The user then requests information that is not contained in its entirety within the host on which the user is signed (i.e., the data is distributed among multiple host processors). The host that the user has currently an established session with is now responsible for forwarding the user's authentication information to the other hosts on the network contributing data for the composite request. The host process (acting on behalf of the user) passing the user's authentication information to other nodes on the network must be trusted and have a high degree of assurance relative to proper operation. In addition, the process acting on the request from the host and accepting and processing the authentication data accompanying the request must also be trusted. It could even be said that this receiving process must be trusted to the level of the requesting process, since its activities will include accessing objects based on the authentication information of the ultimate user of that data.

As authentication cascades, trust and assurance must also cascade in parallel and in number. Heterogeneous hosts, operating systems, levels of trust, accreditation ranges, and the particulars of the security mechanisms implemented will all impact the ability to propagate trust and assurance to support cascading authentication.

In a distributed environment where complete trust is not ensured between active and passive entities, there are specific security issues that arise. Each system, application, and mission will have a different threat portfolio that must be examined and dealt with. For distributed systems without trust between components, things like access controls, accountability, and authentication become mandatory security constraints on the system. Authentication is the first step to ensuring access controls and accountability and therefore must be implemented accurately in the distributed architecture. The threats against authentication can be numerous and can include masquerading, spoofing, replaying information that was used correctly by someone else, or even by modifying the authentication messages as they are transmitted over the network.

The mechanism that facilitates secure cascading authentication is called a "passport."[8] Passports are passed along with each stage of the cascade and digitally signed at each transition. The information thus signed is that which is critical to the authentication. Authentication in this discussion also depends on the use of pairwise authentication between communicating participants. This concept and passport mechanism are planned to be implemented in an existing, heterogeneous distributed system called the Mercury System at MIT.

Goals

The goals that must be achieved by an authentication mechanism in a distributed system are taken from Sollins[9] and listed below.

1. Authentication cannot be forged. It is important that something be passed to the final destination to be used for access control and accountability and that there be a mechanism not only for trusting that information be tamper-proof, but also to be verifiable. This is achieved through the use of private keys (encryption) of the partici-

pants or transit points. A trusted authentication server is used to verify the identity of a participant based on a private password.

2. Accountability. It is often necessary to be able to track the route of cascading requests as part of providing access control. Therefore, identification of each participant in order of his or her participation is important. For example, it is important to the accounts payable office that the requests from the car rental agency and hotel have come originally from the traveler and then through the travel agency. Accountability is achieved through the inclusion of the participants' names (or even device addresses) and encrypted for protection.

3. Discretionary restriction. At each transit point, the client at that point may want to restrict access privileges of any service further down the route before the final destination. For example, returning to the example of travel arrangements, if the traveler has given permission to charge up to a certain amount for the trip, the travel agency may want to restrict further the amounts that the car rental agency and hotel can charge, keeping the remainder for air travel. This is achieved through an ability to include constraints or limitations at each transit point.

4. Modularity. It is important, especially in a widely distributed environment, that a client not need to know the internal structure and implementation of the services it invokes. In a situation such as a global network, remote services at autonomous but loosely cooperating organizations may either be hidden for local security reasons or may change unpredictably. Returning to the traveler's example, the traveler should not need to know whether the travel agency will bill the accounting office for the car and hotel or pass those actions off to the respective organization. Modularity is achieved by superimposing digital signatures on the passport in such a way that verification is done only at the end. Each transit point needs to know only about the one to which it is sending the passport and does not need to know about how that transit point will achieve its job.

5. Independence. One of the advantages of a distributed environment, especially when cascading authentication is available, is that the client need not be available when the request is being acted upon. Therefore, a goal may be to permit independent activity, even when authentication is required. In the case of the traveler, the client should not need to be available for verification of requests, since wait lists of reservations may cause those to occur at any time. The client may not

only go home in the evenings expecting the travel agency to continue working on the travel arrangement, but may even turn off the workstation. One should not need to depend on later verification from the originator or any other participant. Independence is achieved by superimposing digital signatures and permitting such constraints as time limits on a passport's validity.

6. Combining of identity. It is often necessary to act as a combination of oneself and a client. This was the case of the travel agency requesting payment from the accounts payable office. Only because a request comes from the travel agency on behalf of the traveler might the charges be accepted. This is achieved by cascading and superimposing digital signatures. It is possible to identify all the participants in a request, thereby allowing the trusted authentication server to accept requests only when the required combination of principals is involved.

Trusted Path Propagation

If processes are permitted on behalf of users to communicate and pass identification and authentication information to other processes and components, a propagation of a trusted path is assumed. This assumption, however, does not mean that a trusted path exists or has been designed. To support ever-increasing distributivity and cooperation among processing entities, the ability to propagate a trusted path with a high degree of assurance is required.

Privilege Passing

The concept of privilege passing is not a new one and can be said to be only an extension of the notion of a subject acting on behalf of a user. However, as systems become increasingly distributed, cooperative, and intelligent, the need to restrict the propagation of privileges becomes necessary. If privileges are permitted to propagate without being controlled, many additional security risks become evident to system resources and data.

Network Security Mechanisms—Authentication

There are numerous choices for network security authentication services. The application of a particular network security mechanism/service should be driven by the environment in which the mechanism/service will operate.

Authentication services and their level of implementation detail and sophistication should be driven by two major factors:

1. The level of trust and confidence in the way in which information is communicated and the communications services used to provide the service

2. The level of trust and confidence that exists between the peer-to-peer entities that communicate over the network

If there is a substantial lack of trust between peer-to-peer communicating entities and the communication services provided by the network, then very robust and sophisticated authentication mechanisms may be required. These may include the use of nonrepudiation services and digital signatures. On the other hand, when peer-to-peer communicating entities have a strong and consistent level of trust and have a high level of confidence in the communication services provided by the network, then the use of simple user ID and password schemes may be sufficient to identify and authenticate the originator of a message. Passwords, however, are vulnerable to replay attacks. A perpetrator can capture a data stream containing log-on and password information. By replaying this information, the perpetrator can masquerade as a legitimate user and thus gain unauthorized access to network resources. In situations where trust exists between peer-to-peer entities, but the communication services of the network are not trusted, the use of passwords should be augmented with the additional use of encryption. Replay attacks can also be thwarted by using three-way handshaking protocols and/or time stamping with trusted network clocks.

Network security mechanisms and approaches commonly used to support authentication services include public key encryption and digital signature. The digital signature can be used to support data origin authentication. The sender of a message uses private information in the form of a private key to produce an encrypted form of the message, which is referred to as the "signature." This signature, in combination with the plain-text data unit, is sent to the authorized recipient. The recipient can then authenticate the data origin by comparing the received plain-text data unit with the information obtained through decrypting the signature using the public key of the sender.

4.6 ACCESS CONTROL SERVICES

Access control services are used to protect network resources, files, data, and applications from unauthorized access. Access control services are probably the most commonly thought of service in computer and network security. In the context of networking, access controls can be used to restrict access to network resources, applications, and services as well as information. Access control services are closely tied to identification and authentication services. A user or process acting on behalf of a user must be identified and authenticated before the access control mechanism can effectively mediate access to network resources, services, and information. Access control services are commonly provided through one of five mechanisms:

1. Access control lists
2. Information/data labels
3. Capabilities/functions–based access control
4. Logical networking controls
5. Technical incompatibility

Mandatory Access Controls

Mandatory access controls (MAC) are a global set of rules that implements a consistent and globally applied security policy across all system resources and users. MAC is necessary when there are identifiable information categories that must be consistently separated and protected from disclosure. For example, certain information that traverses the system may never require access by certain employees. If this information and its user can be specifically identified, then a MAC policy can be implemented. The MAC policy represents those access control rules that are consistent and cannot be modified by the general user community.

Distributed MAC

As systems become more distributed and users may require access to processing and data on a number of hosts and workstations, and from communication services, the ability to distribute MAC credentials rapidly and securely becomes increasingly important.

Discretionary Access Controls

Discretionary access controls (DAC) are typically provided to permit the separation of data through what is commonly referred to as *need-to-know*. A DAC policy is just that, discretionary, and it is commonly left to the discretion of the users to provide or deny access to data that they own. For this reason, DAC policies are often circumvented because they are neither universally nor consistently applied, as are those found in a MAC policy.

A network DAC policy, however, is a very important service and capability and can be used to support the separation of privacy, proprietary, and program-specific data to specified granularity within each category. A DAC policy can be established to ensure that only a single user, group of users, or groups of users are permitted access to identified data sets, files, and applications.

Countermeasures used to enforce DAC are readily available with many of the software add-on packages having been certified at either the C1 or C2 levels by the National Computer Security Center (NCSC) of the National Security Agency (NSA).

Distributed DAC

As systems become more distributed and users may require access to processing and data on n-number of hosts and workstations and from communication services, the ability to rapidly and securely distribute DAC credentials becomes increasingly important. The idea of each node that stores data being responsible for maintaining an access control list based on individuals and their privileges will be difficult to manage, if not impossible.

Access Control Lists

Access control lists are used to maintain a list of all individuals or processes that are authorized to access specific information, applications, or network resources. Access control lists are the most common form of access control in networks today. Most intelligent networking components, workstations, hosts, and PCs provide access control list capabilities.

ACL Issues

Standard access control lists (ACLs) for distributed systems where control and security have a high degree of distributivity may be inadequate. Clients cannot easily transfer their privilege to access an object with ACLs because that privilege is stored in the reference monitor with the object. A client could transfer its identity to a manager, but this gives the generally untrusted manager access to all of the client's objects. Yet privilege transfer is critical for nested operation invocations, which are a very important part of systems with a high degree of distributed control and security.

The following printing example explains this point. File F and printer P are two objects. A client prints a file by invoking a print operation on printer P and passing the file name F to the printer. The print manager invokes repeated nested read invocations on file F. Assume the print manager was developed by an applications programmer and cannot be trusted to perform properly. In an ACL-based system, the print manager may access the file F only if one of the following conditions is met:

- The print manager is given read access to all objects and is trusted to access the objects properly. Since peripheral managers are commonly developed by applications programmers, this solution imparts too much privilege on untrusted code and is generally unsatisfactory.

- The client process transfers its identity to the print manager. This gives the print manager far too much privilege, as it now may access any object available to the client.

- The client modifies the ACL of the object for the print manager before invoking the printer operation. This is probably the most secure, but suffers from poor performance.

This problem is dealt with by allowing clients to transfer special identifiers that allow the receiver to access only a specific object and no others.[10] Dividing a client's identities into smaller units ensures that their use by untrusted managers is more constrained. These special identifiers, termed "proxy contextual identities,"[11] provide some of the benefits of capabilities, including privilege transfer, in the ACL approach to DAC. However, they do not provide the fine-grain control over privileges that capabilities offer on a process-by-process basis, nor do they incur the expense of establishing separate protection domains. Privilege transfer through the transfer of identities allows a manager to invoke operations on behalf of a client. In the above example, the printer manager is reading the file on behalf of the client. The file manager would use the client's identity for access authorization.

A second issue is the ease with which the privilege to grant privilege to clients can be distributed.[12] The problem with ACLs is that any client with the privilege to modify the ACL for an object may give any other client any privilege to the object (including the privilege to modify the ACL). Most ACL-based systems do not provide any mechanism to restrict use of the privilege to grant privilege. A solution to this problem is to separate privileges into two categories: regular and restricted. Hence, the ability to modify restricted privileges is greatly restricted. This is obviously an application-dependent issue, but it can be used to further restrict unnecessary or malicious privilege transfers.

A common issue arising in the design of DACs for distributed systems is where to locate the access control lists. In Vinter,[13] the decision was made not to put the ACLs in the kernel primarily because the access control is a type-dependent function in object- oriented systems, and the kernel was specifically designed to provide type-independent services (e.g., message routing and object-to-location binding). The ACLs are also large, creating additional data management services not otherwise required by the kernel. Maintaining consistent copies of the ACLs for replicated objects also complicates the kernel. The solution arrived at was to place the ACLs in each object manager.

The model of privilege transfer allows the proxy identities to be usable for accessing a limited set of objects. However, the implementation requires that the objects be parameters in the invocation. This requirement is a major limitation for applications with highly nested objects. For example, a document object might consist of paragraph, figure, and table objects. Passing the privilege to a manager to access a document object might not be adequate because privilege might be needed to access the paragraphs, figures, and tables. Since the structure of a document (and therefore its nested objects) is generally hidden from the client, there is no way for these to be included in the invocation on the document. The requirement that the proxy CCI objects list be included in the invocation parameters may be awkward for some applications, too. More work is needed to investigate the usefulness of the proposed privilege transfer mechanism with specific applications.[14]

Information/Data Labels

Information and data labeling is a common form of access control employed across networks that use trusted networking components or frontends and networks that support secure protocols. The Internet Protocol Security Option (IPSO), Revised Internet Protocol Security Option (RIPSO), Commercial Internet Protocol Security Option (CIPSO), DODIIS Network Security for Information Exchange (DNSIX), the Trusted Socket model used in the MaxSix (Project Max), and Trusted Socket (Trusted Systems Interoperability Group or TSIG) are examples of protocols capable of intimately associating a label with the information being transmitted within the packet. IPSO, RIPSO, and CIPSO are all approaches to using the Internet Protocol Security Option field to provide a way to control access across a network based on informational content of IP packets. DNSIX is a specification published by the MITRE Corporation under the direction and sponsorship of the Defense Intelligence Agency (DIA). MaxSix is being designed and developed by an industry consortium: Project Max. The TSIG and Project Max have both been working to develop and implement a security model based on a trusted socket that will be used to define and specify both the socket and stream interfaces. Each of these secure networking architectures provides trusted services that are transparent to an application.

There are also trusted networking components and front-end devices that are employed within the typically classified government/intelligence networks that enable information to be output by a host device, captured, and buffered by the networking component/front end, augmented with a label, and transmitted over the network. The information is typically encrypted by the trusted networking component/front end with the label left in the clear. Other trusted network components/front ends can then read the header/label to determine which devices are authorized to access the protocol data unit. Boeing has developed a multilevel trusted LAN that has been certified by NCSC at the A1 level of trust. This multilevel network employs front-end devices capable of labeling to provide a consistent trusted environment for heterogeneous network environments.

Capabilities/Functions–Based Access Control

Access control can be implemented through defining access and authorizations to capabilities and functions provided in the network. A capability is normally implemented through the use of a token that serves as an identifier for a resource. If a user or process possesses the token, then that user or process is assumed to have authorized access to the associated network resource. Capability- or function-based systems can be very effective from a network security implementation perspective because work functions and the tools, applications, resources, and information to do those work functions can be defined on an individual basis. For example, if an individual has responsibility for invoicing customers, that person may not require access to marketing or technical information of the organization. In addition, the person can be granted access to only those network resources and applications that are required to do his or her specific job function. Capability-based access control systems fall short when the environment is highly dynamic where individuals have numerous and continuously changing responsibilities. Critical to the success of capability-based systems is their ability to be implemented and managed in a consistent and trusted manner.

Logical Networking Controls

Access control can be supported through the use of logical network controls. For the most part, the inherent attributes of network components provide the means to separate users, resources, services, and entire networks logically—thereby limiting and controlling access to network resources. Bridges and routers are good examples of network devices that can be very effective.

4.7   CONFIDENTIALITY SERVICES

ISO/IEC 7498-2 defines four forms of confidentiality services. The purpose of confidentiality services is to protect network information from unauthorized disclosure to individuals, processes, and entities.

- *Connection confidentiality service* provides confidentiality of data in an N-connection.

- *Connectionless confidentiality service* provides confidentiality of a single connectionless data unit.

- *Selective field confidentiality service* provides confidentiality of specific fields within the data during a connection or in a single connectionless data unit.

- *Traffic flow confidentiality service* provides protection of information that may otherwise be compromised or indirectly derived from the observation of information traffic communicated over a network.

Network Security Mechanisms—Confidentiality

To a large degree, network confidentiality services are provided through the use of encryption. For example, connection confidentiality can be provided by the sending node/process encrypting the data with a key private to the receiving node/process. Connectionless confidentiality service can be achieved through the use of encryption and a private key from the originator of a message to the intended recipient of the message. Connection and connectionless confidentiality services may both be supported through the use of routing control mechanisms. Through the application of defined rules during the routing process, routing control mechanisms can provide more secure data transmission routes.

Selective field confidentiality service can be provided through the use of selective encryption (i.e., only encrypting a specific field of a message) and the use of a private key. Traffic flow confidentiality service can be achieved though the use of encryption between the sending node/process and the receiving node/process. In this way, encryption services can be used as a means to scramble the traffic on a network to preclude a would-be perpetrator from being able to discern intelligence from traffic patterns and other indicators. The use of encryption requires the use of keys, and, thus, a key management scheme is required. Encryption keys must be protected with great care. In most instances, encryption keys are at their most vulnerable when they are communicated to the devices on the network where they will be used. As a result, a secure means for key distribution is very important.

A perpetrator can use traffic analysis techniques to infer information such as the presence of traffic, the lack of traffic, the frequency of traffic, the consistency of traffic, the level of traffic, and the direction of traffic. Such information may disclose some very useful information about function, intention, or activity. Traffic flow confidentiality services can be provided through the use of traffic-padding mechanisms. Traffic padding involves the padding of protocol data units to a consistent length and the introduction of spurious traffic.

Network security mechanisms and approaches commonly used to support confidentiality services include routing control mechanisms and encryption.

Fundamentally, encryption is typically provided in one of two forms: link encryption or end-to-end encryption. Link encryption provides security for message transmission over an individual communication link between two nodes on a network regardless of the source or destination of the message. It is very common for messages to be passed between numerous network nodes before finally arriving at its intended destination. As a result, each network node in the route decrypts the message and then encrypts the message again with the key for the next point-to-point link. A single message transmitted from one origin to a final destination may be encrypted and decrypted many times, using different encryption keys and possibly heterogeneous encryption algorithms. The contents of each message are normally encrypted, including the destination address. As a result, a perpetrator cannot intercept a message stream and determine the destination address of a message. In addition, link encryption masks message attributes such as frequency, message length, traffic presence, traffic absence, and traffic flow because a continuous flow of information always exists between transmitting and receiving communications components. A major disadvantage of link encryption is that it requires all network nodes involved in the encryption/decryption process to be physically protected. Another substantial cost driver in the application of link encryption is key management and distribution. Link encryption normally uses the same key to encrypt and decrypt the message stream. As a result, coordination and key management is required to ensure that nodes in the network possess the same key at the same time. In addition, most link encryption devices require the manual loading of keys. If keys are required to be changed on a regular basis, this process can be very time consuming and risky to the overall protection of the network.

Link encryption is applied in networks where a collection of nodes are interconnected through the use of communications links, each of which may be independently protected. End-to-end encryption mechanisms, on the other hand, are used in networks for transporting information in a secure fashion from origin to destination. Encryption typically occurs once and the message is then decrypted at the intended destination. As a result, the contents of the message are not compromised if a node in the communications path of the message is subverted. End-to-end encryption mechanisms are much simpler to implement and manage. Encryption keys must be negotiated, stored, and managed only at the origin and destination nodes where the protection of information is required. The network over which the messages travel does not have to be secure, greatly reducing the cost of providing an encryption capability. Unlike link encryption, end-to-end encryption is required only for those users/nodes where security is required. As a result, end-to-end encryption can coexist in a network environment without every device possessing the capability. Overall, end-to-end encryption is far more cost effective in a network environment.

On the downside, traffic flow analysis is a substantial threat to networks that employ end-to-end encryption. Depending on the network security attack, the mere existence of network traffic in a network may provide substantial information to a perpetrator. Traffic flow analysis is one of the easiest ways to compromise a network. For as little as $250–$300, a perpetrator can purchase a very commonly available network management and trouble-shooting software package that can be used to capture information over a network. The software and process are designed to be passive and nonintrusive, so it cannot be detected. These types of packages are meant to assist in troubleshooting and diagnosing network problems. However, because they perform these functions by monitoring network traffic, a perpetrator can just as easily use the package maliciously to compromise information. The frequency, pattern, and level of message traffic may indicate many things to a perpetrator.

The reason for this inherent vulnerability is due to the fact that end-to-end encryption schemes must leave the destination address of the protocol data unit in the clear because networking resources (i.e., bridges, routers, servers) must be capable of properly routing the PDU en route over the network. Network security countermeasures used to combat traffic analysis threats are typically designed to protect data that may reveal useful information to a perpetrator by hiding the length, frequency, and the origin and destination patterns of the message traffic between the layer connections within the OSI protocol model. Link encryption provides all such protection by encrypting the entire message stream and providing a consistent and continuous message stream over the network. However, end-to-end encryption can only limit, and not eliminate, the amount of information available to the perpetrator engaged in traffic analysis attacks. Hiding node-to-node–level communications patterns is not achievable in a network environment using end-to-end encryption. Such protections would require the encryption of all destination addresses and PDUs on the network.

Confidentiality of information en route prevents traffic flow analysis based on information content. There are two common types of encryption algorithms: symmetric and public key or asymmetric. Symmetric encryption relies on the use of a secret key. This secret key is used to encrypt and decrypt the information. Symmetric encryption requires both the sending and receiving devices to possess the secret key. The Data Encryption Standard is the most commonly known symmetric encryption algorithm.

Another very common implementation of symmetric encryption is the Kerberos distributed security system. Kerberos was developed by the Massachusetts Institute of Technology (MIT) as part of the campus-wide Athena networking project. In Kerberos, the client and server share a key used to encrypt and decrypt information on a network. In the development of Kerberos, the key concern was how keys were going to be distributed over an unsecured network to conduct ultimately secure communications. This issue has, and continues to be, the most fundamental problem and challenge associated with the application of symmetric encryption schemes. The most common approach to date has been to distribute keys manually. This is also the most common way in which passwords for new accounts are distributed (i.e., passwords typed on a piece of paper and sent through the mail to the user for initial account activation).

On a common UNIX system, a user is prompted for a user ID and password. The user ID and password would be entered by the user and the system would then encrypt the password and compare the encrypted value against the stored value for the password. In Kerberos, the UNIX system takes the user ID and transmits it to the Kerberos distributed security system. Kerberos then validates that the user is known to the network. If the user is known to the network, Kerberos will send a ticket to the ticket-granting server, alerting the server that a client will be contacting it soon. Next, Kerberos sends a PDU to the workstation that is encrypted with the user's password. The encryption algorithm used for Kerberos is the DES. Inside the PDU is the same ticket that was sent to the ticket-granting server. In addition to the ticket, the PDU will also include a session key. The UNIX system will then prompt the user for a password. The entered password will be used to decrypt the PDU sent by Kerberos. At this junction, the UNIX system is able to engage the ticket-granting server. Once engaged, the ticket-granting server will give the client access to resources and services on the network. The most interesting thing about this approach is that the password never was introduced to the network. Moreover, the password was not even stored on the UNIX system; rather, the password was used exclusively to decrypt the first PDU.

Once the client possesses the ticket, he or she is able to engage the ticket-granting server. The ticket is designed to be usable only for a very limited period of time. The ticket must be renewed periodically, thereby preventing a perpetrator from capturing an old ticket and masquerading as a legitimate client. Every session established between a client and a server includes the name of the client, the server, the client IP address, the current time and duration of the ticket, and a session encryption key. The entire ticket is encrypted with the server's key password. As a result, the server can decrypt the ticket; however, the client is unable to modify the ticket. When the ticket-granting server sends a session ticket back to the UNIX system, there is one more piece of information that is required, which is a copy of the session key. The UNIX system cannot utilize the session key inside the session ticket because it is encrypted with the server's key. Every piece of information received by the UNIX system, including the key for a session and the ticket for a server, is encrypted with the key that is shared between the client and the ticket-granting server.

Kerberos is beset with the same problem that all symmetric key systems have: transmission and distribution of the shared key to the client and server. The key must remain totally secure and secret during the transmission and distribution process or Kerberos cannot be trusted to provide any level of network security protection. As a result, just like other symmetric encryption schemes, Kerberos requires a very substantial investment in time, effort, physical security measures, and the management of the key distribution process. Kerberos does not scale up well to very large networks, because there remains a need to transmit keys across different Kerberos network and operational domains.

Public key, or asymmetric encryption, relies on the use of two keys. One key is publicly available and known, while the other key is treated as a private secret key. Public keys are used to encrypt messages, while private keys are used to decrypt messages. These two keys are related algorithmically, but large prime numbers are used, so there is virtually no way to discern one of the keys from the other. This two-key approach provides flexibility with an adequate degree of security for encrypting and decrypting messages. The public key is known and used to encrypt and send messages to the owner of the public key and then the owner's private key is used to decrypt the messages.

A common public key encryption algorithm is the Rivest, Shamir, and Adleman (RSA).[15] The RSA algorithm is very powerful, but when compared against DES,[16] its performance (actual encryption and decryption process) is substantially slower. This algorithm is based on the fact that it is much easier to multiply two large numbers together than it is to factor the product of the multiplication operation. Using RSA, keys range from 512 to 1,001 bits in length, or 150 to 301 decimal points. Massively parallel processors have provided substantial performance gains of 10 to 100 orders of magnitude over traditional processors; however, the ability to break the RSA algorithm and determine the private key is still several orders of magnitude beyond today's processing capabilities. RSA (the company) has been very aggressive in pursuing software licensing agreements with product vendors in the industry as a way of populating the networking industry with the RSA algorithm. Currently, the RSA algorithm stands head and shoulders above any other public key encryption technology. Examples include:

- Novell uses RSA in NetWare as part of the bindery, a naming service and security subsystem.

- Motorola uses RSA to support its secure voice communications products.

- Lotus uses RSA in its Notes product, a groupware conferencing application.

- Tektronix uses RSA to secure fonts on its printers.

Maybe the most substantial market penetration of the RSA algorithm was accomplished by allowing the free use of the RSA algorithm in the Privacy

Enhanced Mail application for noncommercial users. Trusted Information Systems developed PEM under a paid contract from the federal government of the United States. Electronic mail has become the most predominant application used on networks today. Many companies and organizations have purchased networks and the necessary software for the explicit purpose of being able to provide an electronic mail capability. Because of its tremendous appeal and use, electronic mail is being used for everything from small talk to business planning and contract negotiations. It is the communications application of choice for communicating highly proprietary commercial product information as well as government secrets. PEM provides the framework to protect information communicated via this very important network application.

PEM is built on top of the standard Internet transport mechanism, which is the Simple Mail Transfer Protocol (SMTP). PEM standards have been composed with flexibility in mind. Specifically, different types of encryption can be supported using the PEM standards. The initial implementation of PEM is based on the RSA algorithm, but there is absolutely no reason why other encryption algorithms cannot be used in the generation of interchange keys.

PEM provides three services:

1. Authentication
2. Message integrity
3. Confidentiality

PEM authentication provides the security services necessary to ensure that a peer process is a legitimate and authorized process. Further, PEM authentication provides the security protections to ensure that a message from a user is in fact from that user, thereby reducing the threat of process/user masquerading. Once authenticated, nonrepudiation services are also afforded in that users, or processes acting on behalf of users, cannot refute that they received a PEM message.

Message integrity is a critical capability, especially in highly distributed, large, and complex distributed information systems. Message Integrity Checks (MIC) are used by PEM to ensure that messages are not modified or otherwise tampered with illegally. The Message Digest 4 algorithm, developed by RSA, is a commonly used MIC mechanism.

PEM provides confidentiality by encrypting the actual contents of the electronic mail message so that it cannot be accessed and compromised by unauthorized individuals. Once a message is encrypted, one must possess the RSA algorithm and the correct key to decrypt the message.

An outgoing electronic mail message employing PEM is processed through four representations, beginning with the local message in some internal structure. Second, the message is put into a representation that supports the SMTP transport, based on a 7-bit ASCII and carriage return/line feed for delimiters. Next, the authentication and encryption services are applied to the contents of the message. A MIC is generated for the message. Padding is added to the message to ensure its length is consistent with the requirements for encryption, which require the message to be an integral number of 8-byte quantities. Specific portions of the message may be excluded from the encryption process by accentuating the region(s) with an asterisk; however, authentication services are always applied to the complete message. Two types of encryption keys are used in the application of PEM. The Data Encryption Key (DEK) is used to encrypt the text of a message (or message contents) and also is used to generate the MIC. This encryption process is based on the DES algorithm. The Interchange Key (IK) is used to encrypt the DEK.

Consistent with the application of public key technology, if a mail message is sent to a mail group containing multiple users, each recipient of the message gets a separate DEK, each encrypted with a separate IK. By possessing an IK, the receiving device is able to decrypt the DEK, which can then be used to decrypt the message and MIC. Once the message has been encrypted, it must be put back into a printable encoding so that it can be sent on top of the SMTP. The PEM standard supports this process by taking the bit string (i.e., the message) and converting it to a printable representation by representing each group of 6 bits as a printable character (i.e., an 8-bit octet). As a result, the message increases in size by approximately 33 percent and the results of the encoding are represented as a series of lines possessing 64 characters each. Standard origin and destination address headers are placed around the PEM message and handed off to the messaging system (i.e., SMTP).

For PEM to operate, there must be a method to distribute IK throughout the network. PEM requires that a certificate be acquired prior to communicating with a remote user on the network. A PEM certificate provides the following information:

- Version number
- Serial number
- Certificate signature
- Issuer's name
- Validity name
- Subject's public component

The subject's name is an X.400 Originator/Recipient (O/R) name as specified in the government's Open Systems Interconnection Profile (GOSIP) Version 2 specification. This distinguished name is less than or equal to 259 characters. This name includes a country, a message handling administration, an organizational name, and a personal name. A name may also include zero to four organizational units to define further the organizational name. The certificate provides information from the issuer regarding the attributes being vouched for about the user. Normally, the issuer will vouch for the person's name, the organization that the user belongs to, and the role within the organization that the user performs. The public key component of the subject includes an algorithm identification, and the key varies in size between 320 and 632 bits. The certificate signature is used to validate that a certificate has not been compromised. The signature is an encrypted, one-way hash function calculated on the contents of the certificate. The decrypted quantity is compared to the hash quantity generated at the time the certificate is checked. A certificate is signed using the public key of the issuing organization to vouch that it is real. The issuer's certificate is required to prove that the issuing organization is real. Multiple certification trees exist, and each one is managed and administered by a top-level certification authority (i.e., U.S. government, RSA Data Security, Inc.).

PEM does *not* provide the following services:

1. Traffic flow confidentiality
2. Routing control
3. Access control
4. Assurance of receipt
5. Replay prevention or other stream-oriented services

Consistent with all asymmetric (or public key) cryptographic schemes, PEM header and destination address information is left in the clear. As a result, PEM does not provide traffic flow confidentiality. A passive wiretap would enable a perpetrator to determine that an electronic mail session was occurring and who the participants were. Access control, routing control, and other security services are intended to be provided by other portions of the network. Access control normally will be provided at the application or operating systems level. Routing controls usually will be applied within the routing mechanisms in the network and configured and managed through proactive network management systems. Assurance of receipt, or nonrepudiation services, should be provided by the message handling system.

The Diffie-Hellman public key encryption method,[17] used in Sun's secure remote procedure call (RPC), and secure network file system (NFS), is based on the fact that it is much easier to raise a number to a power than it is to find the root of the number. Sun, using the Diffie-Hellman method, takes a commonly known constant and raises it to the power of a key that produces a 192-bit number. While public key encryption schemes are very well suited for initial authentication services (i.e., user and process authentication and session establishment), symmetric encryption is commonly used to protect the actual information communicated during the session. The combination of the two techniques is very effective in a networked environment because the public key encryption scheme can be used to distribute the symmetric keying materials throughout the network. The ability to combine symmetric and asymmetric encryption mechanisms is highly desirable because key management can be accomplished effectively through asymmetric encryption, and overall network performance is not overly burdened as a result of applying symmetric encryption on the bulk of network traffic. More sophisticated algorithms and the application of error-correcting codes extrapolated from information theory continue to advance and improve public key encryption.

Passive wiretapping is a very common threat in a networked environment. Passive wiretapping occurs when a perpetrator taps into a network and observes the message traffic as it passes over the network. In most instances, the perpetrator will actually capture the information and write it to a storage medium for future reference and observation. The application of encryption can substantially reduce the amount of information that a perpetrator can obtain from passive wiretapping. The protocol layer in the context of the OSI model in which the encryption is applied has a direct bearing on the amount of information and which information is available to a perpetrator employing passive wiretapping. For example, if encryption were performed at the presentation layer (layer 6), then all session (layer 5), transport (layer 4), network (layer 3), link (layer 2), and physical (layer 1) protocol information would be available to a perpetrator. On the other hand, if encryption were performed at the transport layer, then only information at the network layer and below would be visible to the perpetrator. For end-to-end encryption schemes, it is commonly believed that encryption should be performed at the transport layer and above.

4.8   NONREPUDIATION SERVICES

Nonrepudiation services are used to protect against the originator of a message or action denying that he or she originated the message or the action. Nonrepudiation services are also used to protect against the recipient of a message denying that he or she received the message. Nonrepudiation services are provided in two forms.

- Nonrepudiation with proof of origin service: proof of origin is provided to the recipient of the message.
- Nonrepudiation with proof of delivery: proof of delivery is provided to the sender of a message.

In addition to the two nonrepudiation services, notarization mechanisms can be used that involve data registration with a trusted third party (or a notary). This registration process can be used to provide a higher level of assurance and confidence in the accuracy of the data relative to origin, destination, type, and integrity.

Network Security Mechanisms—Nonrepudiation

Network security mechanisms and approaches commonly used to support nonrepudiation services include public key encryption and digital signature.

4.9   ASSURANCE

Finally, assurance is a very important aspect of any network security program. Assurance is a direct byproduct of the security services employed by the network. Assurance is the level of trust that is placed in a security device, software routine, or service so that it will perform the security functions accurately and correctly. Without assurance, the security of a system is not useful because it cannot be measured, nor can it be counted on to consistently enforce a system's security policy.

Assurance can be gained through several methods. One method involves the extensive testing of software, hardware, and the integration of security countermeasures. Testing can support one's belief that a security component does in fact have a high degree of trust. Other methods include penetration testing, system modeling, testing through simulated environments, the introduction of errors, and formal verification. Another measure of a security component's trust or level of assurance can be obtained through the NCSC of the NSA. Products that have been certified by NCSC have been exposed to extensive testing by experts in the field and can in most cases be trusted to perform as advertised.

4.10 SUMMARY

In this chapter, we've discussed the different types of security services pertinent to a network security program. In the next chapter, we'll shift our focus to the different disciplines that apply to network security—physical and personnel security, information and operations security, and others.

END NOTES

1. International Standards Organization, *Information Processing Systems—Open Systems Interconnection—Basic Reference Model, Part 2: Security Architecture* (ISO/IEC 7498-2), February 15, 1989.

2. National Computer Security Center, *Trusted Network Interpretations,* NCSC-TG-005 Version-1, July 1987.

3. National Computer Security Center, *DoD Trusted Computer System Evaluation Criteria,* DoD 5200.28 STD, December 1985.

4. Ibid.

5. Ibid.

6. Ibid.

7. K. R. Sollins, "Cascaded Authentication," in *IEEE Symposium on Security and Privacy,* April 18–21, 1988, 156–163.

8. Ibid.

9. Ibid.

10. S. T. Vinter, "Extended Discretionary Access Controls," in *IEEE Symposium on Security and Privacy,* April 18–21, 1988, 39–49.

11. P. A. Karger, "Authentication and Discretionary Access Controls in Computer Networks," *Computer Networks and ISDN Systems* 10, no. 1 (January 1986): 27–37.

12. Vinter, op. cit.

13. Ibid.

14. Ibid.

15. R. Rivest, A. Shamir, and L. Aldeman, "A Method for Obtaining Digital Signatures and Public-Key Crytosystems," *Communications of the ACM* (February 1978): 120–126.

16. Federal Information Processing Standards Publication 46 (FIPS 1977), January 15, 1977.

17. W. Diffie and M. Hellman, "New Directions in Cryptography," *IEEE Transactions on Information Theory* IT-22(6) (November 1976): 644–654.

5

Network Security Disciplines

5.1 INTRODUCTION— SECURITY ENGINEERING DISCIPLINES

Security engineering is a comprehensive science encompassing multiple disciplines. To be effective, each security discipline must be evaluated and examined in the network security engineering process (Figure 5.1). Security disciplines include physical security, personnel security, TEMPEST, information security (INFOSEC), operations security (OPSEC), communications security (COMSEC), computer security (COMPUSEC), and industrial security. Each security discipline must be evaluated for its relative importance to the security of a network and also for its impact on other security disciplines. Each security discipline must be evaluated in the context of the complete system and never in isolation. This enables the cost-effective application of security countermeasures and precludes redundancy of effort and unnecessary expenditures.

5.2 PHYSICAL SECURITY

Physical security includes those measures designed to protect personnel and to prevent unauthorized access to equipment, facilities, materials, and documents and to safeguard them against damage and theft. Historically, physical security has played a large role in securing systems and networks that

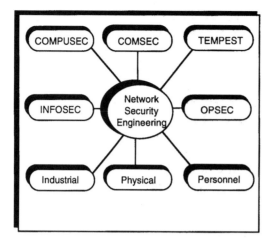

Figure 5.1 Network security requires the comprehensive evaluation of all security engineering disciplines.

process and communicate sensitive information. There are many different types of physical security countermeasures. Examples can include simple countermeasures (such as door locks and physical walls) to sophisticated automated physical entry devices such as retina eye scanning devices and voice recognition. Other physical security countermeasures can include:

- Penetration alarm systems
- Physical construction and barriers
- Clear spaces
- Motion detectors
- Controlled areas
- Alarmed cable plants/networks
- Closed circuit television (CCTV) surveillance systems
- Physical/biometric personnel identification systems
- Guards and patrols
- Emergency response teams

In the vast majority of cases, physical security represents a very substantial investment and recurring cost.

5.3 PERSONNEL SECURITY

Personnel security defines those policies and procedures for recruiting and hiring practices, personnel investigations, and access to information and information assets. Personnel security is often minimized when compared to high-tech security countermeasures. Any decision to minimize the importance of personnel security can be a major mistake. Numerous studies and research have shown that between 70 and 95 percent of all network security incidents are caused by insiders. An insider is anyone who has legitimate and authorized access to information processed, stored, and communicated over a network. This single fact demonstrates the tremendous need for effective and consistent personnel security policies, procedures, and practices.

Of the large percentage of insider security incidents, the vast majority of these are tied directly to user errors, simple mistakes, and lack of network and application configuration management. For this reason, focused management attention on processes, effective configuration management, user/management network security training, and common sense, if properly applied, can dramatically reduce the damage commonly caused by user errors and configuration mistakes.

In government situations, personnel security is a straightforward process for systems that process classified information. Personnel cannot access classified information unless they have a security clearance that is equal to or higher than the information being accessed and possess a valid need-to-know for the information accessed. The security clearance process places additional constraints on the utilization of networks and information processed, stored, and communicated on networks. Specific attributes and relevant activities associated with personnel security include:

- Clearance procedures
- Defining clearance and need-to-know requirements
- Access control list definition
- Security training
- User/personnel security accountability
- User/personnel identification measures
- User/personnel investigations

5.4 INFORMATION SECURITY

Information security deals with those administrative policies and procedures for identifying, controlling, and protecting information from unauthorized disclosure, damage, destruction, or unauthorized manipulation. This protection encompasses how information is processed, distributed, stored, and destroyed. Securing a network must take into account how information will be protected during its entire life cycle. The protection of information, for example, may influence where servers, printers, workstations, and processors are physically located.

Specific attributes of information security may include the following:

- Secure distribution of information (over a network or via hard copy)

- Security education/training to ensure policies and procedures are well understood

- Information tracking and maintenance (i.e., where does the information reside, how many copies exist, and who is responsible for their protection)

- Declassification or desensitivity procedures

- Classification or sensitivity guide addressing what information is sensitive and why

- Consistent and visible marking of information to communicate the level at which the information should be protected

- Production controls

5.5 TEMPEST

TEMPEST is the science that deals with preventing unauthorized individuals or systems from intercepting, interpreting, and ultimately compromising electromagnetic emanations. Providing a TEMPEST-compliant design for networks is more difficult and complex than for stand-alone monolithic systems. This complexity results from the size, distributed nature, and multiplicity of various hardware components that are typically accessible through a network. TEMPEST is a finite science that can be easily measured and tested with appropriate equipment. The cost of TEMPEST compliance, however, is a different story. Significant cost savings can be realized through creative TEMPEST designs, taking into account the physical placement of the equipment, its orientation, and the facility's own ability to impede the propagation of electromagnetic emanations. TEMPEST issues and requirements commonly influence network architectural design. Physical separation can be a cost-effective TEMPEST design alternative, whereby components used to process sensitive information are located a specified physical distance from components and systems that process information that is not sensitive. A common and related problem is electromagnetic interference (EMI) in network today. EMI refers to the emanations propagated by a computer system, communications media, or networking components that actually interfere with the performance of other systems and components.

Many people erroneously believe that TEMPEST is a concern only for super-secret government organizations. This is simply not true. Numerous articles and actual examples point directly to the use of communications equipment by competing businesses to intercept and compromise electronic emanations. The technology and equipment necessary to intercept electromagnetic emanations from computers and networks is very cheap and easily obtained. The biggest culprits for electromagnetic emanations are computer displays. Some computer displays will generate an electromagnetic signal easily intercepted at distances in excess of 3,000 feet.

Common approaches to TEMPEST security include:

- Use of TEMPEST approved equipment. The government maintains a TEMPEST preferred products list (PPL) that lists equipment that has been TEMPEST certified. The PPL is intended for government systems/networks that are used to process classified information.

- Push-to-talk monodirectional microphones and automatic disconnects for phone systems to eliminate acoustic coupling

- Isolators, filters, wave guides, and use of fiber optic cable plants

- Physical separation between components and potential conveyance systems

- Use of low signaling equipment (plus or minus 6 volts)

- Grounding, bonding, and shielding of facilities and computer facilities

- Use of TEMPEST, EMI, and RFI approved computer components, racks, and housing elements

- Defining an equipment radiation transmission zone (ERTZ) and living within the defined boundaries of the zone for equipment location and use

5.6 NETWORK AND COMPUTER SECURITY

Network and computer security refers to all hardware and software functions, characteristics, features, operational procedures, accountability measures, access controls, and administrative and management policy required to provide an acceptable level of protection for hardware, software, and information in a network.

5.7 COMMUNICATIONS SECURITY

Communications security, commonly referred to as COMSEC, is defined as the protective measures taken to deny unauthorized persons access to information that could be derived from communicated information and to ensure the authenticity of these communications. In networks, communications security is the protection of information that is communicated between devices, systems, or users. This protection applies to LANs, metropolitan area networks (MANs), and wide area networks (WANs). All three types of networks may require technically different COMSEC countermeasures to support various media, access technologies, data rates, and degrees of protection.

In most cases, communications security is provided in two forms. The most common form is through the use of encryption. Encryption is very common in networks that communicate information over physically unprotected media. MAN and WAN technology most commonly employ encryption for communications security. In the case of LAN technology, general physical security countermeasures are still the most common type of protection. Basically, the cable plant is physically protected so that unauthorized personnel cannot tap the network and extract information.

5.8 INDUSTRIAL SECURITY

Industrial security embodies the rules, policies, and regulations that contractor and partnering company personnel and organizations must abide by when storing, processing, or otherwise using sensitive information. It is becoming increasingly common for multiple companies to form strategic relationships and leverage their strengths in developing a product, attacking a vertical market segment, or in developing a proposal for a large government procurement. It is also likely that the strategic partnership is established for a particular program or effort and may be disbanded at the end of the defined activity. Moreover, it also may be possible for two or more companies to form a strategic relationship to pursue a certain portion of a marketplace together, but still aggressively compete against one another for the other portions of the market.

In the government marketplace, industrial security refers to the protection of classified or sensitive information in the possession of U.S. industry and encompasses any number of key attributes, including:

- Government regulations
- Facility clearances
- Facility security officer
- Accountability of information maintained in the facility
- Training requirements for users of the information and systems that process the information as well as training directly related to security requirements and guidelines
- Control of all sensitive and classified information
- Periodic government audits by the Defense Investigative Service (DIS)

5.9   OPERATIONS SECURITY

Operations security is the process of denying unauthorized individuals information about capabilities, intentions, and strategies by identifying, controlling, and protecting indicators associated with the planning and conduct of operations and other activities. Elements of operations security protection may include:

- Threat/vulnerability analysis
- A concept of secure network operations
- User/management training and awareness
- Tiger teams to determine actual information that is being potentially communicated by the operations of an organization

5.10   LIFE-CYCLE SECURITY ENGINEERING

As a result of classified processing, the system will be continuously responsible for securing the data and resources of the system. Security must be a continuous and consistent discipline for the system. In addition, there are specific government regulations that require periodic updates to security documentation, risk analysis, reaccreditation, and the like. These activities are required on a recurring basis once a year, every three years, every five years, or when the system experiences major modifications.

5.11 SUMMARY

In this chapter, network security was looked at in the context of the various disciplines that comprise security programs. In the next chapter, the services discussed in the previous chapter and the various disciplines from this chapter are combined into an overall, multi-layered approach to network security, particularly under the ISO/OSI Reference Model.

6

Network Security Approaches and Mechanisms

6.1 INTRODUCTION

In this chapter, we'll focus on the International Standards Organization (ISO) Open Systems Interconnection (OSI) approach to multilevel network security. We'll first take a quick look at the OSI Reference Model,[1] and then see how the various network security services discussed in Chapter 4—and the mechanisms that can be used to deliver those services—apply to the various model layers.

6.2 THE ISO/OSI REFERENCE MODEL

The OSI model began in March 1978 and the seven-layer model was adopted by spring of 1983.[2] Despite these dates of 15 and 10 years ago, respectively, OSI-based networking still has the connotation of the emerging networking standard. Products have been somewhat slow in coming, primarily due to the entrenchment of SNA and DECnet and the use of TCP/IP as a surrogate open systems network foundation, despite a lot of corporate proclamations about "OSI as part of our strategy."

The beginning of the 1990s should see a further increase in products based on the OSI protocols for several reasons:[3]

1. Federal agencies are now required to use a subset of OSI (GOSIP, discussed next).

2. Multinational corporations prefer to use an internationally approved standard for their global networks.

3. OSI compliance and interoperability tests are available, easing the introduction of new products.

There are, however, some downsides to OSI:[4]

1. It sometimes takes too long to translate standards into products (reference the 1978 and 1983 dates discussed previously).

2. There is no compelling reason to switch from the TCP/IP protocols to OSI. Even though TCP/IP is closely coupled with the UNIX operating system, there are many interface mechanisms to PC LANs, SNA, DECnet, and other communications facilities.

3. OSI-compliant products may not even interoperate with one another due to the variety of protocol options available under the OSI umbrella.

The OSI model consists of seven layers. The seven layers of the model were derived according to the following criteria:[5]

1. A new layer should be created when a different level of abstraction from those currently available was needed.

2. Each layer should perform a well-defined function.

3. The function of each layer should be chosen with an eye toward defining internationally standardized protocols.

4. All communications between identical layers of the protocol stack in cooperating systems should occur on a peer-to-peer basis.

5. Layer boundaries should be chosen to minimize information flow across those boundaries.

6. The number of layers should be chosen carefully. The number should be large enough so distinct functions are not grouped together in the same layer out of necessity; it should not be too small as to make the architecture unwieldy.

The seven layers of the OSI Reference Model are shown in Figure 6.1. Let's take a closer look at the various functions among the layers.[6]

Physical Layer—Layer 1

This layer transmits bits over a communication channel. The purpose is to provide a physical connection for data transmission and a facility to activate

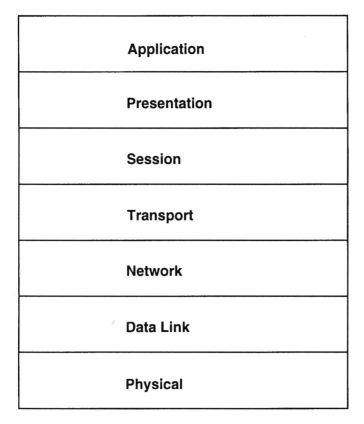

Figure 6.1 OSI Reference Model layers

and deactivate physical connections. The issues dealt with at this level include:

- the number of volts used for "0" and "1" representation
- timing issues
- simultaneous transmission model (full-duplex, half-duplex, simplex)
- the procedures to initialize and terminate physical connections
- pin numbers and assignments

Data Link Layer—Layer 2

We talked about data link layers in conjunction with SNA earlier (SDLC). The data link layer sits above the physical layer and is charged with transmitting data reliably across a physical link. Data is divided into frames, which are transmitted sequentially for regrouping at the recipient.

The data link layer must determine how frame boundaries are designated and recognized, and this can be accomplished through special bit patterns (example: the SDLC "01111110" flag or an STX ASCII character) or some other manner.

Retransmission and duplicate frame management must be handled at this layer. Counters of frames must be maintained. Speed control over messages (e.g., don't send them too fast) is also accomplished. The entire purpose of the data link layer is to give the network layer the impression that an error-free line is present; therefore, problem resolution at this layer is critical.

Network Layer—Layer 3

This layer is responsible for defining how—by what route—information is *routed* from one system to another. This routing may be done by static tables built into the network or, in robust environments, can be dynamically determined due to real-time statistics and other algorithmic information. Bottlenecks must be avoided wherever possible.

There are four sublayers to the network layer:

1. The access sublayer—this provides link services across an interface to the data link layer; no routing is necessary.

2. The intranetwork sublayer—all message routing within networks of a single type is performed here; an example would be in a homogeneous LAN environment.

3. The harmonizing sublayer—this provides harmonization of the intranetwork and internetwork layers.

4. The internetwork sublayer—this is where global message routing across heterogeneous networks is accomplished.

Transport Layer—Layer 4

The transport layer is intended to provide network-independent transport services to the session layer (layer 5). Data is accepted from the session layer, divided into manageable portions, and passed to the network layer, which in turn manages the successful transmission of the data to the recipient(s).

The transport layer is charged with creating the appropriate number of network layer connections, including any necessary multiplexing, subject to parameters such as traffic load.

The transport layer is also responsible for managing the routing of messages in multiprogrammed hosts—those computers running more than one application—and ensuring that messages are sent to the correct application.[7] This requires a name service of some type (the concept is discussed later) through which the sender of a message can specify which recipient is to receive that message.

Transport layer services fall into two general categories:[8]

1. *Connection Management*—these services permit a transport layer user to create and maintain a data path to another transport layer user. The specific services included are:

    a. *Establishment Service*—this provides for the establishment of transport layer connections.

    b. *Close Service*—this provides for an orderly shutdown of transport layer connections.

    c. *Disconnect Service*—this is basically the same as a close service, but data may be lost.

    d. *Status Service*—this informs the user about the status of any transport layer connection.

2. *Data Transfer Services*—these services are used actually to exchange information among the participants in a transport layer connection. These include:

    a. *Data (Normal) Service*—this permits a user to transfer data under normal circumstances.

    b. *Expedited (Urgent) Service*—a limited amount of data may be transferred outside of the normal data stream.

    c. *Unit Service*—this permits the transfer of data without first establishing a transport layer service.

Session Layer—Layer 5

The session layer is where the user interfaces with the network. Negotiations must be undertaken to establish a connection with another machine. Once that connection has been established, dialog can be managed in an orderly manner.

The term "session" is used to define a connection between two users. Examples of sessions include remote log-ins (such as TELNET in the DDN protocol set) and file transfer (such as using FTP in the DDN suite).

Session addresses are different than those that apply to the transport layer, so an address conversion scheme must be used to ensure that a requested communication with another user is translated into the correct transport address. Additionally, high-level message control is done at the session layer (above that done at the packet formation level) to support data integrity, message ordering, and similar functions.

Presentation Layer—Layer 6

The presentation layer includes facilities for such application-oriented functions as data value representation, data structure management, and abstract syntax notation. The OSI Reference Model provides no generalized specifications for the detailed implementation of these facilities; rather, it simply recommends that such functions be performed at the presentation layer.

Application Layer—Layer 7

The application layer contains application entities that employ application protocols and presentation services to exchange information; that is, such functions as application-to-application communications facilities are handled at the application layer.[9] Enterprise architectures can establish a formal set of these guidelines based on remote procedure calls (RPCs), messaging, or other guidelines, and these can be implemented.

At different levels, a variety of protocols may exist. Some may be *connection-oriented*—that is, a formal logical connection is established before some data transfer occurs and information about communications partners is maintained and controlled—and others are *connectionless*, where data are transferred on sort of a one-shot deal approach without the need formally to establish a relationship.[10]

6.3 NETWORK SECURITY SERVICES REVISITED

As part of the formal specification of the OSI Reference Model, a set of security services—indeed, an entire security architecture—is defined. As part of the security architecture specification document a set of services is listed.[11] These services—which were discussed at length in Chapter 4—include:[12]

- Authentication—These services are provided to authenticate some peer entity and the source of data. Peer entity authentication provides corroboration that a peer entity in some association is the one claimed. Data origin authentication provides corroboration that the source of data is the entity the source is claimed to be.

- Access control—These services ensure that there is no unauthorized use of OSI-accessible resources (whether those resources are OSI-based or non-OSI but accessible via OSI protocols).

- Confidentiality—There are several types of confidentiality services, including: connection confidentiality, where OSI connections (recall our earlier discussion of connection-oriented and connectionless protocols) are protected; connectionless confidentiality, the same types of services for connectionless communications; selective field confidentiality, where selected fields within some user data are protected on either connection-oriented or connectionless communications; and traffic flow confidentiality, which protects against information that may be derived from observation of traffic flow (see our discussion of covert channels in Chapter 9).

- Data integrity services—These services are used to counter active threats in a variety of modes: connection integrity with recovery, connection integrity without recovery, selective field connection integrity, connectionless integrity, and selection field connectionless integrity.

- Nonrepudiation services—These services may be of two types: nonrepudiation with proof of origin, where the recipient of some data is provided with proof of the data origin as protection against the sender's false denial of sending the data, and nonrepudiation with proof of delivery, which provides the data sender with proof of delivery (and, therefore, protects against false denials of never having received the data).

6.4 NETWORK SECURITY MECHANISMS

The various services discussed in the previous section may be viewed as generic in nature; that is, they are necessary and, as we shall see, apply to various OSI Reference Model layers.

A network security approach must go beyond the generic consideration of security services, though, and the OSI security architecture document also includes definitions of mechanisms by which the various services may be delivered. Let's take a brief look at the various mechanisms.[13] Some of these services are incorporated into one or more appropriate model layers in a formal sense, while other services are considered to be pervasive security mechanisms—that is, they aren't specific to any particular service nor are they explicitly defined as being in any particular layer but rather pervade the overall security approach.

Specific Security Mechanisms

Figure 6.2 lists the various security mechanisms. Let's look at each type individually.

The first mechanism is *encipherment*, which provides confidentiality of either data or traffic flow information. There are two types of encipherment algorithms. The first type—reversible algorithms—are either symmetric in nature (example: knowledge of the encipherment key implies knowledge of the decipherment key) or asymmetric (example: public key encipherment, where knowledge of the encipherment key does not imply knowledge of that used for decipherment).

The second type of encipherment algorithms—irreversible ones—may or may not use keys and, when keys are used, they may be either public or private.

Digital signature mechanisms are used to define two procedures: signing some data unit and verifying a signature on a data unit.

Access control mechanisms are used to ensure that an entity neither accesses some resource that is unauthorized nor accesses an authorized resource in an unauthorized manner. The access control may be accomplished through mechanisms such as access control lists (Chapter 4), authentication information such as passwords, security labels, timing and routing information, or duration of access information. Access control mechanisms may be applied at either end of some communications association, at some intermediate point, or any appropriate combination of the above.

- Encipherment
- Digital Signature Mechanisms
- Access Control Mechanisms
- Data Integrity Mechansims
- Authentication Exchange Mechanisms
- Traffic-Padding Mechanisms
- Routing Control Mechanisms
- Notarization

Figure 6.2 Specific security mechanisms of the OSI security architecture

Data integrity mechanisms are used to ensure the integrity of a single data unit or field within that data unit. Alternatively, the integrity of a stream of data units or fields may fall under the control of the integrity mechanism. In the case of a single data unit, some quantity that is a function of the data itself is appended by the sending entity to the data unit and is checked by the recipient against a corresponding quantity generated at that end. This is basically the same as a checksum orientation, though the checksum (or block check code) may itself be enciphered as an additional layer of protection. Streams of data units typically require additional control such as sequence numbering or time stamping.

Authentication exchange mechanisms are used to provide authentication services through some type of information exchange (example: passwords, cryptographic techniques, or some "possessions").

Traffic-padding mechanisms are used to provide protection against traffic analysis and the traffic padding must be protected by a confidentiality service.

Routing control mechanisms are used either to choose routes dynamically or by some prearrangement that uses only physically secure subnets and links. Among the components may be instructions that data carrying certain security labels be forbidden to pass through specified subnets, relays, or links because of suspected or documented compromises.

Finally, *notarization* mechanisms are provided by a third-party notary that ensure various communications properties (such as origin, time, and destination) between two or more entities.

Pervasive Security Mechanisms

Figure 6.3 lists those security mechanisms which, as we mentioned earlier, are pervasive to the entire principle of network security and therefore don't apply to a specific service or implementing layer.

These include:

- Trusted functionality, a general concept that specifies that any functionality used directly to provide or to provide access to security mechanisms itself be trustworthy.

- Security labels, such as those used to specify the security level of a particular data unit.

- Trusted Functionality
- Security Labels
- Event Detection
- Security Audit Trail
- Security Recovery

Figure 6.3 Pervasive security mechanism in the OSI security architecture

- Event detection, which specifies that apparent violations of security as well as possibly normal events (such as log-ons, log-offs, accesses to specified resources, etc.) be detected, logged, and possibly reported. Additionally, appropriate recovery action must be part of the event handling system.

- Security audit trail, which is used within independent reviews and examinations (audits) of a given system or an entire enterprise.

- Security recovery, which specifies that recovery actions be applied as necessary according to specified rules. There are three types of recovery actions: immediate, temporary, and long term. Immediate actions—such as disconnecting a security policy violator—immediately abort some operation. Temporary actions tag some entity as temporarily invalidated. Long-term actions may include placing some entity into a security violator black list or changing some key.

6.5 LAYERING AND PLACEMENT OF NETWORK SECURITY SERVICES AND MECHANISMS

So far, we've discussed security services and mechanisms within the framework of the OSI Reference Model security architecture. How do these two classes of items relate to one another?

Figure 6.4 illustrates the "appropriateness" of the various OSI security services against the specific mechanisms discussed.[14] Remember that the pervasive security mechanisms apply to multiple layers and multiple services and therefore aren't included in Figure 6.4 because of their pervasive, automatically included nature.

Now, on to the layered approach. As we discussed above, the OSI Reference Model is built on a seven-layer model. In this section, let's take a look

	Encipherment	Digital Signature	Access Control	Data Integrity	Authentication Exchange	Traffic Padding	Routing Control	Notarization
Peer Entity Authentication	√	√			√			
Data Origin Authentication	√	√						
Access Control Service			√					
Connection Confidentiality	√						√	
Connectionless Confidentiality	√						√	
Selective Field Confidentiality	√							
Traffic Flow Confidentiality	√					√	√	
Connection Integrity with Recovery	√			√				
Connection Integrity without Recovery	√			√				
Selective Field Connection Integrity	√			√				
Connectionless Integrity	√	√		√				
Selective Field Connectionless Integrity	√	√		√				
Nonrepudiation, Origin		√		√				√
Nonrepudiation, Delivery		√		√				√

Figure 6.4 OSI Reference Model: security services and mechanisms cross-reference

at which of the various services and mechanisms discussed in the earlier sections of this chapter—and elsewhere throughout this book—are applicable to the various layers.

Physical Layer

The objectives of physical layer security are to protect the entire physical service data bit stream and to provide traffic flow confidentiality. Services include connection confidentiality and/or traffic flow confidentiality. Traffic flow confidentiality services may be used on a full basis for various types of transmissions (e.g., synchronous) while limited traffic flow confidentiality may be applied to asynchronous transmission. These services may be applied to either point-to-point communications or multipeer communications and are restricted to passive threats.

The primary mechanism that applies to the physical layer to implement these services is total encipherment of the data stream.

Data Link Layer

Either of two types of security services are applicable to the data link layer: connection confidentiality or connectionless confidentiality. Encipherment is used to provide these services, which brings up an interesting point. We mentioned in the previous section that encipherment is also used for physical link security. The OSI security architecture document includes an annex that describes the selection process of choosing the exact position(s) of applications' encipherment.[15] Most applications don't require encipherment to be used at more than one level, and therefore an appropriate level must be selected.

The guidelines include the following points:

1. Physical layer encipherment is used when full traffic flow confidentiality is required. Adequate physical security and trusted routing (along with those attributes at relays) can satisfy confidentiality requirements.

2. For cases when a high granularity of protection is required (example: separate keys for each application presentation) *and* nonrepudiation or selective field protection is also required, then encipherment should occur at the presentation layer. This will allow for integrity without recovery, nonrepudiation, and all confidentiality.

3. When all end system-to-end system communications need bulk protection and/or an external encipherment device is desirable, then network layer encipherment should be selected.

4. When integrity with recovery is required along with a high granularity of protection, then encipherment should be done at the transport level.

5. "Encipherment at the data link layer is not recommended for future implementations."[16] (Contrast this statement, a direct quote, with the specifications for encipherment as the only mechanism used to provide data link layer security services. Clearly, the encipherment should occur elsewhere.)

Network Layer

The following security services may be provided within the context of the OSI network service:

- Peer entity authentication
- Data origin authentication
- Access control service
- Connection confidentiality
- Connectionless confidentiality
- Traffic flow confidentiality
- Connection integrity without recovery
- Connectionless integrity

The mechanisms used to provide these services can include:

- Cryptographically derived or protected authentication exchanges, protected password exchange, and signature mechanisms (for peer entity authentication)
- Encipherment or signature mechanisms (for data origin authentication)
- Access control mechanisms (for access control service)
- Encipherment and/or routing control (for both connection and connectionless confidentiality services)
- Traffic-padding mechanisms in conjunction with a confidentiality service at or below the network layer and/or routing control (for traffic flow confidentiality service)
- Data integrity mechanism, possibly in connection with encipherment (for both the connection integrity without recovery service and the connectionless integrity service)

Transport Layer

Services at the transport layer include:

- Peer entity authentication
- Data origin authentication
- Access control service
- Connection confidentiality
- Connectionless confidentiality
- Connection integrity with recovery

- Connection integrity without recovery
- Connectionless integrity

Since the only additional service beyond the network layer is that of connection integrity with recovery (traded for traffic flow confidentiality), and the mechanisms used for the other seven common services are the same as we discussed in the previous section, we'll mention only the mechanisms for connection integrity with recovery, which are the same as that of connection integrity without recovery (data integrity mechanism possibly in conjunction with encipherment).

Session Layer

No security services are provided within the session layer (and, therefore, no security mechanisms apply).

Presentation Layer

There are three services applicable to the presentation layer that are mandatory:

- Connection confidentiality
- Connectionless confidentiality
- Selective field confidentiality

Additionally, the following other services may be provided:

- Traffic flow confidentiality
- Peer entity authentication
- Data origin authentication
- Connection integrity with recovery
- Connection integrity without recovery
- Selective field connection integrity
- Connectionless integrity
- Selective field connectionless integrity
- Nonrepudiation with proof of origin
- Nonrepudiation with proof of delivery

The various security mechanisms (which also may be used in conjunction with those of the application layer) include:

- Syntactic transformation mechanisms such as encipherment for peer entity authentication

- Encipherment or signature for data origin authentication
- Encipherment for both connection and connectionless confidentiality
- Encipherment (again) for both selective field confidentiality and traffic flow confidentiality services
- Data integrity and possibly encipherment for the following services: connection integrity with recovery, connection integrity without recovery, selective field connection integrity, connectionless integrity, and selective field connectionless integrity service.
- An appropriate combination of data integrity, signature, and notarization mechanisms used for the two types of nonrepudiation services (proof of delivery and proof of origin).

Application Layer

The services include:

- Peer entity authentication
- Data origin authentication
- Access control
- Connection confidentiality
- Connectionless confidentiality
- Selective field confidentiality
- Traffic flow confidentiality
- Connection integrity with recovery
- Connection integrity without recovery
- Selective field connection integrity
- Connectionless integrity
- Selective field connectionless integrity
- Nonrepudiation with proof of origin
- Nonrepudiation with proof of delivery

The mechanisms used to provide these particular services include:

- Authentication information transferred between application entities, protected by presentation or lower-layer encipherment, for peer entity authentication
- Signature or lower-layer encipherment for data origin authentication
- Access control mechanisms in the application and lower layers for access control service

- Lower-layer encipherment for either connection or connectionless confidentiality

- Presentation layer encipherment for selective field confidentiality

- Traffic padding at the application layer in conjunction with a lower-layer confidentiality service for a limited traffic flow confidentiality service

- Lower-layer data integrity possibly in conjunction with encipherment for both connection integrity service types (with and without recovery) as well as connectionless integrity service

- Presentation layer data integrity possibly in conjunction with encipherment for selective field connection integrity and for selective field connectionless integrity

- Signature and lower-layer data integrity mechanisms, possibly in conjunction with third-party notaries, for both types of nonrepudiation services

Figure 6.5 summarizes the information from this section with respect to the services and their appropriateness to the various layers.[17]

6.6 AN EXAMPLE OF A NETWORK SECURITY IMPLEMENTATION

Let's take a brief look at an example of a network security implementation for a specific application: in this case, the X.400 electronic mail standard (1988 version of the message handling system, or MHS).

First, here's some brief background on the terminology used within X.400.[18] An X.400 environment consists of:

1. MHS users—These are actually external to the MHS environment and represent either a person or some application that originates and receives messages.

2. User agents (UAs)—UAs act on behalf of users, executing the desired messaging function. There is one UA for every user of the X.400 MHS.

3. Message stores (MS)—Message stores were added in the 1988 model, with the responsibility of providing for "short-term, stable storage of messages received . . . probably the single most significant enhancement over the 1984 MHS architecture."[19] The UAs can use MS facilities to control how messages are retrieved for users, and the P7

Layer

	1	2	3	4	5	6	7
Peer Entity Authentication			√	√			√
Data Origin Authentication			√	√			√
Access Control Service			√	√			√
Connection Confidentiality	√	√	√	√			√
Connectionless Confidentiality		√	√	√			√
Selective Field Confidentiality							√
Traffic Flow Confidentiality	√		√				√
Connection Integrity with Recovery				√			√
Connection Integrity without Recovery			√	√			√
Selective Field Connection Integrity							√
Connectionless Integrity			√	√			√
Selective Field Connectionless Integrity							√
Nonrepudiation, Origin							√
Nonrepudiation, Delivery							√

Figure 6.5 OSI security architecture: services and layers cross-reference

protocol (discussed later) was added to enable communications between UAs and MSs.

4. Access units (AUs)—Also added in 1988, an AU is used for access to MHS services by indirect users (those from some other type of communication system).

5. The message transfer system (MTS)—The MTS is the guts of the MHS and contains message transfer agents (MTAs), which are discussed in more detail later.

X.400 security is based on the X.509 authentication framework (part of the X.500 directory services standards). Within X.509 there is support for asymmetric encryption that is used for both peer-to-peer authentication as well as digital signatures.

The directory stores certified public keys of MHS users. The keys are stored in the form of encrypted certificates. Three basic security services are used by all application layer OSI services, including X.400 electronic mail services. These security services include:

- Simple authentication, which, even though it is the least secure authentication form, is often sufficient for many environments. There are three different options within X.509 for simple authentication, ranging from unenciphered user name and password transmission (the least secure) to the transfer of a secure token, which is protected by two different hash functions (the most secure—the intermediate type—uses only one hash function).

- Strong authentication, which uses asymmetric public key encryption key techniques such as RSA (described elsewhere in the book)—RSA isn't specifically named, but is heavily implied.

- Digital signatures (also described elsewhere in the book).

Within the X.400 environment, there are various security services specified. These are:

- Security labels, which are used to classify all types of electronic mail (messages, probes—which are queries as to status information—and other types). The various attributes of the labels are defined (policy identifier, classification, privacy mark, and security categories).

- Message origin authentication service, which enables a recipient to verify the origin of the message's originator

- Proof of submission service, which allows the submitter to verify that a message was submitted to the message transfer system

- Proof of delivery service

- Secure access management service, which provides authentication between peer entities for the balance of an exchange

- Content integrity service, which is used to verify that the original content of a message hasn't been altered or otherwise corrupted

- Content confidentiality service, which is used to prevent unauthorized disclosure

- Message sequence integrity service, which verifies that the original message sequence still has been maintained

- Nonrepudiation services discussed earlier (proof of delivery and proof of origin) plus another: proof of submission

- Message security labeling service, which is used to categorize messages for conditional or varying handling
- Double enveloping, which enables a message to be completely embedded within the body of another

6.7   SUMMARY

In this chapter, network security mechanisms have been examined in the context of the OSI Reference Model. As noted, a security architecture consists of both services and the various mechanisms through which those services are provided. Because of the widely accepted layered approach to networks and communications, certain types of services are applicable to certain levels but not necessarily to others. As in the case of the X.400 security architecture, an application (including a system application, such as electronic mail) may pick and choose among the various service types at the different layers to provide appropriate levels of security (including various options, depending on how stringent security must be) for users.

END NOTES

1. James F. Doar, "An Overview of Standards and Protocols," *Open Systems Interconnection Handbook*, Gary McClain, ed. (New York: Intertext/McGraw-Hill), 1993, 6.
2. Dennis Livingston, "Here Comes OSI . . . Sort of," *Systems Integration* (September 1991): 43.
3. Ibid.
4. Doar, op. cit., 6–7.
5. Ibid., 7–14.
6. Ibid., 10.
7. Ibid.
8. Ibid., 13.
9. Alan R. Simon, *Implementing the Enterprise* (New York: Bantam Books/Intertext), 1993, 81–82.
10. International Standards Organization, *Information Processing Systems—Open Systems Interconnection—Basic Reference Model, Part 2: Security Architecture* (ISO/IEC 7498-2), February 15, 1989.
11. Ibid., 4–5.

12. Ibid., 5–8.

13. Ibid., 9.

14. Ibid., 2.

15. Ibid., 16. Note: A breakdown of services applicable to connection mode communications and those for connectionless mode communications may be found in Adrian Tang and Sophia Scoggins, *Open Networking with OSI* (Englewood Cliffs, NJ: Prentice Hall), 1992, 56. Some services, such as peer entity authentication, apply only to connection mode while others (data origin authentication, for example) are used only for connectionless mode communications. Others, such as the two types of nonrepudiation services, apply to both modes.

16. Ibid.

17. Ibid.

18. Sara Radicati, *Electronic Mail: An Introduction to the X.400 Message Handling Standards* (New York: McGraw-Hill), 1992, Chapter 9.

19. Ibid., 110.

7

Personal Computer Networking—Security Issues and Approaches

7.1   INTRODUCTION—THE PC NETWORKING REVOLUTION

With the advent of PCs and local area networking came dramatic reductions in the cost of information processing. These cost reductions were substantial when compared with similar processing capabilities provided by large mainframe computer systems or even departmentalized minicomputers. Cost reductions have been accompanied by unwanted decentralization of control and structure within organizations. Loss of control has been one of the most difficult human and emotional issues during this information revolution.

During the 1980s, many organizations lost complete control over the development of software applications resulting from the substantial development of applications by end users on their PCs and/or workstations. Since most users had little or no formal training, the majority of the applications were developed ad hoc and without such proven methods as structured programming and top-down design. In addition, many of these applications were developed for personal gain or enjoyment, thereby reducing the level of productivity actually achieved by the employee. While most organizations were realizing a substantial cost savings in the actual cost to develop applications, by the end of 1980s, they were also realizing a substantial increase in cost to manage and maintain those applications. The situation was complicated further by the diversity of applications. Mainframe applications, minicomputer applications, and applications developed for the PCs all existed, but were not designed to interoperate or coexist with one another.

Today, organizations are attempting to migrate to an enterprise-wide network computing environment requiring much tighter integration and use of standards across all information resources in the corporation. This migration or transition is being achieved through the use of open system standards such as the UNIX operating system (some with POSIX extensions), TCP/IP protocols, SQL, and other standards that enable applications to coexist and operate in harmony. Applications are now being developed using defined structure and interface specifications such as standard libraries (i.e., Sybase public and open libraries for relational database development) and common application programmer interfaces (APIs).

It is possible that a department may still own its own network, applications, and data processing personnel resources; however, the information that is developed, maintained, manipulated, and managed by that department must be accessible by other authorized users within the organization. The ability to share information and knowledge effectively and quickly will continue to be an increasingly important competitive factor in the information age. As we are seeing currently in both the commercial sector and in government, the rightsizing or downsizing of organizations is occurring at a very rapid pace. This organizational transition is fundamental and is a step the United States must take to remain economically viable in a world economy. This transition is both painful and very necessary. In most cases, the middle management within an organization is being removed, retrained, or otherwise asked to do other job functions. This is the most common form of rightsizing today.

In the past, these middle managers served a very useful purpose in taking information from the workers and passing that information up to top management. The information flow was most always only in one direction: up. Today, rapid and effective knowledge sharing, both vertically (up and down) and horizontally (across organizational elements) is at the heart of the competitive and successful organization. The question is how are the functions of communications that have been supported for many years by middle management being provided? The answer is through an information infrastructure. The information infrastructure is enabling organizations to rightsize and flatten and provides the ability to communicate information effectively both vertically and horizontally. Such an information infrastructure is based on open system standards and embraces leading-edge processing strategies such as client/server computing. PC networking is fundamental and key to this entire organizational transition process and technology movement.

For many years, data security was controlled in the mainframe environment, where it could be easily controlled by the operating system and operating system security utilities in conjunction with the application. In addition, nearly all of the responsibility for physical and data security rested in the arms of the data processing department or a specifically defined group of security engineering professionals. In today's distributed processing environment, information can be manipulated and processed across multiple platforms. This processing paradigm and capability has prevented the data processing department from maintaining security. From the very beginning, the PC and its operating system were designed for a single user on a stand-alone system. As a result, the need for security was minimal and usually neglected. Simple security schemes were employed, such as physical security (i.e., locks on doors preventing access to the PCs), and this level of protection was considered adequate.

When LAN technology became popular and accepted as a proven business technology, many user-developed applications were transitioned from PCs to shared file servers and bulletin boards, which enabled access by multiple users across an entire enterprise. The vast majority of these applications were not designed with security in mind. As a result, network administrators relied heavily on the security services and capabilities provided by PC network operating systems (NOS) and other PC-capable add-on security software packages. Common network operating systems can include Novell's NetWare, Banyan VINES, LAN Manager by Microsoft, and the Network File System (NFS), which is used most commonly in UNIX environments. In most cases, individuals serving in the capacity of network administrators were familiar with PCs but not with NOS security features or deficiencies. NOS were also very limited in their application of security. For example, standard NOS security provided protection only at the file level and did not provide protection down to the field level within a file. This required a complete redesign/reengineering of those applications, which proved to be quite costly.

Substantial effort has been focused on securing centralized, mainframe computer systems; however, very little effort and investment has been made to secure PCs. For the most part, PCs have been designed and developed without much (or any) consideration for network security. There are also other contributing factors to the lack of effort/investment in securing microcomputers. First, it is very important to understand that if it were a straightforward process to secure microcomputers, there would have been many vendors investing lots of money in providing the necessary security. This is obviously not the case. In fact, because of the advent of MS-DOS, the ability to secure MS-DOS–based machines is extremely difficult. Given the sheer density of the MS-DOS operating system market and market penetration that continues, it is unlikely that we will see any major advancement in the near future.

In the very early years, PCs were developed with the thought of being a single-user system rather than a shared or networked computing resource. In this context, PCs were designed and deployed with good intentions. Times and computing have changed dramatically, and this has had a tremendous impact on PC security and one's ability to secure PC networks. As a result, vulnerabilities exist that can threaten the integrity, confidentiality, or availability of PC networks and the information they store, process, communicate, and manage. Other operating systems provide promise of securing the local PC environment. Examples include Microsoft multiprocessing NT operating system and Sun's latest UNIX operating system: Solaris—which sports a true easy-to-use user interface.

Many of these common problems can be minimized through a focused and well-integrated network security strategy that is supported from all affected elements of the organization. If common objectives and policies are defined, and, more importantly, embraced, network security can be integrated effectively into the overall enterprise-wide information infrastructure instead of being force-fitted as an afterthought. The development of a comprehensive network security policy is the critical first step in providing effective and consistent protection for information and networking assets.

7.2 PRACTICAL GUIDANCE FOR PC NETWORKING

Before elaborate security concerns are even considered, it is appropriate and well worth the time to investigate PC security fundamentals. These fundamentals include such issues as physical access to PCs, network access, and general protections.

7.3 PC PHYSICAL SECURITY CONCERNS

If possible, it is strongly recommended to restrict physically access to PCs to only those individuals who have a valid need to access the PCs and require access to them to conduct their job or business function. It is common for users who are either untrained or malicious to use PCs for purposes for which they are not intended. It is recommended that PC components and software be protected so that they cannot be easily stolen. PCs can be protected by securing the rooms where they are located and also by securing them physically to tables or work areas so that special tools are required to remove them from the premises.

Electrical phenomena are an important consideration. Static electricity can damage PC components. Consider the use of special carpets, pads, and antistatic sprays. Eating and smoking should be restricted from areas where PCs are used. Such activities can have detrimental effects on the performance and longevity of the PCs. Surge protectors should be used to minimize the risks associated with power surges, lightning, and other quality of power issues. It is also recommended that PCs be powered from a source isolated from heavy appliances or office systems.

The protection of magnetic media for PCs is very important given that the vast majority of data storage is still accomplished via magnetic media. Floppy disks should always be protected through the use of protective jackets, gentle handling (i.e., not bending), storage within acceptable temperature ranges of 50–120 degrees Fahrenheit, and other common-sense methods. Devices and network components that contain hard disk drives should be handled with care and treated gently. Floppy disks that contain sensitive or classified information should be treated with caution. Common methods for removing sensitive information from magnetic media include degaussing, overwriting numerous times, reuse of media, or destroying through burning or shredding. Care should be taken to ensure that damaged magnetic storage devices are not serviced or returned to a vendor until they are properly degaussed or otherwise removed of the sensitive information. Many PC erase commands do not actually erase files and the intended information. For example, the DOS erase command performs only a logical erase function through erasing the file name and erasing sector pointers in the file allocation table. The actual, potentially very sensitive information remains unchanged until the specific portion is reused. As a result, logically erased files can be easily recovered through the use of special utility application programs such as the Norton Utilities.

7.4 IDENTIFICATION AND AUTHENTICATION— NETWORK OPERATING SYSTEMS

Novell's NetWare and Banyan VINES are explored in the remainder of this section due to their overwhelming dominance in the PC networking environment today. Both network operating systems provide some degree of server-based security features and functionality.[1,2]

Passwords

The first line of defense for the organization at the NOS level is the use of user IDs and passwords. User IDs and passwords are very commonly mismanaged; however, there are no technical reasons for this to occur. If properly managed, NOS user IDs and passwords provide a solid protection for information stored and maintained on network file servers and PCs. The two most common NOSs, Novell's NetWare and Banyan VINES, provide several options that promote the effective management of user IDs and passwords. Nevertheless, most of the features and possibly all of them are disabled when the software is installed and configured for operation. Unlike many operating systems, neither NetWare nor VINES can generate passwords on behalf of users or require a specific format for the passwords; however, both provide the capability to force users to change their passwords at predetermined time intervals (i.e., once every 30 days). Both NetWare and VINES can be used to require a minimum length for a password. NetWare has a default password length of five characters, but the default for VINES has no minimum. As a result, users of VINES networks could select passwords one character in length, making the penetration of such networks very easy to accomplish. Again, the issue becomes the proper management of NOS passwords schemes.

The most effective application of user IDs and passwords provides the capability for users to change their own passwords. In situations where network/systems administrators have attempted to centralize the control of establishing and maintaining user IDs and passwords, excessive support calls from users and wasted time are experienced. Users are more aware of potential compromises or unusual events and developments with the data and information with which they work on a daily basis. As a result, users are much more in tune with when and how often their passwords should be changed. Since user IDs and passwords are universally the first line of defense in networks today, it is very important that NOS capabilities and functions associated with this protection be continuously invoked.

Both NetWare and VINES allow voluntary password changes and mandatory password expiration. The responsibility for changing passwords defaults to the user, not the network or system administrator. It is recommended that the user's password be kept secret, even from the network/systems administrator. Each user password should be unique and there is no valid reason for anyone to know any user's password. This is the fundamental reason why network operating systems never display user passwords to the network/systems administrator. This is also the reason why computer operating systems provide one-way password encryption as a very common feature for password protection. Nevertheless, it is very common to find network/systems administrators who maintain an active list of all user passwords. The excuse is commonly made by the administrator that he or she must maintain user passwords in case a user forgets his or her password or in the event that specific user files are required for immediate access for other purposes.

These situations can be easily remedied by putting the responsibility for these actions on the shoulders of the users. If a user forgets his or her password, the network/systems administrator can simply assign the user a new password. In these instances, the user should be forced to change the password the first time he or she logs on. Users must also ensure that files that should be accessible by multiple users be set up for general access by those users. Group access can be granted to files based on workgroup activity, department, or project. It is important that the user who creates the file be the one held responsible for its protection.

In NetWare, when a network/systems administrator sets a password on an account that requires periodic password changes, the new password is immediately marked as expired, and the user is prompted to change it as soon as he or she first logs on. In VINES, the network/systems administrator must activate one-time passwords when creating the user's profile.

Users should change passwords periodically because the longer a password is used the more likely it is to be compromised. The NOS should ensure that the users are not permitted to simply use the same passwords again when requested to change their passwords based on a predetermined period of time. NetWare can be configured to preclude users from utilizing their eight previous passwords. VINES is even more restrictive by precluding users from utilizing their previous ten passwords, and this feature cannot be turned off, but rather is a de facto security default.

In order to minimize damage, network operating systems should provide the capability to limit the number of inaccurate logon attempts. In Novell's Netware, the LAN administrator can configure the NOS with the number of log-on attempts before the would-be intruder is locked out of the system. The network/systems administrator also has the ability to define the number of minutes, hours, or days that the specific user ID will be locked out of the system. Given that such a restriction could adversely impact authorized uses, it is important to provide enough room for normal mistakes in typing and general log-on procedures to be tolerated. In Banyan VINES, the number of inaccurate log-ons permitted before lockout is set at five. The problem, however, is that this feature can easily be defeated by simply rebooting the PC and trying again. These features do a very effective job against the common threat of a brute force penetration attack.

Before such capabilities existed, it was very common for would-be intruders to write/code simple log-on programs that would attempt hundreds or thousands of log-ons to a network or computer system using commonly used passwords and known user IDs. This penetration technique, which was quite common and successful for a number of years, can be minimized today through the capabilities of lockout and user ID restriction capabilities. Another effective approach for automated user ID/password penetration techniques is to increase the log-on time for every inaccurate log-on attempt. For example, if the first three log-on attempts are inaccurate, then the time between the user ID prompt and the password prompt can be increased. A simple algorithm of doubling the time between each log-on attempt has worked well for many networks. This approach has also been very effective in finding and exposing dial-in network intruders who let their automated systems and penetration programs do the dirty work in their absence.

In a network environment, it is quite possible that numerous and different password management schemes will exist. This results from the fact that numerous systems may exist in a network, including multiple network operating systems, multiple operating systems, and multiple application security measures. The ability to control access to network resources for all users can become a very challenging management task. Fortunately, network operating systems provide default user profiles. These default user profiles can be tailored to reflect the access control policy for the organization. When organizational access control policies exist, it is possible to develop and implement common user profiles across the organization. An established access control policy facilitates consistency and allows a common approach to be leveraged and managed across the organization.

When organizations do not take the time to establish access control policies, policy is normally established by each division or multiple communities of interest within each organizational division. In addition, a standard approach to access control allows the network/systems administrator to develop user profiles and replicate those profiles for other users with similar requirements. This allows the network/systems administrator to maximize his or her time more effectively. Most importantly, the use of a standard access control policy enables the network/systems administrator to manage the upkeep of overall network security access controls better. It is normal to find a common set of user profiles reflected in any given organization. This occurs because certain groups of individuals within an organization require similar access to information. As a result, common workgroup profiles can be developed and replicated for users.

When additional users are added to the network within the functionally defined workgroup, the network/systems administrator need only replicate the profile and add the user to the system. For example, the profile for the sales division within an organization can be established to restrict the display of certain information to certain workstations on the network. As networks grow in size and scope, the network/systems administrator, having established user and workgroup access control profiles, is in a much better position to effectively manage the access control policy of the organization. In addition, the network/systems administrator is much better prepared to delegate security management responsibilities to individuals within certain workgroups once workgroup security profiles are established. These individuals could be delegated the responsibility for adding and deleting users within the workgroup and for day-to-day general maintenance of the workgroup security controls, such as reestablishing passwords forgotten by users in the workgroup. These individuals most likely should not be delegated the responsibility for the modification of user or workgroup profiles.

Mandatory Access Controls

MACs are defined as part of the overall organizational, workgroup, and user access control policies. Mandatory access control implies those controls that cannot be changed or affected by users on the network. MAC policy is static for at least a defined period of time. MAC policy is enforced by the network/systems administrator and not by users.

Discretionary Access Controls

Unlike MAC policy enforcement, DACs are defined and enforced by users. Simply stated, the access to information, applications, and files created by a user is at the discretion of the user. DAC enables users who create information or have direct responsibility for information to define who can access the information. Users who establish DAC for their data are assumed to be authorized to access the network and to define access to the information that they have direct responsibility for. The ability for network users to define and enforce who can access certain information creates the most fundamental vulnerability of networks today.

Numerous studies have indicated that between 70 and 85 percent of all network security penetrations are caused by authorized users who possess legitimate access to the network. For this reason, it is important that users make informed decisions concerning which users are allowed to access their information and files and what actions those users are allowed to take with the information. The most difficult challenge in network security today is how to control and minimize the damage caused by authorized network users. Additional studies indicate unanimous evidence that most network security incidents are caused by user errors (i.e., unintentional or accidental user actions).

Using NOS features, DAC can be implemented by using directory and file access rights and attributes. Novell's NetWare and Banyan VINES NOS security attributes are unrelated and unique to MS-DOS file attributes. This characteristic is very important when dealing with computer viruses. Many computer viruses have been specifically designed to modify MS-DOS file attributes, but have not been successful to date in modifying NOS file or directory attributes.

Novell NetWare File and Directory Security

NetWare possesses two levels of security for the file and directory levels. The first level of security in NetWare is known as trustee security. For trustee security, the user or workgroup is given certain rights in a given directory. These rights include:

Rights	Description
Read	Right to read/review contents of an open file
Write	Right to modify the contents of an open file
Open	Right to open a file
Create	Right to create a file
Delete	Right to delete a file
Parental	Right to create, rename, or delete subdirectories if the user has create, modify, and delete rights. User can also assign other users to the directory and assign restrictions.
Search	Right to list files in a directory. Without this right, the directory will be displayed to the user as empty.
Modify	Right to modify the read/write attributes of a file and rename directories and files

Normally, users are given a specific subset of these rights. The network/systems administrator, however, can retain the option of restricting one or more of the trustee's rights in the directory. In such a case, no user would be assigned the right. For example, the network/systems administrator may want to enable users to write to files but not to delete them. Much like user and workgroup profiles, the profiles defined for rights will follow a similar consistent application, which easily can be replicated based on the needs and security requirements of specific groups of individuals in an organization.

The second level of file/directory protection available in NetWare is attributes. The network/systems administrator or the owner of the information can mark individual files with the following attributes:

Attribute	Description
Execute-only	Prevents executable files from being copied or modified
Read-only	Prevents a file from being modified
Nonsharable	Only one user at a time can use the file
Normal	Indicates a file that is nonsharable and read-write
Hidden-system	Prevents a file from appearing on a listing

Banyan VINES File and Directory Security

Banyan VINES provides only two attributes at the file level: the execution and sharing attributes. At the directory level, VINES controls access to files by assigning an access rights list (ARL) to every directory. Each ARL can contain different access-level characteristics. VINES provides the following four levels of access:

Attribute	Description
Control	Users can control access rights for directories and subdirectories. Users can create, delete, modify, and read files and subdirectories.
Modify	Users can control access rights on subdirectories, but not to the directory itself. Users can read, create, delete, and modify files and directories.
Read	Users can read and copy files and subdirectories contained in a directory.

Attribute	*Description*
Null	Users do not have any rights or privileges with files or subdirectories contained in the directory. Any user or workgroup not included in directory's ARL defaults to a null access to the directory.

Simultaneous Log-ons

Another very important network security feature is the ability to restrict the number of simultaneous user log-ons. This feature is especially effective against those individuals who attempt to log-on to multiple network machines for the purpose of simultaneously penetrating multiple systems in parallel. The user can use an automated process to act on his or her behalf to knock on the door of systems throughout a LAN. As a result, the ability to restrict such an approach effectively is very important. This security feature also discourages users from giving their passwords away and from leaving computers unattended without logging off. The reason this security capability is effective is because it discourages users from letting someone else get their password, since such a compromise could prevent them from doing their work.

Network/systems administrators commonly use multiple log-ons to perform tasks that require them to access multiple systems on a network. This is a major concern, given that virtually any user could gain access to virtually any network node through a system console, terminal, PC, or workstation that is left unattended by the network/systems administrator. Most network/systems administrators are overworked and have continuous demands on their time. As a result, it is very common for a network/systems administrator to be working on a specific problem and be called away for a higher-priority problem. In most cases, the network/systems administrator does not take the time to log off the system he or she was previously attempting to fix or configure; rather, the administrator leaves his or her post to work on the most pressing problem—leaving a wide open security hole in the network for an undetermined period of time. Both NetWare and VINES default to allow simultaneous user log-ons. Since very few users ever require simultaneous access to multiple networking devices, it is recommended that this NOS security default be configured to "no." Simultaneous user log-ons should be allowed only on an as-needed basis and only after the requirements for simultaneous user log-ons are verified by the network/systems administrator.

When protecting very sensitive information, it is also possible for the network/systems administrator to restrict the access to such information to a limited number of network PCs or workstations. This protection capability enables information to be restricted to a set of physical systems. Those systems can be protected through the use of physical security measures. This is often very effective within organizations that are grouped physically based on job function. For example, it is likely that a finance department will require access to personnel information in order to conduct payroll; however, the same personnel information most likely would not be required by the marketing department to conduct its daily business activities. Given that most departments within an organization are physically grouped together, the restriction of specific types of information can be very effective. In addition, by limiting the number of network nodes that can access sensitive information, the chances of an information compromise of the information is reduced.

Both Novell NetWare and Banyan VINES support the ability to restrict which PCs and workstations on a network can access specific types of information. The technique is implemented by Novell and Banyan by "burning in" a unique network addressing identifier on each network interface card. This unique identifier is burned into the Read Only Memory (ROM) on the card. Similar protections can also be provided through Ethernet addresses, IP addresses, and other network addresses that can be used to identify a network device uniquely. It is also important to note that the device that is restricted from accessing certain information does not have to be a device that the user interfaces with directly (i.e., PC or workstation); rather, information can be restricted from other network devices as well. Examples may include network printers, file servers, subnetworks, WAN links, or even network CD ROM and other storage devices.

Encryption

A common assumption made for network security is that the network cable plant is secure and protected from penetration. LANs are especially vulnerable to this type of penetration because all information traversing the network is communicated in the clear. The term "clear" refers to information that is communicated in its native form, or information that is not encrypted. Encryption is a process that is used to scramble information based on an algorithm and a unique key. Encryption is not widely deployed for LANs. As a result, information communicated over a LAN is vulnerable to interception and compromise. A perpetrator need only gain access to a workstation on the network and a tool for analyzing network traffic, and all information communicated over the network can be easily captured and analyzed. The typical tools used by a perpetrator would be the same tools used by network management staff or technicians to troubleshoot network performance problems and bottlenecks. If used in a passive capacity, the user need not even be logged into the network to monitor the communications occurring over the network. As a result, the tools often go overlooked as a potential means of compromising the networking environment.

7.5 APPLICATION PROTECTION IN A PC NETWORKING ENVIRONMENT

In order to protect a network application from compromise, modification, or destruction, it can be placed in a read-only directory. Many applications require write and modify access to the directory because of the use of overlay files. This conflict can be mitigated by placing .EXE and .COM files in a read-only subdirectory in the path and executing the application from the directory where the overlay files reside. This enables the application to execute, since it is in the path, while the overlays will be successfully loaded and modified, since they are in the default directory.

The execute-only attribute also can be used to prevent users from copying the application. This feature is effective only when the application is not itself being used as an overlay file. The problem develops when such an application attempts to read the file, and the network operating system thinks the user is trying to copy it. Since this function is not allowed, the system becomes hung. Developers of applications should be encouraged to work with the network/systems administrator to define an equilibrium between application performance and overall system security. One possible approach is to encrypt the application. If encryption is used, even if the application is copied, it cannot be used unless it can be decrypted first.

A network/systems administrator may wish to give a user read-only access while others may have read-write access. This can be accomplished by creating two types of user workgroups. Users with rights only to query the data are granted read-only access. Users authorized to enter and modify data receive read-write access to the directory. Preventing users from copying data can be much more difficult. Encryption can protect against a user copying the entire file and being able to read it. A user can, however, have a buffer turned on at the workstation where the clear, unencrypted data is being captured. The only effective way to prevent this is with sophisticated workstation security or by the use of diskless PCs. To protect the data against accidental or intentional destruction, the network/systems administrator could remove the user's delete right on Novell's NetWare network directory.

Security for Network Applications

Security features can be built into applications; however, it is very difficult to protect files or data from compromise, destruction, or unauthorized modification unless the user is forced through the application to access files or data. The application can protect access to the files if the user attempts to access the data through an application. Outside the application, these protections will not be effective.

Databases compose the largest and most popular type of applications accessed through the use of networks. Due to the extensive use of databases and the sheer amount of data maintained and managed by databases, a substantial amount of development and investment has been made in developing application-level security controls for databases. Most databases today provide three fundamental layers of security. These three layers of security are provided at the application level, table level, and the field level.

At the application level, the user is normally prompted for a password, which is commonly assigned by the developer of the application. The application would then have certain access rights associated with the password. Password management features such as password aging, editing, and defined length and characteristics can be developed within the application. Many of these features may not be necessary, depending on the use of the security features provided through the operating system. At the table level, where the data exists, password protection can be provided in two dimensions. Encryption is commonly used to protect information associated with a table. Encryption can be used to prevent a protected table from being edited from the command line or any other external application or text editor. The most important benefit of using encryption at the application level is that the information remains encrypted, and thus protected, while it is communicated throughout a network. As a result, a perpetrator who taps a network for the purpose of information compromise will not be able to discern any intelligible knowledge from the information acquired. If a network security policy requires users to possess different levels of access within an application, then encryption becomes even more important. For example, if a user is not permitted to view certain fields, the user could exit the application and view the data (including the protected field) from the command line or with a text editor. If the data is encrypted, however, perpetrators will be able to view only unintelligible information. Depending on the level of application integration and the exchange of data between applications, encryption may be effective or may prove to be too cumbersome to be worthwhile. If data must be exchanged between applications, it would be necessary to first decrypt the data to be exchanged and then transmit the information over the network in the clear, losing any security advantage originally gained through encryption.

The second common mechanism used for the protection of database-stored table information is the ability to assign unique access rights within the application to users. Examples may include:

Feature	Function
Read-only	User can read a table, but cannot modify it.
Write-only	User can write to a table, but cannot view the table's contents.
Modify-only	User can modify existing records, but cannot add new records or delete existing records.
Limited update	User can update certain fields in existing records.
Add/Modify only	User can add new records and modify selective fields, but cannot delete them.
Add/Modify/Delete	User can add new records and modify and delete existing records.
All	User possesses complete access to the table.

Developers of applications often want to protect a table against user error, which is the most common form of security breaches in networks. To accomplish this goal, a table password may be included in a script. This procedure is acceptable as long as the script is also password protected. Password protecting a script will protect the table password and prevent anyone from examining or modifying it. It is important to note that users will not need the password to execute the script.

The third common level of access available to users within databases is at the field level. This is the level of access where NOS security is not sufficient.

Network level security provides protection only at the file level, not at the field level. Common features available for field-level protection include:

Feature	Function
Feature	*Function*
None	A user cannot view or change information in a field.
Read-only	User can view the information in a field, but cannot modify the information.
Read/Modify only	User can view and modify information in a field, but cannot delete the field.
All	User can view and modify information in a field.

7.6 SUMMARY

In this chapter, network security has been looked at from the perspective of PCs. In the next chapter, malicious software, such as Trojan horses, time bombs, and the ever-popular viruses are discussed.

END NOTES

1. David Bittle, PC Networking Conference; comments during a formal presentation, Denver, CO, October 19, 1992

2. *DataPro*, "Network Services," (New York: McGraw-Hill): 1992 edition.

8

Controlling Viruses
and Trojan Horses

8.1   INTRODUCTION

One of the most substantial threats to computer networks today is malicious software. For years, the actual instances of malicious software have increased dramatically. The use of viruses, Trojan horses, and other malicious software attacks has become very popular due to their consistent visibility in newspapers and on news shows such as CNN.

Common malicious software attacks can be categorized as follows:

- Virus—software that copies itself into any software program it can modify
- Worm—software that plants copies of itself in remote networked computer systems
- Logic bomb—software that does sudden and comprehensive damage to information
- Time bomb—software that does sudden and comprehensive damage to information based on a predefined time (i.e., explode on July 21, 1993, at 2:00 P.M.).
- Trojan horse—harmful software concealed within an attractive software program or application
- Covert channel—a disguised software program that modulates information on an information channel to convey information contrary to the

security policy of a system/network and contrary to the original intention of the information channel

Some of the best known "viruses" have actually been worms because they have spread throughout networks versus modifying programs. Nothing in the definition of worm or virus denotes harm or injury. This fact contributes to the complexity associated with defending against their potential harm. A virus or a worm can actually serve a useful purpose in a network. It is important to note that the difference between a virus and a worm is that a virus requires a host software program to live and execute, while a worm does not. This distinction parallels in biological terms as well in that a virus invades a cell and forces the cell to make copies of the virus in other cells, while a worm does not need a host (i.e., a cell) to invade; rather, a worm can live by itself without need of a host organism.

8.2 VIRUSES

A virus is a software program that can infect computer systems and networks in much the same way a biological virus infects humans. The formal definition of a computer virus is a piece of software code with a self-reproducing attribute that attaches itself to other programs. A computer virus cannot exist on its own. In many ways, a virus can be thought of as a parasite in that a virus requires a host (computer program) to survive, and its survival can ultimately harm or kill its host.

To date, the perpetrators of virus attacks have typically been individuals experimenting with technology or for the purpose of malice. To create a virus, the perpetrator must possess programming skills. It is highly unlikely that anyone with intentions of greed would ever employ the use of a virus. Clearly, anyone wishing to steal something does not need to go to the trouble of designing, developing, and implementing a virus to accomplish his or her goal.

A virus can spread expeditiously and comprehensively in a networked environment. Consider the role of a system editor in the context of virus infection. Assume that the editor of a system is infected with a virus and that every software program that ever used the system editor would become infected. Since every program is likely to be susceptible to modification by some user of the editor, infection soon becomes universal.

Viruses are typically capable of searching through computer application and system software and infecting them by attaching themselves to the program. The infection process can take a fraction of a second and is typically not noticeable to the user of the system. This process is replicated and replicated until the virus is detected and stopped. Virus programs are very dangerous in the context of network computing. In a networked environment, virus programs have a much larger population of computer systems to infect and damage. To date, virus programs have been used as a practical joke and for academic experimentation. As a result, the damage has been tied almost exclusively to lost productivity resulting from loss in network performance and operational anomalies. The potential risk posed by virus programs is much more than just performance and productivity related. For example, a virus program could easily be programmed to search through specific application and system software and erase designated files. Theoretically, a virus could literally destroy an entire network. Several virus programs have been discovered that have been programmed to do such severe damage. In most cases, these virus programs did not execute properly or were discovered prior to their activation.

Virus Advancement

The first generation viruses have possessed the following types of attributes:

- They achieve access to a system through the system's boot process, or through a user running an infected program (intentionally or unintentionally).

- They achieve control of system processing time through the activation of virus code. This activation normally occurs only when an infected program is running.

- They achieve access to other software and storage media by intercepting input/output activity through a system's interrupt subsystem and then by locating the desired targets (i.e., executable files).

- First generation viruses have avoided detection because of inadequate or totally absent security countermeasures, the lack of security policies and procedures, and failure to adhere to established security procedures.

As a result, first generation virus delivery approaches have not been extremely complex and have possessed limitations in their execution. Delivery approaches refer to the way in which virus code is introduced and executed on a system or network. In the vast majority of cases, product and software vendors have rapidly produced virus prevention/detection software to combat each type of virus introduced. To avoid starting from scratch, most virus developers have relied on existing virus code and delivery approaches in their development of new virus software. As this development process has evolved, viruses have become increasingly difficult to detect.

The second generation virus, or the advanced virus, appears to be much different. These advanced viruses present a new and challenging problem for networks. The most fundamental difference between first and second generation viruses is the level of detail, attention, and complexity surrounding the protection of the malicious virus code from detection. This development has presented new challenges to the antivirus software development vendors. Without effective, implemented, managed, and monitored network security programs, second generation viruses present a tremendous threat to network computing environments.

The focus and intention of the second generation virus is to go completely undetected. For example, antivirus programs that detect changes to program files by calculating a cyclic redundancy check (CRC) or a checksum and comparing the result to a previous value have proven ineffective to many of the second generation virus programs. Many of these viruses intercept all file input and checks to see if the input file contains its own code from the file before presenting the file to the requesting program. As a result, a CRC or checksum appears to be totally normal, and the infection is not revealed. Advanced virus programs are also aimed to infect every file in the system that is open during its execution. If a computer system possessing the virus program is in an active state in its memory, executing a CRC or checksum or any type of virus-scanning signature software that evaluates every program in a system would not protect system information, but rather would infect every file in the computer system or network.

Second generation advanced virus programs can be dealt with through a fundamentally secure system/network. The best defense is to ensure that adequate security countermeasures are being used properly. Operational procedures are also critical in the protection of network information. For example, procedures should be in place and enforced, including:

- Access control to systems and the network
- Rigorously enforced backup procedures
- Restrictions on external interfaces to other systems/networks and services

- Procedures for the introduction of any software into the operational environment

- Software testing procedures before full operational utilization

Even if these countermeasures and procedures are implemented and followed, they are still not sufficient to protect against the advanced strain of virus programs that is common today. Highly reliable virus prevention and detection software should also be utilized as the third line of defense.

Virus Protection

Virus protection against harm can include preventing the harm from ever occurring, restricting the extent of damage, or recovering from harm after the damage has been done. The real threat of a virus or a worm is that they can both spread very quickly and cover numerous systems, making it very unlikely that the origin of the virus or worm can be found. A virus protection approach must include the capability to react more expeditiously and on a larger scale than in the past.

Viruses and worms have actually created more publicity and anticipation than actual harm. In fact, much greater damage would result if viruses were to inhibit or preclude the use of information processing and networking technologies. If the use of networking were to be curtailed as a result of the fear of virus attacks, tremendous capabilities, services, and resources would be lost to the entire information processing industry. Given the virus attacks to date, such a reaction would be totally unwarranted. Most companies that have been hit by virus attacks have been able to recover most of everything that was lost. The reason for this effective recovery has been the fact that these companies have had good backup and recovery procedures in place and have been able to reload a networked environment totally with minimal loss defined in days or hours of processing time.

To be harmful, a virus must execute under conditions that allow it to copy its code and to modify one or more software programs other than the one in which it originally resides. When a virus spreads, it in fact modifies programs by attaching itself to the programs and thus infecting them. It follows that preventing a virus from spreading and causing potential harm involves either preventing it from copying itself or preventing it from modifying any program in which it does not reside. As a result, a virus infection can be detected by recognizing that a software program or application has been modified. If it is not possible to prevent or detect the spread of a virus, then the best solution is to work very hard never to acquire any virus-contaminated software in the first place.

Software Acquisition

What used to be reliable channels for acquiring software may no longer be. There is a lot of progress needed in the process of providing assurances to end users that software products and applications are not contaminated with virus code. The National Institute of Standards and Technology (NIST) continues to warn government agencies against relying too heavily on virus scanning software. Antivirus software is a useful detection tool, but it often takes too long to use and does not solve fundamental problems.

Secure Systems

An effective approach to combating the virus problem is to build hardware and operating systems that are less vulnerable. For example, vendors can isolate the boot sector of a hard drive to guard against virus infection. But organizations tend to shy away from such security measures, because they force managers to make hard choices about system functionality and user requirements. The technology exists to do what is necessary; however, the actual price to the end user for such protection may end up being too expensive. The other question deals with functionality and performance.

Network Performance Alarms

Ways and means for proactively monitoring resources to determine load and capacity are very common to network management systems today. These same tools can be used to detect proactively the presence of a virus in a networked environment. The Internet worm provided an outstanding example of what malicious software launched against a network can do relative to performance impact. Capacity and performance thresholds can be established and set for networking components and computing resources. If these thresholds are exceeded, then alarms can be sent to a network management station to be processed and interpreted. Assuming a large number of alarms are received, one could postulate the existence of a virus, worm, or other substantial network problem. One of the greatest benefits of this approach is that the components sending the alarms can be identified immediately so that a subnet or other physical/logical portion of the network infected with a virus can be immediately taken off line to prevent further infection.

Preventative Program Utility

A preventative program utility is software that can help prevent a virus from reproducing and modifying programs. Controls on program modifications are included, but they are not the only countermeasures of this type. Another could be a tool that establishes a unique environment for the execution of a software program where there is not a high level of confidence that the software does not contain malicious software. Within such an environment, system clocks could be advanced to uncover the existence of any time bombs or logic bombs. In addition, such an environment should make it possible to detect any attempt to learn of the existence of a modifiable program. Any programmed attempt to learn of the existence of modifiable programs would suggest the existence of a virus in a program being tested and would alert the software tester to the need for further investigation and evaluation of the software.

Gateways and Filters

When an administrator recognizes a threat to the network, he or she must have a means for dealing with the problem. Gateways that can serve as chokepoints through which network traffic must traverse can serve effectively in this capacity. Network security administrators can concentrate their energy on a much smaller set of components, rather than having to address every component on the network. The administrator must act quickly by inserting software into the network that will locate and kill the malicious software expeditiously.

Detective Software

Since a virus modifies software programs and applications, detective software could be used to detect irregular modifications of programs. Irregular modifications would be those that occurred outside established procedures and control mechanisms. One way to accomplish this would be to make a backup copy of every software program every time it is modified in accordance with established software development procedures and controls. This protected copy could then be checked periodically against the production version of the software for modification. The vulnerability to program comparisons is due to the fact that the program, when copied, may already be infected with a virus. As a result, the program comparison approach must be augmented with other virus security countermeasures.

Computer Emergency Response Teams

The Michelangelo virus, even though it did not cause catastrophic problems, did do a lot to undermine overall consumer confidence in software products. The Michelangelo virus was effectively contained because of widespread media coverage and national attention. In addition, government computer emergency response teams (CERTs) were formed to conduct analyses and dispose of virus software. CERT activities were coordinated through the Forum on Incident Response and Security Teams, or FIRST. The Michelangelo virus incident has proven beyond a shadow of a doubt that effective and expeditious communications are a critical element of diffusing virus security emergencies.

In the case of the Internet worm, a fundamental lesson was learned. Network administrators of systems on the Internet had become dependent upon the network as the means for communicating among their peers to resolve network problems. The Internet worm caused total disarray of this common communications method, which severely hampered a coordinated approach to control and kill the Internet worm. Since the Internet worm experience, many network administrators have put emergency procedures in place and have defined specific expert teams to deal with similar threats.

NOS Virus Protection

Intel Corporation has developed a server-based software package (LANProtect) that helps protect users of Novell NetWare 3.1 NOS from the effects of more than 850 common viruses that threaten networked data. LANProtect installs as one NetWare loadable module on the file server and scans incoming and outgoing files continuously for viruses. LAN managers can view the activity of the software from a central server without installing a terminate-and-stay-resident (TSR) program on the client platform. When LANProtect detects a virus, it creates an alarm, which is an on-screen message and a beep at the workstation, and moves the infected file to a private directory. The program also logs information about the virus, such as where and when it was detected and where it originated on the network. LANProtect uses 275KB of RAM on a file server. This product is different from other products that use TSRs at the client station, including scan programs that must be run manually every day. The problem with these other products is that if the virus is smart enough, it can look to see if there is virus protection in memory and it will look for a way to beat it. The Intel product requires no RAM at the workstations and files are scanned when they are opened or closed (transparent to the end user). As a result, most users are unaware that virus scanning occurs.

Practical Virus Advice

A true assumption is that any infection discovered on any computer, whether it be networked or not, poses a potential threat to all computing activities and data storage of this unit. Any computer virus infection should be treated as a security violation, as it is—because someone has gained access to your data, only by a different means.

A single infected diskette left undiscovered for a few days will destroy weeks, even months of work. The establishment or improvement of any present scanning policy is not wasted time. This effort should be given serious thought and company resources in developing suitable protection.

Since viruses cannot spread until activated, scanning at any computer is relatively safe. With the proliferation of computer viruses, it is safer to perform local scanning than to use a disk that never gets scanned. The diskette that is too much of an inconvenience to scan is the most likely diskette to infect a network.

It has been documented that where the ADP departments established a single scanning point and/or made diskette scanning an inconvenience, less than 40 percent of newly introduced diskettes were ever scanned. It was found that some departments in these companies hadn't scanned a diskette in months. This should worry anyone concerned about the possibility of an undiscovered virus infection. When you stop and think about the fact that 90 percent of all infections to date are traced to a commercial source, shrink-wrapped commercial software is the number one infection media.

Practical Virus Prevention

The following practical virus prevention tips are provided to help network administrators, operators, and technicians effectively combat the virus threat.

1. Never use any demonstration or game software that comes as part of a computer system (i.e., resident on the hard disk of the system).

2. Spend time to get to know the vendors providing hardware and software. Do not purchase hardware or software from a vendor that you do not know or one that does not have a solid track record in the industry.

3. Use only bulletin board services that are reputable and those that have defined procedures for testing software prior to making that software publicly available to other users.

4. Do not use nonlegitimate copies of software programs (i.e., nonlicensed).

5. Establish a comprehensive set of backup procedures and define specifically who is responsible for making sure the procedures are adhered to. The most recent backup will provide the means necessary to have an aggressive restoration in the event of virus infection. Backup procedures should include backup of all software applications (both system and network), user files, and any other software including operating systems, operating system utilities, file systems, device drivers, and any boot software. These backups should be kept in two separate safe locations.

6. Never boot or initialize a system from a diskette that is not trusted to be free of malicious software.

7. Never accept free or public domain software that is not trusted to be free of malicious software.

8. Establish a central software check-out function where all computer diskettes to be used on the network are examined for viruses prior to being used on any production system attached to the network.

9. Never use unsolicited demonstration software contained on diskettes.

10. Ensure that the vendors and service providers that you work with are aware of the virus threat and implement specific policies and procedures to reduce the introduction of malicious software in the products and services they provide.

11. Ensure the the write protect tab is always activated on system boot diskettes.

12. Use intrusion detection security countermeasures.

13. Use encryption. The use of encryption to protect against virus attack can be very effective by providing authentication services during the distribution process. Basically, the vendor generates a numerical signature that is verified by the user who customizes the software, pro-

ducing user locally executable software, under the direct control of a device named as the authenticator.

14. Use optical write-once-read-many (WORM) media. Information stored on WORM media is inherently protected from virus attacks because it cannot be modified.

Specific and Practical Actions

Once a virus has been detected, or when one is believed to exist, the following practical actions should be considered.

1. Establish a well-defined virus prevention action team.

2. Determine the type, name, and method of infection.

3. Separate infected portion of network (i.e., logical or physical subnetwork) from the rest of the network to limit further propagation of the virus.

4. Suspend processing for the infected portion of the network.

5. Use the approved company write-protected antivirus software. Scan the shared computer resources in that area and section, deleting infected files as they are found.

6. Lock up all diskettes. Start scanning diskettes after you have collected them. Scan and mark as clean, if scanned and found so. Resecure the diskettes until they are all scanned. This way you're not chasing the tail of the dragon by scanning diskettes, only to have someone reinfecting them as quickly as you do.

7. Document as much information as possible, but do not hinder efforts to control the spread with an overabundance of paperwork.

8. Scan all user accounts. This includes all directories, all files, all shared resources (i.e., databases), and other mounted drives and backup file servers. If it's accessed at any level, scan it. Delete infected files as found.

9. Expand the scanning to all new files in the network.

10. Determine the damage caused.

11. Document any steps taken, and provide senior management with an overview briefing. This is a companywide problem and the team should be allowed freedom of movement. All reports should go to everyone on the team and to anyone involved, using everybody's un-

derstanding and knowledge of the network and applications installed on the network.

12. Have the team meet immediately after the analysis and scanning process to prepare a detailed assessment of the situation. Also arrange an after-action meeting to discuss further activity.

13. Set up an after-action meeting immediately. The team will turn over documentation to personnel directly affected and responsible for the portion of the network infected by the virus.

14. Notify company personnel of progress, but waste no time tracking down hard-to-find people who fail to answer repeated pages or respond to beeper calls.

15. Have the director of MIS keep company management apprised of the progress of containment, status, and/or damage caused by the virus.

16. Reinstall application/network software as soon as possible from write-protected originals. Data files are seldom infected, but when they are, they can be cleaned safely, provided certain common-sense precautions are taken.

Ongoing Activities

Viruses have been taken very seriously across a number of government and commercial organizations. The following sections discuss some activities in certain organization classes with respect to virus activity and prevention.

Government

Major U.S. government agencies involved in training, awareness, policy, and the development of guidance for the virus threat include the DoD, NCSC of the NSA, Department of Commerce (DoC), and NIST. NIST and the NCSC are contributing a substantial amount of time and money to research and policy direction to fight the virus threat.

Commercial

Numerous commercial vendors and commercial organizations have worked together to develop working groups, technical interchange conferences, mail groups, and response teams to deal with the virus threat. Today there are many conferences, working sessions, and seminars available that address malicious software in networked environments.

Summary—The Virus Threat

The virus threat is substantial. As systems continue to get larger, networked, and interoperable, the virus threat will continue to increase. To date, virus programs have caused substantial harm due to down-time and loss of productivity; however, the damage to date is nothing compared to the potential damage that could be caused by a more malicious strain of virus. There are numerous software utilities that can be used to catch common viruses and these are highly recommended. There are also fundamental policies and procedures that, if implemented and managed, can substantially reduce the risk of a virus attack. In the next section, we describe the threat of and protection against Trojan horse attacks.

8.3   TROJAN HORSES

A Trojan horse is "a computer program with an apparently or actually useful function that contains additional (hidden) functions that surreptitiously exploit the legitimate authorizations of the invoking process to the detriment of security."[1]

Introduction

The major characteristic that separates a Trojan horse from other penetration techniques is its inherent ability to perform both overt and covert operations. The overt function of a Trojan horse serves as the visible bait or useful function that attracts a user to the program containing the Trojan horse. This portion of the Trojan horse may be a compiler, assembler, sorting utility, or other useful program commonly desired by system users. Since these programs are executed by a user, they are able to act on behalf of the user and, in doing so, assume all access privileges of that user. Through the useful or overt function of the program, the covert portion also gains access to any information or application that is available to the user. To ensure access to information or resources otherwise inaccessible to the Trojan horse perpetrator, the covert portion is used simultaneously with the overt function. The information available to the Trojan horse is any information that would be normally available to the unsuspecting user (not just the information required to perform the intended application). More importantly, data to which the user has access, but may not be aware of, can now be accessed by the Trojan horse. An example of a Trojan horse implementation is a text editor program that legitimately performs editing functions for the unsuspecting user while browsing through his or her directories looking for files to copy. This is particularly effective for the perpetrator because, as far as any internal protection mechanism of the computer system is concerned, there are no unauthorized actions in progress. The Trojan horse (e.g., text editor) is simply a user program, executing in user address space, accessing user files, and performing legitimate and authorized system service requests such as giving another user (the perpetrator) a copy of his or her files.[2]

Types of Trojan Horses

A Trojan horse is effectuated when hardware and/or software are covertly modified. In subsequent processing, unauthorized functions are performed alongside normal ones. Trojan horses can come in various sizes and appearances and can be used to perform an array of malicious functions. Whether it be hardware, compilers, assemblers, log-on programs, application programs, operating system utilities, editors, or other functions, a Trojan horse can be used to exploit information or cause other damaging effects.

A taxonomy of Trojan horses is provided in the following sections. Generally, Trojan horses can be categorized by the way in which they are implemented. An objective for using a particular Trojan horse may be shared among different perpetrators, but the way in which a particular Trojan horse is implemented will probably vary.

Trojan Horses in Software

The most prevalent and well known Trojan horse programs are those developed through software techniques. Since a tremendous amount of software is developed every year, the risk of Trojan horses within programs has increased dramatically. Whether the perpetrator is developing a unique application or enhancing a commercial database application, creating a Trojan horse with programming techniques is relatively simple. Unique applications, user programs, commercial software packages, and updates and enhancements to existing software are all potential breeding grounds for Trojan horse development. Software updates are particularly attractive since the user has little reason to suspect a program that has never caused trouble in the past.

Trojan Horses in Hardware

Trojan horses also may be implemented in hardware. The advent of microcircuitry and the ever-accelerating evolution of hardware processors has facilitated the ability to perform an enormous amount of processing within the confines of a single chip. An entire microprocessor could be modified to include the addition of malicious instructions. Since these chips are very small and intricate in nature, they could be replaced without notice. The comprehensive utilization of hardware by many programs within a computer system increases the complexity associated with implementing and using a hardware Trojan horse.

Viritic Trojan Horses

A virus may act as a Trojan horse.[3] This phenomenon was referred to as a viritic Trojan horse in Israel in 1987.[4] A specific virus may act as a Trojan horse if, while performing an overt action, it also performs a covert action and then propagates itself to other areas in the file system, taking advantage of the executor's privileges and rights. Because the viritic Trojan horse has the ability to flow through the system, it may increase the likelihood of execution and number of executions.[5]

A virus program can be categorized as a Trojan horse when its implementation includes a useful or seemingly useful function. A virus is not considered to be a Trojan horse when its implementation is accomplished without utilizing an overt or legitimate function.

Trap Door Trojan Horses

A trap door is a hidden software or hardware mechanism that permits system protection mechanisms to be circumvented. It is activated in some nonapparent manner (e.g., special random key sequence at a terminal, special password, an event, or time).[6]

A Trojan horse may be used to create a trap door or a trap door may be used to allow a convenient, nondetectable entry to implement a Trojan horse. Probably the best known fictitious use of a trap door was portrayed in the motion picture *War Games*. In *War Games*, a young hacker uses a special password to gain access to a highly classified computer system. While trap doors can be used in conjunction with a Trojan horse, they themselves are not Trojan horses.

For the most part, trap doors are used for legitimate purposes. Trap doors are commonly used by maintenance personnel for software enhancements, testing, or troubleshooting. In addition, trap doors have been used by programmers for many years to facilitate a simple entry access method. Nevertheless, if the programmer who created the trap door becomes disillusioned with his or her job or is fired, the trap door may become a vehicle for revenge and a simple entry point for the insertion of a Trojan horse program.

8.4 TECHNIQUES FOR INTRODUCING A TROJAN HORSE INTO SYSTEMS

A Trojan horse may be implemented through software or hardware techniques. A Trojan horse may be used as a virus by propagating itself or it may be used in conjunction with a trap door to gain unauthorized access to a system. The Trojan horse perpetrator will want to ensure that the strategic placement of the Trojan horse will achieve the desired results and that the risk of being caught is minimal. The criteria for introducing a Trojan horse into an automated data processing environment are predicated primarily on two considerations:

1. Where the Trojan horse should be inserted to gain access to the targeted assets.

2. Where the Trojan horse can be most effectively placed for the greatest benefit with the least amount of risk to the perpetrator.

Based on the two aforementioned considerations, a system vulnerability is targeted and the Trojan horse is introduced. The individual responsible for the placement of such a mechanism is likely to have knowledge of the system, programming abilities, and a knowledge of the types and interrelationships of data processed by the system. The perpetrator must have access to a computer testing facility to ensure the Trojan horse operates correctly and, if the attack is designed to compromise information, must have a means to obtain the results of the attack.

Introducing a Trojan Horse in Hardware

Modification of computer hardware is one avenue used to introduce a Trojan horse into a processing environment. Hardware may be removed from a processing component during a period of down-time or inactivity, modified, and then returned to the system when operations are reinitiated. The perpetrator may also choose to modify an independent element of circuitry, choosing one that is electronically and physically compatible with existing circuitry. During a standard preventative maintenance visit, the perpetrator replaces the existing circuitry with the "new-and-improved" version—and a very dangerous Trojan horse is born.

Introducing a Trojan Horse in Software

The most common means of introducing a Trojan horse is through software techniques. A software Trojan horse may be introduced by inserting logic into a program during development, by inserting logic during a later enhancement in the original form in which the software was coded (source), or, with more difficulty, logic may be inserted in machine-language form (object). All phases of the entire software development life-cycle are subject to attack.

A programmer responsible for the development of software can be the agent for the introduction of a Trojan horse. By simply adding a few lines of code to an existing application, the programmer may be able to implement a Trojan horse successfully. A Trojan horse may also be introduced into a processing environment via commercial-off-the-shelf (COTS) software (i.e., compilers, assemblers, editors, etc.).

The most obvious way to introduce a software Trojan horse is the blatant modification of user or system programs. However, a modification to a program might be uncovered if the program were examined manually or a computer were used to compare it automatically with the original. To elude discovery, a more complex method of inserting a Trojan horse can be used. A Trojan horse could be placed into a utility program that is used continuously. When this program is executed, the Trojan horse modifies the operational program before the changed part is executed and then removes it after execution.

A perpetrator may also attempt to lure the unsuspecting user into using enticing software created or modified by the perpetrator, often as public domain software on computer network bulletin boards. The overt capability of the advertised software may provide a large enough piece of bait for the unsuspecting user to use it. If the software contains a Trojan horse, the perpetrator may now have access to sensitive information while the user remains in the dark. The capabilities of the advertised program and the methods to market this program have direct effects on the success of the perpetrator. The security, literacy, and knowledge of the targeted user community also affects the success rate of the perpetrator.

A Trojan horse can also be constructed in such a way that it creates the unauthorized activity routine from seemingly innocuous data and erases them after use. In this instance, a programmer searching for the Trojan horse must look for instructions that create the instructions that perform the ultimate unauthorized act. Hence, a recursive pattern is possible; the instructions need not be located adjacently but can be sprinkled throughout the program where they are executed. Each instruction preserves partial results for the next instruction when it is executed. Alternatively, each instruction may be followed by a transfer of control to the next instruction, or they may all be assembled in physical sequence momentarily (while executed) and then erased. Another method entails the use of encryption. The main body of the Trojan horse instructions may be encrypted using a key and then decrypted only when it is used. Finally, Trojan horse instructions may be disguised as inconspicuous little subprograms or as data that look as if they have some other, legitimate purpose.[7]

Introducing a Viritic Trojan Horse

A viritic Trojan horse[8] may be introduced using the same methods and techniques mentioned above. Basically, the only difference between a Trojan horse and a viritic Trojan horse is the degree of infection. A viritic Trojan horse may perform the identical function of a single-program Trojan horse; however, the virus element of the attack may allow the malicious program to propagate itself throughout a system.

For a viritic Trojan horse to be implanted successfully, the following two conditions must occur:[9]

1. The target program must remain operational.

2. The virus must be put into a location such that the entire viritic element is guaranteed to be executed.

A viritic Trojan horse may also pose the threat of propagation in a communications system. If a packet-switched network—specifically, a packet assembler and disassembler (PAD)—were infiltrated with a viritic Trojan horse, the virus attribute of the Trojan horse would propagate itself over a period of time into every PAD, into every host processor, and finally into every workstation on the entire network. A second example illustrates the use of a viritic Trojan horse in a LAN environment. Many vendors of LAN components offer downline loadable software for their network products. This allows a substantial cost savings, since servers and other devices do not require disk drives to load operational software. Updates and enhancements to the operational software can be loaded onto one machine and then distributed to the entire network. Generally, a single device is used to download software to all network equipment. If this device were penetrated with a viritic Trojan horse, it would then be possible to infect the entire network with malicious logic.

Introducing a Trojan Horse through the Use of a Trap Door

A trap door may provide the entry point for the introduction of a Trojan horse. Through the use of a special password, event, or specific time designation, a perpetrator may gain unauthorized access to a computer system or network via a trap door. If successful, the perpetrator may then compose and introduce a Trojan horse program. If the Trojan horse is designed to gain access to sensitive information and store the information to a hidden directory, the perpetrator may be able to use the same trap door to remove the compromised information.

Methods and techniques available to the would-be perpetrator for the introduction of Trojan horse programs are unlimited. However, for a Trojan horse to be successfully introduced into a system, the perpetrator must be able to exploit a vulnerability. This vulnerability may be poorly managed password accounts, insufficient security policies and procedures, or insufficient internal security controls.

8.5   EXPLOITATION

A Trojan horse has a specific objective to achieve: to subvert the system's security policy. This objective is achieved through the identification and exploitation of a vulnerability. One perpetrator may want to compromise sensitive information, while another may want to contaminate information. Still another objective may be to prevent authorized users from accessing information over a network. All of these objectives have one common ingredient: to be successful they must first subvert the security policy of a system. A Trojan horse can be used to exploit a variety of system vulnerabilities, the result of which can be categorized into three areas:

1. Violation of the secrecy policy—information compromise
2. Violation of integrity policy—unauthorized modification or deletion of information

3. Denial of service—the prevention or intentional delay of processing, functions, missions, or the intentional denial of information to authorized users

Commercial and corporate organizations have much to lose if their computer systems are attacked with Trojan horse programs. Personnel data, trade secrets, marketing strategies, and many other information-related assets are all subject to attack. It was once possible to separate data from users within a corporation by using physically separate machines within each department or division. For example, a company may use one computer system for marketing, one for sales, one for manufacturing, personnel, and so on. In today's information revolution, the need for sharing information among departments and divisions within an organization has required that these once-isolated devices be interconnected through local and wide area networks. The distributed use of computer systems and networks has enabled great gains in performance and productivity and has substantially reduced computing costs. This technology, however, may also allow a perpetrator to have a greater span of entry points to introduce malicious software.

The multitude of threats posed by the use of Trojan horse programs is staggering. The most serious side effect of their use is their ability to operate without notice. The appeal of free or public-domain software will continue to lure many unsuspecting users into the grasp of a Trojan horse.

System Vulnerabilities Exploited by Trojan Horses

If a vulnerability exists, it is safe to assume that there is someone who has the knowledge, drive, and ability to exploit it. Generally, a Trojan horse is most effectively used against system vulnerabilities that are not common knowledge. If a system vulnerability is not commonly known, the perpetrator can continue to exploit that vulnerability without risk of being identified. The following provides a practical overview of the most common network security vulnerabilities.

Absence of Security Policy

The most commonly exploited vulnerability of a network involves the absence of a security policy. For many networks, a security policy is never established and there are no clear guidelines for the protection, dissemination, use, storage, or processing of information. Users and administrators are forced into a position of making impromptu decisions and decisions under pressure regarding the protection of data and resources. Without an established security policy it is impossible to prevent or deter the introduction of a Trojan horse.

Inadequate Security Policy or Countermeasures

It is possible that an established and supported security policy will not properly address the Trojan horse threat. Once vulnerabilities have been identified through risk analysis, a security policy and measures to enforce that policy are designed and implemented. It is possible that certain vulnerabilities will be ignored either because they are too expensive to remedy or because their associated risk is low. Generally, this process is repetitive until a target residual risk factor is realized. It follows that a Trojan horse may be used to gain access to information via a method that is *not* specifically addressed by the current security policy of a system. For example, a system certified at the B1 level may be penetrated through the use of a covert channel in conjunction with a Trojan horse. B1 denotes a set of requirements contained in the TCSEC.[10] At the B1 level, however, the system is not trusted to protect against a Trojan horse that uses a covert channel to convey information to a lower access class. The security policy for a particular system may require that users in the manufacturing department of a company be prevented from accessing information from the personnel database. However, the policy does not prevent the introduction of a Trojan horse through shared public domain software. Hence, the policy is inadequate since it does not specifically address the Trojan horse threat.

A security policy may specifically address the Trojan horse threat, yet may employ inadequate countermeasures to implement the policy. The policy is implemented through countermeasures. The selected countermeasures may not provide the required functionality to prevent a Trojan horse attack. For example, a system may implement a user authentication scheme based on user IDs and passwords. Each user is given a separate user ID and password. A malicious user of the system is able to write a Trojan horse program that emulates this mechanism and compromises the user IDs and passwords of network users. It is evident that an effective security policy must be comprehensive, globally applied, and employ the *correct* countermeasures to defend against a Trojan horse attack.

Lack of Support for Security Features

The selection and use of security countermeasures is effective only if their implementation is supported and properly managed. Since many network administrators and data processing managers view security protection as just another performance limitation, they may be unlikely to support and manage the security aspects of their network. If rules are bent, massaged, or otherwise not used, the Trojan horse perpetrator may find the opening he or she has been waiting for. The lack of support for security countermeasures is a serious and exploitable vulnerability. Audit trails are commonly available and are used to support the security policy of numerous secure network implementations. Yet, how many of these audit trail printouts are later examined? If the would-be perpetrator knows that the security administrator doesn't even look at the audit trail records but rather throws them away after they are printed, he or she is given a license to challenge the security of the system without being monitored.

Having an established security policy and implemented countermeasures to support that policy does not prevent the introduction and use of a Trojan horse. Without support and continuous application of those controls, a Trojan horse can easily exploit many network vulnerabilities.

Discretionary Access Controls

One common vulnerability exploited through the use of a Trojan horse is discretionary access controls (DAC) (discussed in Chapter 4). The implementation and application of DAC is fundamentally flawed with respect to the Trojan horse threat. DAC normally permits the owner/creator/possessor of the data to decide who may access it. By placing the decision process in the hands of the users, as opposed to a universally applied policy that dictates who may see what, it then becomes possible for users to share data and programs that may contain one or more Trojan horses. A Trojan horse, by mimicking a legitimate user, may pass access authorization of that user to itself. The use of a DAC policy against a Trojan horse threat is a futile countermeasure. Security administrators who oversee computer networking environments where a DAC policy is used are cautioned to be aware of a continuous and permanent Trojan horse threat.

Mandatory Access Controls

Networks that implement mandatory access controls (MAC—discussed in Chapter 4) are more resistant to Trojan horse attacks than networks implementing only DAC protections. MAC provides increased protection because it is consistently applied and universal. A Trojan horse can be used in conjunction with a covert channel to penetrate a MAC environment.

Individuals with access to systems that implement MAC may not be authorized to access all information contained in a network. Even though it may be far easier to introduce a Trojan horse into a network providing only DAC protection, the successful introduction of a Trojan horse program into a network providing MAC protection would have much greater consequences. For example, assume that a government network is used to process information simultaneously at the unclassified, confidential, and secret levels. Some of the users who have physical or logical access to the system do not possess a clearance (uncleared status). One particular uncleared user, through programming techniques, is able to introduce a Trojan horse into this environment. This Trojan horse is embedded within a system editor. Since the editor is used to modify documents and data for the entire system, it has default access to the level of the user using it. When the editor is used to modify a secret document, the Trojan horse portion of the editor reads the data and conveys that data through the use of a shared resource. The shared resource (covert channel) is modulated to convey the secret information to the uncleared perpetrator's receiving process. The information conveyed through the shared resource is not detected or under the purview of the MAC, since it is system information and not a user file, resource, or application.

Programming Environment

A major network vulnerability commonly exploited through the use of a Trojan horse is the programming environment. Without consistent policies, procedures, and verification techniques in place, the would-be perpetrator has a much easier time achieving his or her aspirations. Nonstructured software development, the absence of documentation, inadequate testing procedures, and inadequate configuration management and control policies are all exploitable vulnerabilities in the programming environment.

For many networks, continuous software development and enhancements are commonplace. These software development activities can be used to subvert the security policy of a network. In order to meet tough schedules, mission requirements, or reporting criteria, many programming activities may be managed haphazardly without proper testing or review. There may not be time to test for the absence of malicious code before the software is loaded and executed. If this is the case, an individual is in a position to develop and implement a Trojan horse without challenge.

The Insider Threat

It is recognized widely among individuals and policy makers in the information security (INFOSEC) community that managing the risks arising from insiders on sensitive computer systems is of major and growing importance. Numerous studies and comprehensive research suggest that insiders account for 75–85 percent of all network security breaches. An insider is defined as anyone who has authorized access to the automated facilities and to the resources they manage. Access limits for each insider are set by the security policy and enforced by the network access control mechanisms. The degree of trust placed in an insider may vary from organization to organization and is generally a consequence of a formal review of the person's background, intended job function, and required access to specific types of information. Inappropriate conduct of an insider in the use of an automated system constitutes a threat of potential damage. This inappropriate conduct may be characterized as any use of the system that violates the security policy of that system. Unauthorized persons who may penetrate the access controls of a system are referred to as intruders. Intruders have the same potential for damage to the system as do insiders who engage in inappropriate conduct.[11]

The threat posed by an insider is large relative to that of a would-be perpetrator who does not have physical or logical access to the computing resources. The methods and techniques of compromise available to the insider are much greater. Once an individual is cleared to a certain level and given access to sensitive information, the ability exists for that individual to compromise information. Memorizing a screen of information containing a trade secret, a special chemical compound, or a code word can be easily accomplished without requiring the insider to steal a disk or a printout or illegally penetrate a network resource.

Mandatory and discretionary access controls are one common form of protection, and by using these methods the security administrator limits the range of potential damage from the insider. Additional countermeasures to restrict the unauthorized activities of the insider include surveillance, either by passive or active activities.[12]

Passive detection is an in-depth analysis of surveillance data to detect an insider threat during offline, after-hour activities. Active surveillance is a proactive detection whereby surveillance data are tested in real time for certain events. If specified events are detected, procedures can be immediately put in place to stop the event. Many of these approaches include the use of comprehensive audit data.

Probably the most effective and least complex approach to dealing with the insider threat is to employ the principle of least privilege. This requires that a person be given access only to information required to perform his or her job function. This would also include application and network resources.

8.6   EXAMPLES OF TROJAN HORSES

Few actual Trojan horse cases have been publicly reported. Whether the reason is embarrassment, the protection of the nation's security, or a lack of understanding, few actual Trojan horse case reports exist. Nevertheless, the amount of information written about the potential threat of Trojan horse attacks has spawned increased awareness.

It is difficult to estimate the actual amount of destruction and information compromise caused by Trojan horse attacks. The number of reported Trojan horse cases is estimated to be only a fraction of their actual number. In the commercial sector, for example, if a Trojan horse is uncovered it may make better business sense not to disclose the event. If a Trojan horse found in a banking system was being used to extract money from the bank, would it make better business sense to tell all bank depositors about the incident or to ignore it completely? More than likely, the latter. A large percentage of Trojan horse cases are not disclosed. Therefore, the knowledge gained from the discovery of and techniques used to identify Trojan horses is not widely discussed. Most papers written on Trojan horses discuss their ability to subvert specified security model implementations and ways and means to prevent their use. But very few articles or papers discuss successful methods that have been used to identify the actual existence of Trojan horses.

There are two philosophical approaches to this problem and they both have merit. The first approach is termed "the open approach." The open approach requires that *all information relating to computer crime, computer vulnerabilities, and threats to computer resources be made publicly available.* The public information would include actual penetration methods, systems penetrated, and the specific system vulnerability exploited. The merits of the open approach include:

- Public attention, concern, and activity
- Users' and system administrators' awareness of the problem(s)
- Ability to analyze the real scope of the problem

- Ability to react with information and knowledge to support other similar threats and vulnerabilities

- Historical data and experience

The potential disadvantage of the open approach is that it may cause widespread exploitation of all publicly identified vulnerabilities.

The second approach is termed "the closed approach." The closed approach requires that *any computer security incident, which may be replicated on another system, be restricted from public dissemination or be classified.* The merits of the closed approach are that it:

- prevents other perpetrators from attacking publicly identified vulnerabilities in similar or identical systems,

- instills a feeling that the problem is not as big or as dangerous as it really is, and

- keeps the malicious user and perpetrators ignorant of the security flaws and vulnerabilities existing in systems today.

Many have determined that the public release of information concerning Trojan horse attacks could be more damaging than keeping it under wraps. This may be one of the major reasons why information about Trojan horse attacks is not more widely available. If a Trojan horse is used to exploit a vulnerability in a commonly used system, the information concerning the incident may not be released. This decision is justified, since the release of this information may cause extensive and widespread use of malicious logic against that vulnerability in similar systems. Until a fix can be made, the information concerning a vulnerability is generally not released. The problem with this logic is that it restricts the resolution of the problem to a very select group of individuals. If Trojan horse incidents are restricted from the public and continue to be so, the lack of public awareness and support coupled with the limited supply of expert talent for problem resolution could have a detrimental effect on the research and development of Trojan horse countermeasures. The following examples of real-world Trojan horse events provide insight into the methods used to subvert systems.

Case 1—Space Physics Analysis Network

Date: September 16, 1987
Location: Bonn, West Germany
Penetrated Organization: National Aeronautics and Space Administration (NASA)

For more than three months, a group of West German computer hobbyists rummaged freely through data on the Space Physics Analysis Network. This group was able to install a Trojan horse and gain access to over 135 computer systems on the network. The Trojan horse program provided the means to bypass security controls of the network. The network was used to provide post-flight data analysis information to researchers, scientists, and other NASA agencies in the United States, Britain, West Germany, Japan, and five other countries. Information communicated over the network and contained within the penetrated computer systems was unclassified. Nevertheless, if data were modified, the monetary loss relative to NASA research and statistical analysis programs could be tremendous. One security investigator said that to his knowledge this was "the most successful running of a Trojan horse."[13]

Case 2—A Money Order Trojan Horse

Date: August 1980
Location: Southern United States
Penetrated Organization: Money Order Company

In an attempt to pay back gambling debts, an individual created and profited from the use of a Trojan horse. A money order company was in the middle of a transition to a new computer system. The perpetrator was contracted as a consultant to program a new money order package. While performing his job, he also added additional covert code to the program. This change provided additional functionality to the program. He added six commands that performed branch testing and transfer of control functions. The program instructed the computer to store a record of each money order sold, read in from data forms filled in with pertinent information. Additional data were read in when the money order was returned. Three of the data fields in each record were for indicating the status and action to be taken such as active, cancel, missing, delete, refund, and a special new category, expropriated. Actually, the purpose of the new feature was simply to input money order records, but, by classifying them as E, they would never be printed out.

The effect was that E-marked money order records went into the system, were debited and credited, but never came out of the system. The perpetrator proceeded to steal money order blanks, fill them out with an E, and cash them. Records of them existed only in the system. This caused the ledger to be out of balance by the accumulating total of the perpetrator's money orders. He counted on the fact that the ledger was out of balance during the confusion of changing systems. The blank money order forms were carefully controlled by recording the preprinted serial numbers on them. The money order forms that he stole were discovered to be missing, but, again, they were thought to be lost in the conversion confusion or in the mail.

Since the out-of-balance condition continued, it was reported to an outside accountant. The accountant agreed to help and the day of the audit was established. The night before the audit the perpetrator broke into the computer room and stole the incriminating documents, including listings of the Trojan horse computer program and some blank money order forms. The burglary was immediately reported to the police. After a series of investigations the perpetrator was confronted and he confessed. Once the manager read the program while looking for fraud, the E-field control of suppression of printing was simple to find and understand. If he had not been suspicious of fraud, he said, the real purpose of the instructions for fraud would have never occurred to him.

This is a classic and simple Trojan horse case. The perpetrator executed the crime in the way he knew best, as a programmer. Access to the blank money orders and production computer operation facilitated the crime without the need for collusion. This was not a fraud to end in a mystery of where the money went. It was merely a means of delaying a search for the missing money until the perpetrator had a chance to restore it. The accounting program subverted by a Trojan horse made the computer a hiding place for stolen money orders. The records were in there, but there was no routine way for them to be seen and questioned.

This case may be indicative of why so few Trojan horse cases are known. The Stanford Research Institute (SRI) Computer Abuse Project receives occasional confidential reports of Trojan horse cases, but details are rarely revealed. Many cases probably involve circumstances in which the victim has a choice of reporting it or not. Few people would ordinarily know about or even understand such technological crimes. Relatively low-level managers who might discover penetrations can easily cover them up until the loss can be restored or relegated to operations errors. In addition, as in the money order case, there may be intent to restore the loss before it is discovered. In many cases, the perpetrators might be successful in doing this, and any evidence of temporarily missing and restored assets is dismissed as an unexplained aberration of the system.[14]

Case 3—A Trojan Horse in a Pharmaceutical Company

Pharmaceutical Company A developed a new drug and was making preparations to patent the formula. Management anticipated that this drug would make many of its competitors' drugs obsolete. A rival company learned about the new drug through the industry grapevine. An executive of the rival company bought time on Company A's computer through use of a fictitious business. Through network connectivity into Company A's computer resources, the rival company was able to install and effectively activate a Trojan horse program. The program (and Trojan horse) they ran, ostensibly for business purposes, actually caused Company A's online files to be read onto a tape. The executives of the rival company then searched through the tape on their own computer system. They were able to find the formula they sought and patent it for their company several days ahead of Company A.[15]

8.7 IDENTIFICATION OF TROJAN HORSES

This following information is used to provide information for identification and does not specifically provide guidance for prevention. Prevention techniques are discussed in a subsequent section. It should be noted, however, that methods used to prevent the introduction of malicious code often provide the means to identify their existence.

Observation

The term "observation" includes many techniques and management processes. Network administrators, security administrators, and users of secure networks should be encouraged to report variations in processing characteristics. Generally, Trojan horse code is found through observation in one fashion or another. The negative aspect of identification through observation is that the Trojan horse normally has been used to compromise the system before one observes its activity. Observation can be an effective deterrent to the Trojan horse threat; however, in many cases a well-designed Trojan horse will not exhibit any unusual behavior to the unsuspecting user. More often than not, the observation process is completely manual and relies on the users of the system to gather information and point out anomalies.

The network administrator can promote effective observation by educating users on specific processing characteristics or variations to watch for. Once the users are educated, the network administrator should take time to question the users periodically about these areas of interest. This periodic questioning will serve two purposes: 1) it will instill a degree of assurance, since the would-be perpetrators will be less likely to use a Trojan horse if they know they are being watched, and 2) it demonstrates to the user community that the identification of security-relevant events has legitimate value since the network administrator is taking the time to ask the questions.

Automated observation techniques also can be effective in network computing environments. If the legitimate and nonlegitimate use of network resources and services can be quantified, and a means for detecting and reporting the difference can be implemented, then a Trojan horse can be identified through automated observation.

Automated Comparison Assessment

Identification through automated comparison assessment techniques is a formal process and requires additional time and resources to be effective. Automated comparison assessment is the process of identifying malicious or potentially malicious modifications to operational software and network applications. The intent of this technique is to deter the Trojan horse perpetrator and quickly identify any modifications to software that may include a Trojan horse. Complete automation of this process is recommended to ensure accurate and concise reporting and to minimize time and resource requirements.

One simple method of automated comparison assessment is provided through the use of standard compilers. A compiler is used to create object code that is directly processed by a computer system. Once this code is created and tested and found secure (relative to the associated security policy), the operational module(s) can be validated periodically by direct automated comparisons with the original copy. For example, if no modifications, additions, or testing of the code were scheduled, one would assume that no size differential in the operational code should occur. It is useful to compare the compiled size of the original code with the size of the operational code to determine if the size of the program (in bytes or bits) has increased or decreased. Likewise, the number of executable lines can be compared. This same process can be effective in identifying network viruses. It is important to note that a decrease in size (bytes) or in the number of lines of code does not preclude the use of a Trojan horse. The perpetrator could simply remove or reprogram certain sections of the code and then, with the additional space, introduce a Trojan horse. Any unplanned modifications to the program should be noted and investigated. Most standard commercial compilers or compiler utilities provide many of the automated comparison functions discussed above.

The use of automated comparison assessment techniques is not a total solution to the Trojan horse threat. It is theoretically possible that a Trojan horse could be created and introduced without affecting either the size or the number of lines of code within a program. It then becomes necessary to implement a utility that can perform a direct comparison between the original code and the current executable version. This utility provides the ability to perform a line-by-line comparison of the program in question and provides an output, which delineates any changes. To provide additional assurance, the actual binary code could be examined and compared.

A more innovative automated comparison assessment technique is referred to as integrity assessment. The objective of integrity assessment is to determine whether software has been modified in any way. To ensure that the integrity of software can be trusted, a checksum or some other type of integrity label is associated with protected software modules. This checksum or integrity label will be the result of processing the binary code through a special algorithm. The resulting integrity label can be stored with the software and used as a verification stamp. During a comparison assessment, the algorithm is used to recompute the checksum and compare it with the stored checksum. If the checksums do not match identically, the module should be tested immediately for the presence of a Trojan horse. When using this technique, it is imperative that the integrity label and the algorithm are protected from modification or destruction. The integrity label, once generated, could also be encrypted to ensure further its consistent accuracy and protection from clandestine modification.

A simple comparison program designed to identify code common to two programs can be used to find a viritic Trojan horse. If common code is found, it is necessary to review the identified code manually to confirm or deny the presence of a viritic Trojan horse. Many times, common code has a useful and legitimate function. The objective here is detection of similarities in code that, in principle, should not exist. This method is independent of the function of the viritic Trojan horse. A comparison program used to find common code within multiple programs would not be effective against a nonviritic Trojan horse program for obvious reasons (i.e., only one copy of the Trojan horse may exist).[16]

Identification of Trojan horse programs using automated comparison assessment techniques offers benefits to both the software development manager and the network administrator. One assumption required for the use of automated comparison assessment techniques is that the original code, program, or system does not contain a Trojan horse. If this assumption cannot be made with confidence, utilization of these techniques is useless and could actually be helpful to the perpetrator because they may ensure the continued existence of a Trojan horse. More research is required in this area to develop more effective automated tools that will expedite the process to ensure accuracy of the comparison and reporting procedures further.

Audit Control

The use of auditing systems is a passive approach to Trojan horse identification. For many years, audit trails and auditing controls have been used to support backup procedures and security requirements in automated processing environments. The greatest benefit of any security audit trail is that it permits the network administrator to reconstruct the events leading up to a compromise or crime. Auditing differs from many of the techniques discussed here because it is truly an after-the-fact technique. Specifically, audit trails reinforce the use of security countermeasures by giving the security administrator a list of evidence to use in the prosecution of computer crime. An effective audit trail serves as the detective and the information gathered by the audit trail provides the eye witnesses and fingerprints.

The network administrator should maintain audit records so that once a security problem arises the event can be tracked to the perpetrator. More importantly to the identification of Trojan horses, the audit trail can provide insight into software development activities, both authorized and unauthorized.

Auditing can be an effective tool in identifying the introduction of Trojan horse code. The two most important aspects of an effective audit trail are the creation of usable reports and generation of alarms based on preestablished thresholds. A third critical element of an effective network auditing system is global incorporation and support. So many times the processing and performance overhead associated with auditing is too overwhelming to be beneficial. In addition, the sheer mass of reports generated and the volume of data to be analyzed will cause the average network administrator to find more productive things to do. To be effective, the auditing system must be supported by the network administrator; it should not overburden the system, and it should provide condensed, usable reports that can be easily read and evaluated. The current state of the art in auditing systems does not support these objectives to the necessary degree.

Centralized Control

Many of the techniques used to identify Trojan horse programs assume that there is a facility that maintains and protects original versions of software.

Without a baseline from which to make comparisons and decisions, it becomes impossible to maintain successfully and control a secure software environment. A centralized control facility can be used to protect, control, maintain, and restrict access to developed software and network applications to only a single person or a select group of persons. Once an authorized modification is made to an existing program and has been thoroughly tested, the network administrator should log this modification to the centralized control facility. Complete and comprehensive documentation of the modification(s) also should be maintained. A network server also may be used to control access to software applications used on the network. For example, a centralized server can be used to store physically applications used on the network and users of the network can be forced to access the server to gain access to the application desired. The client (i.e., user) requesting the application can then be authenticated at the server and given access to only those applications for which the user is authorized. The user workstations can act as true clients and never possess the actual application software on their workstations. This can be accomplished through read-only applications as well as diskless workstations. Finally, the actual number of authorized application licenses can be enforced through the use of a centralized server by limiting the number of applications that can be used simultaneously at any given time on the network.

8.8 PREVENTION

The identification of Trojan horse programs is secondary in importance only to the prevention of their introduction. This discussion provides guidance on techniques and methodologies that can be used to prevent the introduction of Trojan horses. In this section, many of the countermeasures commonly used in secure networking environments are examined for their utility and relevance to the prevention of Trojan horse attacks.

Mandatory Access Controls

The use of MACs is the single strongest Trojan horse prevention mechanism, and it can be used to significantly lessen the damaging effects of Trojan horse programs.

Secure networks that correctly implement a MAC policy provide universal and consistent mediation between subjects and objects within various access classes. Mediation is generally implemented through the use of a reference monitor. A reference monitor that implements MACs will prevent a Trojan horse from passing data from a higher access class to a lower one. Generally, MACs are used for networks that process multiple levels or sensitivities of information and are accessed by users authorized at various levels. The separation of data, functions, and network processes may be separated by classification level, sensitivity, value, or purpose. MAC is used to ensure that a user or a process acting on behalf of a user cannot gain access to information at a higher access class than the user's current access class. The mediation between subjects and objects is generally facilitated by the use of data/file labels and indicators.

A trusted path is required to ensure that a user, when logging on to a network resource, is interfacing with a secure process (e.g., security kernel). A trusted path can provide protection against Trojan horse attacks caused by users responding to requests from application software that masquerade as the operating system. A trusted path is important in the design and implementation of MACs, since the MAC could be circumvented by a masquerading program.

An example of a security model that delineates and supports the use of MAC is the Bell and LaPadula model.[17]

Implementation and enforcement of the Bell and LaPadula model protects systems against the unauthorized transfer of information from a higher access class to a lower access class. The Bell and LaPadula model implements the simple security property and the *-property (pronounced the star property), which are used to enforce mandatory security policies. The implementation of the simple security property dictates that (READ) access is granted only when the subject's access class is equal to or greater than the object's access class. This property prevents users from accessing data that they are not authorized to access. The implementation of the *-property dictates that (WRITE) access is granted only when the access class of the object is greater than or equal to the access class of the subject. The purpose of the *-property is explicitly to address the Trojan horse attack. Using the *-property, information cannot be compromised through the use of a Trojan horse program, since a program operating on behalf of one user cannot be used to pass information to any user with a lower access class.

If a MAC policy is properly implemented, as in the Bell and LaPadula model, a Trojan horse would require a covert channel in order to transfer data from a higher access class to a lower one. These covert processes would also be required to work in harmony. Through the support and implementation of MAC security policies, the DoD as well as commercial industry could lessen the damage potential of Trojan horse programs.

Integrity Controls

If the purpose of a Trojan horse is to violate the integrity of a system or the data it contains, a policy implementation that enforces only the Bell and LaPadula model will not be sufficient. To avoid an integrity violation, Biba suggests that integrity attributes may be assigned to each subject and object.[18] The subject receives his/her current integrity attribute based on the lowest integrity attribute of all items to which he/she has read access (the low-water mark for subjects); he/she may either be fully restricted for writing into an area with higher integrity attributes or output may be labeled by the current attribute (the low-water mark for objects).[19]

Additional concepts and specific implementation techniques have been postulated and include spray painting[20] and Boebert's types and domains. When implemented concurrently, a security policy (MAC) and an integrity policy together provide a reasonable countermeasure against Trojan horse attacks.[21]

Discretionary Access Controls

Many processing environments do not require mandatory access controls. For many installations, a discretionary security policy provides the required level of security and assurance. Mandatory and discretionary policies are differentiated in a number of ways. Mandatory polices mandate that various types of information be separated from various types of users. This distinction is generally reflected by the sensitivity level of data and the authorization or privilege level of users. A discretionary policy allows for the owner/creator/possessor of the data to decide who may access it. Many times this decision is based on a user's need for the information in question. Therefore, mandatory policies, which are consistent and all-encompassing, are definitive restrictions, whereas discretionary policies allow for the owner/creator/possessor to decide the rules and access rights of other network users.

Although DAC policies have been shown to be fundamentally flawed against Trojan horse attacks, DAC is mentioned here because it is a predominant security measure. The Trojan horse threat to a DAC environment is increased or decreased depending on the target network and the users and administrators of that network. If users are properly trained and administrators properly manage, a DAC policy can be implemented to provide a very limited degree of protection against Trojan horse attacks. This minimal protection is afforded through separation of users and data based on intelligent and competent discretionary decisions.

Management of Software Development

The competent management of a software development effort is critical to the successful control of malicious logic introduction. Various aspects of management are critical in the prevention of Trojan horse attacks. Often, the first decision mandated is the selection of the staff to perform the work. The manager of this software development effort should be selective when he or she chooses the development team. The selection of competent and trustworthy individuals is one of the most important decisions made by software development managers. This selection process can ensure a professional and competent development team and can also greatly decrease the amount of risk associated with malicious activity.

The manager should immediately establish configuration management procedures and policies and a quality assurance program. Based on the size of the program, the manager may want to divide the development effort into separate groups of individuals. By providing separation, there is a lessened opportunity for collusion between developers, thus reducing the exposure for Trojan horse introduction. As with all management functions, planning is required for a successful development. In addition, planning and milestone performance and deadlines imply a degree of progress, and the would-be perpetrator may not have the time or resources to implement a Trojan horse since there are deadlines to meet. Additional techniques are described below. It is important to note that these ideas will never work without the total commitment and support of the manager of the development effort.

Logic Flow Diagrams

To successfully deter the introduction of a Trojan horse, the technical staff of a software development effort and the management of that staff should be abreast of the intended logical flow of the developed software. This understanding can be gained easily through simple flow charting documentation. The three primary questions answered by this process are:

1. How do software modules interface?

2. Why do they require an interface?

3. If they do interface, what information, parameters, transfers of logic, etc., are being passed between them?

As with the initial software development, subsequent enhancements to software should also be subjected to these questions. In addition, for each proposed software update or enhancement another qualification question should always be asked: What is the purpose of the upgrade or enhancement?

Interrelational Logic Description

Interrelational logic descriptions are a further refinement of logic flow diagrams and they represent a second step in determining the definitive operations associated with a module-to-module interface. Now it is not only important to understand what type of data or parameters is being passed between software modules, but also its content and size. This process is also effective in identifying software interfaces that should not exist.

In many instances interrelational logic descriptions can be more effectively portrayed if the programs are represented in a different format or presentation. Special decompilers, disassemblers, and flow-charting programs can be used to transform a program into another form or into a different language, which might make a Trojan horse stand out and be easier to find.[22]

Eliminations of Software Development Dependencies

As discussed above, one technique to restrict the propagation or introduction of malicious code is the independent development of software functions. There should be a clear and distinct separation of functions and processes between various programmers. Programs can be designed and developed in small modules by different programmers, so that formal interface standards are required between modules. The manager may also want to identify the most critical areas of the development (relative to the security policy) and subdivide those areas between a number of programmers. Programs can be developed and debugged by one team of programmers and tested by another team. These techniques force the need for collusion and make hiding a Trojan horse more difficult.

Documentation

Without accurate and concise documentation, configuration management, quality control, and security assurance are impossible to attain. Documentation should be an integral part of software development and should be a continuous and living representation of the processes performed and their need, justification, and relationship to the network.

Techniques to Eliminate Trojan Horses in User Code

Most networks are not protected against the threat of Trojan horse attacks through the informal user development environment. Perhaps the best example is the academic computing environment. Computer science majors have authorized access to computing resources, are well-trained, and have been known to penetrate internal security protection mechanisms. Normally there are no procedures or policies in place that would prevent a malicious user from sabotaging the network with a Trojan horse program. The problem stems from the intimate knowledge gained during day-to-day interaction with the network. The average user learns tricks and shortcuts, network security flaws, and ways and means to directly access network resources or system software (e.g., operating system). These qualifications make the average user of a network a qualified and competent threat. Most networked environments do not restrict the introduction of public domain or user software. This common lack of control increases the vulnerability to Trojan horse attacks.

Restricted User Software Development or Isolation

The simplest method available to prevent the introduction of Trojan horse programs is a comprehensive policy that prevents users from developing or introducing software into a network. Basically, users are forbidden to develop software or bring software to work and execute it on the network. This technique can be taken to extremes. For example, the network administrator could remove all compilers, assemblers, and separate files containing executable code from data files. For most environments this technique is far too restrictive; however, it can be applied to networks where the users are not required to develop or enhance software. A variation of this technique is to prevent software from being developed on the operational network. A development machine could be used, and only verified and tested user code would be ported from the development network to the operational one.

Manual Review of Logic/Source

Software programs (source and object) generated by users may be examined manually to determine whether a potential Trojan horse program exists.

One of the greatest benefits of this activity is that it instills fear in the would-be perpetrator. If the user knows that all developed software will be scrutinized, specifically for security reasons, there will be less likelihood for covert activity. In many environments, automated assessment tools are not available, and manual review is the only available method of detection or prevention of Trojan horses in user code. The manual review of printouts can be a cumbersome task and often will not provide any additional prevention against the introduction of a Trojan horse program. A Trojan horse program can be sprinkled throughout many programs or may erase itself after execution. Therefore, having and reviewing source code is useful but is not a complete solution to the Trojan horse problem.

Behavioral Observation

The network administrator can generate statistics on user-developed software. Statistics such as processing time, types of resources accessed, memory usage, CPU usage, etc., are all valid ways to measure the behavior of the program. Once this data is gathered, the network administrator is in a position to test and validate the processing characteristics of the program. If a certain threshold is exceeded or abnormal processing characteristics are noted, there may be an active Trojan horse causing the anomaly. With statistics on user-generated programs, the network administrator is also in a better position to understand what is actually executing in the network.

Risk Management Scheme

This technique is implemented "by classifying executables according to the likelihood that they contain malicious code, and giving users a way to avoid unwitting use of high-risk software."[23]

Since software and programs can originate from various places and individuals, it is important to assess their threat potential. The network administrator should attempt to determine the origin of software to be used on a secure processing network. This can be a way to categorize software and to prevent the intermingling of software relative to origin and assessed threat potential. Much like an integrity label, software would be labeled or controlled based on its threat potential. If the origin of the software is such that it warrants significant concern, it should be restricted from entering the system. If the software is from a reputable organization or user who had provided consistently secure and nonmalicious software in the past, it would be much easier to trust. Software categorized as middle-of-the-road should be restricted from interacting with software with a lower likelihood of contamination. This particular technique would be beneficial in a DAC environment.

8.9 MAINTAINING "TROJAN HORSE–FREE" CODE

Once a secure software development effort is completed, the developed software must be maintained and protected against unauthorized modification. A comprehensive configuration management program is required to maintain and protect software. This program can be augmented with user training and specific countermeasures directed at ensuring consistent and accurate software execution. These techniques are discussed below.

Training

Training instills awareness. Users and developers with access to secure networking environments must be continuously trained on the proper procedures for software development and the risks associated with various threats (e.g., Trojan horses). If users and developers are trained continuously on these aspects of secure processing, the likelihood of a compromise or crime is lessened. One hour per month, at a predefined time and place, a training session should take place where users and developers can meet and discuss security objectives. These meetings can also provide the forum for discussing anomalies or concerns with current security practices and procedures.

It is important that this training and awareness is reinforced and that areas of responsibility are clearly delineated. Each individual who has physical, logical, or any other type of influence or control over a secure processing environment must understand the established security requirements and policies. Reinforcement of security awareness can manifest itself in many ways (e.g., additional training classes, videos, documentation, reports, bulletins).

Encryption

Encryption of executable code can be used as a method to protect programs from Trojan horse attacks. When programs are developed and tested and found to be free (to the greatest extent possible) of malicious logic, they can be encrypted and stored in encrypted format. Prior to execution these programs are decrypted. If a Trojan horse attempts to write to an encrypted program, the results would be unintelligible and useless to the perpetrator. However, the program would be subject to Trojan horse attack during its execution (while decrypted) and, therefore, this technique is not foolproof.

Read-Only Memory

When programs are developed and tested and found to be free (to the greatest extent possible) of malicious logic, they can be put into ROM devices to prevent a Trojan horse program from gaining access to them. Programs stored in ROM devices are protected from modification because they cannot be modified. The most obvious example of a read-only storage device is the commonly used CD-ROM. Adequate measures must be taken to ensure that only uninfected programs are stored in ROM. Since the information in a ROM device cannot be changed, ROM should be used only to store final executable versions of software. In this manner, source code would be separate from executable code and would be developed and maintained on a separate system and not on the target system. A ROM device is vulnerable to a perpetrator replacing a ROM device with a contaminated one. Therefore, if executable software is protected by using ROM devices, physical protection of these devices must be afforded.

Configuration Management and Control

The preceding ideas and guidelines are incomplete without the complementary use of a continuous and thorough application of configuration management and control. Without configuration management, software development and software maintainability become nontractable. The configuration management of a secure network is a critical parameter associated with the avoidance of Trojan horses. This is especially true for large software development programs. The intent is to provide procedures and automated mechanisms to promote the consistent knowledge of the current and accurate version of software.

Configuration management is only effective if it is applied throughout the network's life cycle. Therefore, upon development initiation, configuration management must be established, applied, and supported. Once the network is implemented, configuration management remains intact and grows and matures in tandem with the network.

8.10 SUMMARY

A Trojan horse is a potential threat to any network. The most frightening attribute of a Trojan horse is that it is actually a simple mechanism that most computer-literate individuals can implement. Trojan horses are not the tools of hostile intelligence agencies, but rather the tools of the everyday computer user.

Computer systems that implement a DAC policy are fundamentally flawed against a Trojan horse attack. A DAC policy allows authorized users to arbitrarily grant or deny access to information. Since users can stipulate access privileges for individuals and programs, a DAC policy cannot be consistently applied.

Computer systems that implement a MAC policy greatly reduce their vulnerability to Trojan horse attacks. A MAC policy provides universal and consistent mediation between subjects and objects within various access classes. Specifically, the implementation and enforcement of a MAC policy protects systems against the unauthorized transfer of information from a higher access class to a lower access class. If a MAC policy is properly implemented, a Trojan horse requires a covert channel in order to transfer data from a higher access class to a lower one. Therefore, these covert processes would be required to work in collusion with one another.

A common myth surrounding the Trojan horse threat is that a source listing of a program can be an absolute solution to identifying a Trojan horse program. As was shown, a Trojan horse program may operate without notice; hence, no one would take the time to look for it. A Trojan horse program may be embedded within system code consisting of millions of lines. Even if an individual was positive that a Trojan horse existed in a particular program, the probability of locating the Trojan horse would be remote. A Trojan horse program can be sprinkled throughout many programs and may not be represented in its entirety in any one program. A Trojan horse program can successfully perform a malicious act and then erase itself from existence. The perpetrator is presented with many options to avoid being discovered through a review of source code. The bottom line is that having and reviewing source code is useful but is not a total solution to the Trojan horse problem.

Strict enforcement of structured programming techniques, configuration management and control, information flow analysis, logic descriptions, division of responsibility, and the proper selection of personnel all contribute to the deterrence of Trojan horse attacks. However, there is no universal solution that eliminates the Trojan horse threat.

END NOTES

1. National Computer Security Center, *Trusted Computer System Evaluation Criteria*, DoD 5200.28 STD, 1985.

2. P. A. Myers, "Subversion: The Neglected Aspect of Computer Security," Master's thesis, Naval Postgraduate School, 1980.

3. Ken Thompson, "Reflections on Trusting Trust," *Communications of the ACM* 27, no. 8 (August 1984).

4. Howard Israel, "Computer Viruses: Myth or Reality?" in *Proceedings of the 10th NBS/NCSC National Computer Security Conference*, 1987, 226–230.

5. Ibid.

6. National Computer Security Center, op. cit.

7. Donn B. Parker, *Fighting Computer Crime.* (New York: Scribners), 1983, 122-123.

8. Israel, op. cit.

9. Ibid.

10. National Computer Security Center, op. cit.

11. A. R. Clyde, "Insider Threat Identification Systems," in *Proceedings of the 10th NBS/NCSC National Computer Security Conference*, 1987, 343–356.

12. Ibid.

13. "Computer Hackers Crack International NASA Network," *Gazette Telegraph* (September 16, 1987): A8.

14. Parker, op. cit.

15. Peter Grant and Robert Ricke, "The Eagle's Own Plume," in *Navy Proceedings*, July 1983.

16. Israel, op. cit.

17. David Bell and Leonard LaPadula, *Secure Computer Systems: Mathematical Foundations*, MTR 2547, vol. 1, The MITRE Corporation, March 1, 1973.

18. Ken Biba, "Integrity Considerations for Secure Computer Systems," in *USAF Electronic Systems Division*, ESD-TR-76-372, 1977.

19. David Bonyun, "A New Look at Integrity Policy for Database Management Systems," in *Proceedings of the National Computer Security Center Invitational Workshop on Database Security*, May 1986, 1–18.

20. "Multilevel Data Management Security," in *Woods Hole Workshop on Secure DBMS* (Washington, DC: Committee on Multilevel Data Management Security, Air Force Studies Board, Commission on Engineering and Technical Systems, National Research Council, National Academy Press), 1983.

21. Israel, op. cit.

22. Parker, op. cit.

23. Maria M. Pozzo and Terence E. Gray, "Managing Exposure to Potentially Malicious Programs," in *Proceedings from the 9th DoD/NBS National Computer Security Conference*, 1986, 75–80.

9

Covert Channels

The subject of covert channels in networks, once the domain of detached intellectuals, is rapidly becoming the everyday problem of an ever-widening range of professionals both in the network security field and in related fields that include systems engineering, software development, computer acquisition, and others. Both system defenders and attackers are becoming more sophisticated and better armed. With higher expectations and demands from users, the distributed computing industry's next broad target is the mandatory access control environment, where covert channels must be addressed. As networks strive for higher levels of trust and as the more blatant vulnerabilities are eliminated from their design, the continuing presence of covert channels constitutes a proportionately larger vulnerability.

For the system user, buyer, specifier, or administrator, covert channels are among the least understood threats to networks. Still less understood by all but a handful of security experts are the techniques used to identify and measure covert channels. Nevertheless, to develop a secure network capable of enforcing mandatory access control protections, the ability to identify and measure covert channels is important.

9.1 THE COVERT CHANNEL THREAT

There are many other means to penetrate a network than through the use of a covert channel (which we'll "define" at length in the next section). For example, it is probably easier to guess passwords, to sabotage a network

165

physically, or to bribe or coerce personnel to acquire the information surreptitiously than to implant a Trojan horse in a network and launch a more sophisticated attack. Nevertheless, the potential payoff can be very high. The principal advantage of the covert channel is that it is unlikely to be discovered and can thus result in substantial leakage even if the bandwidth of the channel is relatively low.

Unlike more direct compromises, the major damage from a covert channel is its ability to operate 24 hours a day, seven days a week, and to do so with little traceability to a specific individual, in the unlikely event of discovery. Using a Trojan horse within the network and making use of a covert channel to signal information is equivalent to planting a mole inside the enemy's intelligence system and obtaining permission to transmit the stolen information with guaranteed bandwidth.[1] The goal, intent, purpose, and mission of a covert channel is to compromise the mandatory access control policy of a system. The Trojan horse program provides the intelligence and ability to signal information to a lower sensitivity process. The highway, path, or mechanism used to allow the information to be transferred to a lower-level process (thereby compromising the MAC) is the covert channel.

Causes for Covert Channels

There are two possible causes of covert channels: 1) design oversights or 2) weakness inherent in a network design. While covert channels caused by design oversights may be corrected once identified, those that are intrinsic to the network architecture cannot be easily removed without impeding or preventing intended functionality. Therefore, within most networks there will always be at least one residual covert channel. These channels will either be storage or timing channels with certain bandwidth characteristics. After the application of countermeasures, it will generally require insiders, such as system programmers or network administrators in some cooperative fashion, to implant a Trojan horse inside the system to signal information through a covert channel in violation of the security policy.

9.2   GENERAL CONCEPTS

Because the discussion of covert channels hinges upon the notion of a channel, that term is discussed here. This is not so much a search for the right definition as an attempt to establish a common foundation and framework for the discussion of covert channels to follow.

In data communications systems, a channel is a means of transferring information from one entity to one or more other entities. The word system is used here in the broadest sense and can include a single-user computer, a multiuser computer, clustered computers, networks, network components, or combinations of networks. The term entity will herein mean a human or an automated process operating directly or indirectly on behalf of a human. It is also assumed that at least one entity is within the system under observation while the other entities may be within or outside of that system or both.

Intuitively, one normally thinks of a data channel as a confined path where information acts much like a fluid, inserted into the channel at a physical source, confined along its route and forced to take a specific physical path, and removed from the channel at its destination. In data communications systems, several necessary components of a channel can be identified. The most basic component is the medium. Media include devices such as a silicon storage cell on a chip, a magnetic region on a disk, a wire, a beam of light, or microwaves. The medium must have at least one property or attribute whose condition is changeable: the voltage on a wire, the stability state of a memory cell, the magnetic polarity of a region on a disk, or the intensity or color of a beam of light. As long as the condition of the medium remains unaltered, no information can be conveyed.

Information can be impressed upon the medium by changing its condition. In communications, this process is called modulation. Since the change affects the entire medium, a sensor attached to the medium at any point can be designed to detect or notice the change. Depending on design, the sensor may notice only one or two media states or may be able to notice the degree of change over some range. When there is a suitable medium, if its condition can be altered, and if such an alteration can be sensed, it is a communication channel. Typically, communication is thought of as occurring between two, or among more than two, entities. An entity can also communicate with itself. In practice this is usually done to allow the entity to store information for its own later use. The same entity is then the transmitter as well as the receiver. To communicate on the channel, especially between two or among more than two entities, transmitting and receiving entities need only agree upon a convention that establishes the meaning of a condition change. This convention, which is often complex, is called a communications protocol.

Storage and Timing Channels

The condition of the medium and the time at which the medium entered that condition are inseparably related. Without change, time is meaningless and the information contained in the condition or state of a medium is valid or significant only at a specified instant or during a specified period as agreed upon in the communications protocol. Protocols can nevertheless be primarily oriented to either the condition of the medium at a certain time or the time at which a change in the condition of the medium occurs. It is this protocol orientation that distinguishes storage channels from timing channels.

When the receiver is primarily interested in the condition of the medium at a certain instant or during a certain interval at which or during which the protocol says that the state of the medium is valid or meaningful, the channel is said to be a storage channel. Put simply, a covert storage channel is "a covert channel that involves the direct or indirect writing of a storage location by one process and the direct or indirect reading of the storage location by another process. Covert storage channels typically involve a finite resource (e.g., sectors on a disk or portions of main memory) that is shared by two subjects at different security levels."[2] In storage channels, the sensor expects no changes in the medium's condition while the medium is being sensed. A storage channel is characterized by a lengthy period of stability between changes of the medium where the time over which the medium's condition is valid is not particularly critical. The conventional use of a computer's memory is a good example of storage channels. The sensing process is more interested in what the condition of the memory cell is at the time of access rather than when the change occurred.

When the receiver is primarily interested in whether or not the condition of the medium has changed, or how often it has changed, or when it changes, the type of covert channel is said to be a timing channel. Put simply, a covert timing channel is "a covert channel in which one process signals information to another by modulating its own use of system resources (e.g., CPU time) in such a way that this manipulation affects the real response time observed by the second process."[3] The information is contained in the time at which the cell's condition changes rather than in the state of the medium. In timing channels, the sensor expects a change during the interval of sensing. Whereas a change during the sensing interval will confuse a storage channel, that change conveys information to a timing channel. It should be noted that the absence of an occurrence during the period of sensing can also convey information. A serial channel to a peripheral device is a good example of a timing channel. The sensing process is more interested in if, when, or how often the condition of the medium is changed rather than the condition itself. There are timing channels commonly used in computer equipment such as tape or disk systems and networks where the actual condition of the medium is irrelevant. Only the time at which it switched from one state to the other is significant, especially when referenced to a common source of time intervals such as a system clock. Loepere refers to static and time decaying channels as having similar meanings as storage and timing channels, respectively.[4]

Definition of Covert Channels

Although the general notion of a covert channel is fairly consistent among security professionals, the term itself unfortunately has no definition that enjoys universal acceptance. There are at least *eight* definitions in popular literature that contain some distinctions.

In the broadest sense, a covert channel exists any time it is possible to communicate information through a channel for purposes other than those intended by the owner of the channel or the owner of that information, or both. Almost invariably, the channel also conveys noncovert information, which is the reason for the channel's existence in the first place. If the channel served no overtly useful purpose, its very presence would be suspect. The covert transmission then "shares" the channel and could in some sense be considered a parasitic channel in that it usurps some of the legitimate channel's unused bandwidth to convey covert or disguised information.

9.3   COVERT CHANNEL TAXONOMY

There are currently two recognized covert channel types—covert storage channels and covert timing channels. Additionally, there are other covert channels that are undefined, that is, unclassified by other attributes. Let's look at both the defined covert channels as well as the undefined types.

Defined Covert Channels

The TCSEC and the TNI both define a covert storage channel to be "a covert channel that involves the direct or indirect writing of a storage location by one process and the direct or indirect reading of the storage location by another process. Covert storage channels typically involve a finite resource (e.g., sectors on a disk) that is shared by two subjects at different security levels."[5]

The TCSEC and the TNI both define a covert timing channel to be "a covert channel in which one process signals information to another by modulating its own use of system resources (e.g., CPU time) in such a way that this manipulation affects the real response time observed by the second process."[6]

Undefined Covert Channels

Except for the two broad categorizations of covert channels into the storage and timing variety, little work has been done to decompose covert channels further by other attributes. Keith Loepere classifies channels into static and time-decaying as a more precise distinction between storage and timing channels. He also categorizes covert channels by ease of use and bandwidth. Specifically, categorization of covert channels by the kinds of modulation and sensing techniques employed would be most useful to both the designer and the evaluator. There are other fine distinctions in the categorization that would be useful if set forth in a taxonomy. For most attributes of covert channels there are usually only two possibilities. A table of permutations or a matrix of these possibilities could be constructed, providing a useful checklist tool in designs or evaluations.

9.4   EXPLOITATION OF COVERT CHANNELS

The mere presence or identification of a covert channel is not synonymous with its exploitation. Once a covert channel is identified, it means only that a medium suitable for covert exchanges has been found and a vehicle for exploitation exists. To use that vehicle, additional processes are required that are interdependent with the covert channel and must work in close harmony. This section examines these interdependencies and assumptions required before a channel can be exploited in a covert manner. To exploit a covert channel successfully, the perpetrator must employ a number of steps and processes. These processes are discussed below in a step-by-step procedure by which a perpetrator constructs an end-to-end covert communications system through exploitation of a covert channel.

Identification of a Covert Channel Candidate

To exploit a channel, one must first be located. It is easier if the perpetrator has a comprehensive knowledge of the system, but it is not necessary. Finding a channel can be done analytically or experimentally, or both. One of the many myths regarding covert channels is that it takes great skill to find one. This is not to be confused with finding all covert channels in a system, which takes immense skill and knowledge. Analytically, the perpetrator can generate a list of potential covert channels by constructing a shared resource matrix, as suggested by Kemmerer.[7]

Any identified channel must be outside the security domain of the system or network. In other words, the resources being modulated or utilized to support a covert channel cannot be under the control or surveillance of the computer or network reference monitor. Systems that implement mandatory access controls, for example, would not permit information for a higher sensitivity level to be passed to a subject or object at a lower sensitivity level. As a result, a perpetrator must ensure that the composition of the channel selected does not include subjects and/or objects that are mediated by security control mechanisms.

If system/network information and technical specifications are not available, or if the perpetrator does not want to draw attention to himself or herself by showing interest in system documents, covert channels can be found experimentally by feeling out the system. This method is especially practical where the perpetrator has only remote access. It is done by creating two or more processes at the same security level or sensitivity. The perpetrator methodically exercises each system/network–level service or function, including error generation, to see which can be influenced in a predictable way. Then, an attempt is made to sense that influence from a second process. If the second process can sense the influence of the first process on a system/network resource, a potential covert channel has been found. Once the target resources have been identified, the next set of experiments determines whether the test-sensing processes can sense use of the target resources by a process at a higher sensitivity level. If so, the potential covert channel is now identified as an actual usable covert channel.

Channel Exploitation after Identification

Once a covert channel is identified, the perpetrator must quantify the type of information transmitted over the channel. How is the channel currently being used by the system/network? What processes or resources are associated with the channel? What common operations or state changes take place in the channel? What information is available to the channel? These questions must be answered by the perpetrator to understand thoroughly the relationship of changes in the channel in order to assess that channel's value for exploitation.

The shared resource chosen should be used infrequently by other processes. Normal use by other processes constitutes noise to the perpetrator and reduces the channel's effective bandwidth. The shared resource should not be used too seldom by other processes lest the compromising process call the attention of a monitoring routine upon itself by being the only or predominant user of that shared resource. The most exploitable shared resource is one that is used in bursts by one process, then in a burst by another, so that for the time of the burst, the probability of noise is reduced. Application of commonly available error correction protocols can also reduce the degradation effect of noise on the covert channel. Error detection and correction codes can be interspersed into the covert transmissions to allow the receiver to do error recovery or retransmission when noise occurs. This allows the covert channel to compromise information reliably even in the presence of noise.

Channel Access

From a practical network security perspective, it is critical to understand that the ability to use a channel in a covert manner assumes many things, not the least of which is gaining access to the channel. In addition to the existence of a shared resource (the channel) that is not under the purview of the mandatory controls, there must be a vehicle or method of conveying information to the shared resource at one sensitivity (or different) level and to recover it from the resource at a lower sensitivity (or different) level.

Access to the low side of the channel, the side to which the information is to be sent, is relatively easy because it operates at a lower sensitivity level. Users at the lower sensitivity levels are less scrutinized. Access to the high side of the channel is trickier but still not difficult. The most obvious way is to have a user with authorized access plant the program to access the high side of the channel. This scenario must assume an insider threat where a perpetrator has authorized access to the network. The flaw in this scenario is that such an insider would have direct access to the information and can usually remove it in larger volumes through means less convoluted than a covert channel.

The most successful and therefore most common approach that allows the perpetrator access to the high end of a channel generally involves the implantation of a Trojan horse into the system. The program is usually introduced free as a public domain program or an upgrade of an existing program and subverted into a Trojan horse. The objective is to attract a user with a high privilege level to use one of these convenient programs. Upon execution, the program assumes the privilege level of the user executing it. The program is now free to set up housekeeping as the modulator of a covert channel and has access to compromiseable information at the privilege level of the user.

Channel Modulation

When an access route to an identified and useful channel is quantified, the perpetrator must now implement a modulation scheme. Modulation techniques can take many forms. Modulation is a technique that alters at least one attribute of a medium in such a way as to impress additional information onto the medium in a disguised form. To remain covert, the selected modulation scheme must not interfere with information normally transmitted by the channel. For example, if error messages are used, the perpetrator would want to modulate them so that the number of errors would not dramatically increase. If continuous errors were recorded, the system administrator or an automatic security monitor that detects behavioral abnormalities in processes may elect to run extensive tests and in doing so may uncover the covert activity. Almost every modulation technique used in routine data communications can be applied to the modulation of a covert channel.

Covert Protocols

Protocols are the communication rules and conventions between processes or entities stating how the information is to be transferred between them. The term "covert protocol" has been conceived to represent the cooperative, peer-to-peer conventions used to orchestrate information transfer in a covert manner over a covert timing or storage channel. A covert protocol is exercised when two or more peer processes communicate covertly through the use of some medium (the covert channel), contrary to the security policy of a system. As mentioned earlier, these processes are usually instantiations of a Trojan horse. Protocols or processes already implemented within the system to execute legitimate functions may also be modified or subverted to serve this purpose.

Covert protocols operate within the native architecture of the computer system, which makes them especially difficult to detect. Regardless of the resources exploited to transfer information covertly, the problem is not solely the shared resource, but the combination of an exploitable resource with the covert protocols.

Information Reception

If a process is able to modulate a communications channel and transmit data effectively via a common resource (i.e., a channel), there still must be a peer process to receive the data. The receiving process must always be prepared to receive the data or must be awakened in some way. In some cases a specified sector on a disk may be the designated location for the data to be picked up, or it may be a predefined memory location, or even a specified hardware register. Whatever the location for data reception, the receiving process must know where to position itself and when to look for the data. The receiving end of a covert channel is normally in an environment of lower sensitivity and security scrutiny, so it is relatively easy for the perpetrator to implant. For that reason it is desirable that the modulating process be as simple as possible while the recovery process, in a more liberal environment, can be as complex as necessary.

Information Usage and Benefit

Once the data have been transmitted, a receiving process must be able to reconstruct or decode the data. Since the data being communicated over a specific channel is modulated, the ability to decipher it into a useful form is necessary. Again, without cooperative and consistent operations, the use of a covert channel cannot be successful.

9.5 SYSTEM VULNERABILITIES EXPLOITED BY COVERT CHANNELS

This section addresses network vulnerabilities and illustrates how covert channels are used to exploit those vulnerabilities and ultimately compromise sensitive information.

The network vulnerabilities exploited through the use of covert channels are potentially numerous. The first obvious vulnerability consists of the totality of security controls and countermeasures. If mandatory controls within a network are not enforced or do not work correctly, the instances for exploitation of vulnerabilities through the use of covert channels substantially increase. For networks that do not enforce mandatory access controls, the number of avenues and methods that can be used to exploit vulnerabilities within a given system is increased to the point where one could argue that covert channels in nonmandatory access control environments are unpreventable.

If it is assumed that mandatory access controls exist within a given network and that they operate correctly, one can then define certain criteria within which a covert channel is forced to operate. Under this assumption, it is possible to limit, or at least better understand, the potential vulnerabilities within a network. These criteria are assumed here and used to draw certain conclusions. What then are the network vulnerabilities exploited through the use of covert channels? There are three major categories explained below.

1. The incorrect implementation or operation of mandatory security access controls and the inability to provide mediation between subjects and objects

2. The sharing of a network resource by processes accessible to subjects at different sensitivity levels

3. The ability to introduce malicious logic (covert protocols) into a network where an existing channel can be used to facilitate covert information transfer

The vulnerability represented in 1, if true, can act on its own and provide the means for a compromise. On the other hand, 2 and 3 must act in harmony for a compromise to be realized.

Covert Storage Channels—Examples

1. Page faults are a favorite resource for covert channels. Here processes can exhaust the available memory so that the operating system needs to replace an unused memory page with a requested one from mass storage. Two processes, one at a high sensitivity level and one at a lower sensitivity level can manipulate the resource to exchange information.

2. Resource exhaustion is another common technique. Here the higher sensitivity level process intentionally uses the last available sector, block, file descriptor, etc. The lower sensitivity level process purposely tries to obtain the agreed-upon resource. Information can be conveyed depending upon whether the resource can be succesfully obtained or whether it is exhausted.

3. Print spacing manipulation—word processors can use an array of functions to present text on a screen or in printed format. One such attribute of many word processors is their ability to provide spacing justification so that all text is even on the right as well as the left margin. A user at a high sensitivity level could use the word processor to edit a document. The word processor would assume the privileges of the user. While the program overtly accesses only nonsensitive information, causing its output to be labeled nonsensitive, malicious logic could access sensitive information (downgraded previously by a Trojan horse) and modulate the data to convey information. Such modulation could be based on those spacing attributes, and a covert storage channel could result. Say, for example, that for each line of printed text the spacing between the first and second word would represent a bit. If there were two spaces between the first and second word, it would signal a (0); if there were only one space between the words, it would signal a (1). Without going into elaborate detail, one can see how such a simple process could be used to convey sensitive information.

One can, for example, use a space-backspace-space or space-space-backspace sequence or similar technique to accomplish the same thing. A hex-dump would show this to be unusual, if someone thinks of doing a hex-dump. An even more insidious but innocent looking method that does not easily show up even in a hex-dump involves modulation of the spacing between words and even microspacing between letters in a proportionally spaced printout.

The examples above do not actually require a covert channel to extract the information from the system, since the data already has been captured by a Trojan horse and downgraded to to be nonsensitive. In fact, it could simply be printed as nonsensitive and taken from the facility without notice. The benefit, however, is that the covert channel allows the data to be hidden and therefore the chance of the perpetrator being caught is minimal.

4. Disk space available—assuming a group of processes of different authorizations are each allowed to allocate free space on a disk, and each process can query the network operating system for the amount of available space, a potential covert channel exists. In this example, a high authorization process can encode data in the amount of disk space that it allocates, the amount of which can be measured by the lower authorization process through the reduction of available disk space. The point to this example is the fact that the indicator (avail-

able disk space) is not protected by the reference monitor since it is not considered as a normal object.[8] In fact, virtual objects cannot be labeled because this could cause a compromise regardless of decisions. This is a specific instance of the resource exhaustion technique.

Covert Timing Channels

1. Memory paging. One attribute of memory paging is that a page is either currently in memory or is currently out of memory. If a page can be read by processes of multiple authorizations, a usable covert channel exists. This potential covert channel is made possible by using page faults upon the page. A high authorization process has the option to either page in a page, or not. The lower authorization process can then inquire about the page, and, by measuring the time it takes to make the inquiry, determine whether the page was paged into memory by the high process.[9] Similar to the page fault storage channel illustrated above, it shows how the same resource can be used as a storage or a timing channel.

2. Processor availability. The ability to sense the time at which a processor is available could be used as a covert timing channel. If one processor could manipulate and control the availability of a processor and another process could sense that time, a potential covert timing channel would exist.

9.6   COVERT CHANNEL ANALYSIS AND MEASUREMENT TECHNIQUES

Discovery of covert channels only indicates that there are potential leaks in the system but says nothing about the size or flow rate of the leak. To assess the potential damage one must be able to estimate how much sensitive data can be compromised through the use of the channel and at what rates this information can be leaked. Without an accurate assessment of the risk involved, the cost-to-benefit tradeoff to eliminate or restrict the channel cannot be intelligently made. The following methods of covert channel analysis are presented in simplified form to get a flavor of what is involved in bandwidth measurement.

To date, the abilities and methods used to expose or identify the existence of covert channels have fallen short of completeness, especially in networks. Kemmerer submits that, for the most part, methods used to discover covert channels have been system-dependent and that no universal methodology has been successful. The use of formal methods has been restrictive or nonexistent, except for the use of a single specification language. Kemmerer has postulated a method that is effective through all phases of a software development life cycle and provides increased assurance that all covert channels have been discovered. This method is called the shared resource matrix and uses a matrix allocation methodology to represent all shared resources that may constitute an information channel.[10]

The Access Control Method

The access control method, usually implemented through the Bell and LaPadula model,[11] is the most prevalent mechanism to prevent security violations within secure networks. This method is often mistaken by lay persons as a means to detect or estimate covert channels. It is not. Its mention here is solely to emphasize that it is not. In fact, it could be said that while this method works well to model nondiscretionary (mandatory) access control between subjects and storage objects, its inability to deal effectively with covert channels is one of its biggest drawbacks and gives rise to the creation of the other methods mentioned below. Jonathan Millen of MITRE maintains that the access control models (of which the Bell and LaPadula model is an instantiation) have been perceived as inadequate "because of the existence of covert channels in systems that obey an apparently airtight access control policy."[12] He points out that, ironically, the very error messages that deny access to some objects become the vehicle for security policy violations when they are used as covert channels.

Informal Methodologies

Information methodologies expedite the process of identifying the more obvious covert channels in a system. Informal methods can be used to show areas, processes, and functions within a system that do not require increased attention for covert channel identification through formal methods. It is useful to evaluators and developers to employ informal methods first to identify obvious areas of concern and then rely on more formal methodologies for positive covert channel identification, testing, and resolution.

The Information Flow Method

Information flow analysis is a more definite bandwidth estimation. There are several information flow models available to measure the capacity of covert channels. Information flow analysis determines interrelationships that are required for information to be transmitted using a covert channel. Information flow models are able to determine where information flows and which processes (subjects) or data (objects) are affected by the flow. This method has been espoused by Virgil Gligor and others.[13,14] This method first defines all system variables that exist, then does a structured, step-by-step analysis of when, under what conditions, and by which processes those variables can be altered or their condition sensed. In this manner, it can be determined if high-level processes can ever attempt to pass information to low-level processes through such variables. The process is a cumbersome and tedious one, but it is very thorough. Today, front-end analyses have dramatically reduced the amount of flow analysis necessary.

The Shared Resource Matrix Method

The premise behind the use of a shared resource matrix (SRM) is that it identifies in a concise and exhaustive manner all potentially shared resources. The method defines a shared resource as an object or group of objects that can be referenced or modified by more than one process. Further, it defines all resource attributes. When completed, the matrix identifies potential covert channels and how these channels may be used to exploit the security policy of the system.

This method of covert channel discovery and bandwidth estimation was first postulated by Richard Kemmerer in 1981 and further refined in 1983.[15] It defines four conditions that must be met to have a covert channel.

1. Two processes must have access to a common resource.
2. One process must be able to alter the condition of the resource.
3. The other process must be able to sense if the resource has been altered.
4. There must be a mechanism for initiating and sequencing communications over this channel.

The method establishes a matrix in which all objects and their attributes are plotted against alteration or sensing primitives of processes in the system. The entries in the matrix show clearly where processes access objects and whether the access is an altering or sensing access. Once the matrix is filled in, one easily can examine any object to see if alteration and sensing can be done by different processes. If it can, a potential covert channel exists. Next, the processes are examined to see if they could be at two different security levels; if not, that channel is ignored. Finally, the remaining suspect channels are analyzed, using conventional information flow modeling. The use of the SRM greatly reduces the number of channels that need to be analyzed and therefore reduces the total effort. Bandwidth measurement is performed by gross estimation whereby the maximum number of possible accesses is multiplied by the greatest amount of information possible per access. This yields the worst case maximum channel bandwidth. It should be noted that this method greatly overestimates the bandwidth because it does not consider interference (noise from other noncooperative processes that obfuscates the information transferred on the covert channel).

Formal Methodologies

Formal methodologies differ from informal ones in that they allow for greater scrutiny of the system in question, relative to covert channel discovery. Formal methods are generally much more intense and time consuming than informal ones and require greater knowledge and understanding of the techniques used and system being tested. Mathematical proofs, specification languages, and automated mechanisms provide support in this quest for greater assurance and provable security.

Formal Verification

Formal verification is an extension of the above techniques and can be used effectively to substantiate assurance and credibility of the determined measurement. Information flow can be described in detail, then modeled using formal methods and shown to represent or contradict previous findings. Generally, mathematical proofs are the nucleus of the verification.

Formal verification methods are useful in the measurement of potential covert channels. In many cases, the formal verification of a specific TCB may prove impractical due to the size or domain of operation. It may then prove exhaustive to use formal verification for covert channel bandwidth measurement when these channels may potentially span the entire network architecture. The recommended guidance for formal verification in relation to covert channel bandwidth measurement is that it be used on a case-by-case basis and for specific, identified channels.

9.7   PRACTICE AND EXAMPLES

This section presents a brief overview of techniques used to find and determine the bandwidth of potential covert channels.

NCSC Certified Systems

Systems that have been certified by the NCSC at the B2 level and above are required to address covert channels. At this time, only a small number of computer systems and networking components have been certified at the B2 level and above. Many of the methodologies and specific techniques used to support this analysis and the countermeasures and other covert channel bandwidth reduction techniques that were used are viewed as company confidential. The reason for this information being sensitive and viewed as competitive is because it represents a proven advantage over other vendors seeking to develop trusted systems and networks. Systems certified by NCSC and shown to be secure (especially those rated as B2 and above) are in high demand and generally require a large amount of research, development, and manpower expenditures from the vendor. Specific information about the techniques and methodologies used for covert channel bandwidth reduction, identification, or auditing for systems evaluated at the B2 level should be sought from the vendors of those products.

NCSC Practices

The NCSC today uses a combination of the practices cited above for its determinations of covert channels and their bandwidths. To a great extent, the center allows the sponsor of the system under evaluation to determine the exact techniques to be used. The center determines the adequacy of those techniques proposed by the sponsor. Most of the techniques cited above have come to the attention of center evaluation personnel at one time or another. The center does not have a strong preference for any one technique so long as the technique proposed by the system sponsor is deemed to be adequate and well understood by both parties.

9.8   GUIDANCE TO DEVELOPERS AND EVALUATORS

This section attempts to give some practical suggestions to the developer and the evaluator on the practical aspects of implementing the methods and techniques discussed above. Because each system is unique and each configuration of the same system is unique, it should be emphasized that these are only suggestions and are subject to considerable refinement and alterations to suit the specific environment.

It is important to realize that while the operation—or even the presence—of the end protocols was not considered in locating covert channels, such protocols become very important when postulating an environment for bandwidth measurement. How often the condition of the shared resource can be altered is directly affected by the ingenuity and efficiency of the modulation and recovery mechanism.

Another important point, especially for those persons with limited background in computer security, is that bandwidth measurement is not done by attaching an instrument to the channel and reading its bandwidth, the way one would read voltage, current, or temperature. In that sense, the term "measurement" when applied to bandwidth determination is perhaps somewhat misleading.

Measurement of channels can be effected through analytical means and engineering estimates or by actual exercising of the channel and direct measurement. The method of bandwidth measurement utilizing engineering analysis and estimation is the one most commonly used for covert channels. It provides a quicker response than the general identification of channels requiring more formal methods of bandwidth measurement. Both methods are subject to some degree of error due to technological limitations or erroneous assumptions. Although the errors are usually on the safe side, yielding maximum (rather than likely) bandwidths, such overestimation greatly increases system design cost. That is because Herculean efforts may be undertaken to eliminate channels thought to be serious leaks as a result of overestimation, when the actual bandwidth of these channels may represent little—if any—actual vulnerability. Overestimation should be avoided because it results in the expenditure of additional time and cost. Underestimation is more dangerous but less likely with the techniques discussed.

Measurement by Analysis and Engineering Estimate

Probably the most precise analytical measurement technique is the one espoused by Millen.[16] The following observations can be made. Using Millen's mathematical derivation, one can establish several bandwidth values of interest. The worst case maximum value is established when the rate of the modulating process and the rate of the receiving process are theoretically maximized, while the amount of interference from other processes is minimized. Interference can approach zero in some systems if it is assumed that the input from other users is either known and can be accounted for or that the perpetrator can control the input from other processes. The resulting value places an upper bound on the channel's bandwidth. This worst case estimation must be tempered by assumptions of real-world conditions that prevail in a system under actual operating conditions.

Because each case of actual operation is different, Millen provides the mechanisms for postulating the condition of several system effects and then allows the analyst to insert values for these assumptions. Bandwidths can then be established for any combination of circumstances that appears consistent with actual system operation to the analyst. These operation-relative values can also be obtained by observing and measuring those values in systems under actual operation.

The three most important of these parameters are the number of times that shared resource can be altered by the modulating process, the number of times that the receiving process can sense the shared resource, and the amount of interference that is present from other processes. Introducing reasonable postulated or observed values will yield an accurate measurement of the expected bandwidth of the covert channel under scrutiny. The bandwidth thus found provides a reasonable basis on which to estimate the degree of effort that should be expended in its reduction or elimination.

The noninterference model cited above also can be used as a bandwidth estimation tool. It can cross-validate the bandwidths estimated by other methods. It also shows promise of being automated in the future.

Less finely grained, but still adequate for first cut estimation, is the gross estimation process such as that used by Haigh and Kemmerer.[17] This method estimates the maximum number of state transitions per second that can be expected of the shared resource, then multiplies that value by the number of times that the value can be sensed by a receiving process, all under ideal conditions.

There are several effects that influence the covert channel bandwidth. Their combined influence can change the estimate by several orders of magnitude and therefore cannot be ignored.

The first effect, noise, has been touched upon above. Fairly accurate estimates of the influence of noise can be obtained by using Shannon's probabilistic theory of communications over noisy communications channels.[18] It deals with the effects of postulated noise and the effectiveness of protocols designed to counter the effect of noise. It allows computation of the maximum possible amount of information that can be transferred with the desired degree of reliability in any given noise environment.

Another effect influencing bandwidth is parallelism. It can take two forms. Several drivers/receivers can use the same shared resource or a single driver/receiver pair can use several shared resources, or both. Experience indicates that parallel use of a shared resource is subject to the law of diminishing returns, meaning that for each added driver or receiver, the incremental amount of bandwidth gets progressively smaller until adding the next driver or receiver will not return enough added bandwidth to make it worth the effort. Similarly, parallel use of drivers/receivers on a single resource is also subject to the same law. It should be noted that in some cases, this law may not be effective until a certain threshold is reached. If a process has only an occasional chance to modulate a shared resource, then several processes can modulate the resource before the law of diminishing returns takes effect. The analyst must determine if the bandwidth is limited primarily by the bandwidth of the modulating process, the alterability/sensibility of the shared resource itself, the receiving process, or noise.

The law of diminishing returns is explained in the following example of achieving reliable information transfer over a covert channel. Another factor that is often overlooked is the ability of the driver/receiver to influence other processes or to predict their activity so that its own transmissions are made at those times when there is a low probability of interference. Interference (noise) exacts a triple penalty. First, the original message is garbled and bandwidth is lost. Second, error detection or correction protocol must be added to messages, further reducing bandwidth. Third, when a garbled message is detected, a retransmission must be made, further wasting bandwidth. Therefore, if messages are transmitted only half as often, but have a higher probability of success, the total effective bandwidth is actually increased, even though the total covert traffic is diminished.

Measurement by analytical method is preferred where an order of magnitude estimate is needed to get a first cut approximation of the degree of exposure that a channel represents. Although there are several formal and informal automated methods available for finding covert channels, there are as yet no good methods available for automated bandwidth estimation. Should they become available, most bandwidth measurements would be done by analysis instead of experiment.

Measurement by Experiment

The actual implementation of a covert channel and its exercising constitutes measurement by experiment. The experimental approach has been used by Pozzo[19] in monolithic systems and Girling[20] in LANs.

Once the channel to be exercised is identified, several scenarios yielding the highest bandwidth are proposed, preferably by different individuals. Next, the channel is implemented in hardware and software and control conditions are established. They include the number of potentially interfering processes operating during the experiment, the access to the shared resource, and the hardware characteristics that affect bandwidth and similar factors. Instrumentation is inserted at critical hardware points and measurements are taken.

If software instrumentation is used for measurement, such as software timers or counters, the experimenter must be cautioned to ensure that the instrumentation either has no influence on the bandwidth of the channel under observation or that such influence can be fully and accurately estimated and taken into account. Analysis of the experimental results must factor in the effects of parallelism and other factors discussed above.

Measurement by experiment will be far more difficult and time consuming to automate and eventually will be used only under two conditions: 1) to validate the results that are obtained with analytical methods and 2) to determine the bandwidths of those channels that are not tractable to analytic evaluation.

Bursty Channels

The covert channels considered thus far have been assumed to leak at a rate that is relatively constant. There are other kinds of covert channels whose leakage rates vary dramatically. It is conceivable that, for very short intervals, the leakage rate can approach the bandwidth of the backplane. Such channels, which display high bandwidths or very short intervals interspersed by little or no leakage, are called bursty channels because they operate in bursts. Guidance for bursty channels has not been established but there are several ways to deal with them. In the absence of official guidance, the choice of approach will be determined by the kind of information processed by the system.

The first approach extends the bandwidth guidance of the "Orange Book." One could use a conservative or liberal approach. The conservative approach says that the Orange Book bandwidth guidelines apply to the instantaneous leakage rate of a covert channel over several (perhaps a dozen) bit times. This would be the most stringent interpretation and would be appropriate if data in the system changes in value to the adversary and becomes very concentrated at predictable times. For example, troop statistics or sales figures could be collected during the month and concentrated into a troop strength status or sales status report at the end of each month. Since one bit per second is 3,600 bits per hour, 86,400 bits per day, 2,592,000 bits (324 kilobytes) per month, it can be seen that a short burst of 100KB at the end of the month can be of more value to an adversary than the equivalent average continuous rate of 0.3 bits per second maintained throughout the month.

A less stringent interpretation of the Orange Book bandwidth guidelines might say that the average leakage rate of bursts must conform to the guidelines. In this interpretation, a channel that can provide 5,000 bit per second bursts every 1,000 seconds would have an average rate of 5 bits per second and must meet the guidelines of a 5 bit per second continuous channel. The Orange Book equivalent bandwidth could be computed by multiplying the instantaneous bit rate time (in bits per second) times the length of the burst (in seconds) times the number of bursts per interval of interest (minute, hour, day, month) divided by the number of seconds in the interval of interest. This yields the average number of bits per second for the interval of interest. While this interpretation would be clearly inadequate for the case in the preceding paragraph, it may be appropriate to systems in which data maintains a relatively low level of concentration.

In a bursty channel environment potential damage caused by a covert channel is much more difficult to assess than with a steady rate channel. The primary factors are:

Actual and average bit rates of the bursts

Concentration and frequency of burst occurrence

Predictable or determinable points in time when data becomes more concentrated or more valuable

In addition, all other factors related to bandwidth usage—such as parallel channels, effects of noise, and transmission reliability—must be considered.

Considerations in Design

At the initiation of a development effort, specific attention must be applied to associated policies and procedures to ensure that covert channels are not introduced arbitrarily. This is the best time, while the design is still on paper, to analyze the cost and performance tradeoffs regarding covert channels. A search for covert channels and bandwidth estimation for them should be conducted as close to finalization of the design as practical. Shared resources identified in high-level pseudo-code can be analyzed. The methods and techniques to be used in the location and measurement of covert channels should be determined in advance in order to produce a consistent strategy that will be applicable from the top descriptive design document as far down toward object code as possible. Careful consideration should be given to the tools available that will allow covert channel modeling in the programming language of choice for the system in design. The designers should familiarize themselves with the tools available (as cited above) that may greatly reduce the analysis effort by eliminating from actual analysis all but the most likely areas in which convert channels may exist. Parallel use of channels must be considered. Interference from noncooperating processes and other sources of channel noise must be considered. An important consideration often overlooked is the total amount of time during which the Trojan horse driving the covert protocol can exercise the channel, in conjunction with how long an external adversary has the opportunity to monitor that channel. The aggregate amount of information released by a system through covert channels is the total of the number of alteration/sensing trials, the frequency of these trials, the effectiveness of the covert protocol at maximizing the transfers, the effectiveness of the covert protocol in receiving the transfers, the amount of interference on the channel, the bandwidth of the resource, the number of parallel channels exercised, the number of parallel processes cooperating in the aggregate channel, and the amount of time in which these mechanisms jointly operate. It may well turn out that numerous channels, each of whose bandwidth is well under even the 0.1 bits per second monitoring threshold, may represent a far greater vulnerability than one or two channels of a few bits per second each. Bandwidth measurement is necessarily confined to the use of analytic versus experimental techniques described above.

Considerations during Implementation

As the system is implemented, paper estimations obtained during design can be validated. Channels that did not yield to analytical scrutiny now can be constructed and directly measured. Physical access paths to physically shared resources can be scrutinized. Electronics and other logic within the physical path can be analyzed for their ability to support covert channels.

Identification of Covert Channels

Channels may be identified using any of the techniques discussed above, either singly or in combination. Identification is a necessary first step in determining the potentially usable bandwidth of the channel. The best and most currently supported combination method is as follows. First, use the SRM to determine the potential existence of covert channels. Next, use combinations of the other techniques to eliminate all but the most likely and potentially widest bandwidth channels. Last, use the information flow or noninterference method to determine the actual potential of the channel to be used covertly. If the language has an applied analysis method, use that method to search the source code in the areas indicated by the SRM.

9.9 COUNTERMEASURES

It should be self-evident that the earlier in the life cycle countermeasures are considered and implemented, the lower will be the effort and cost needed to implement them. This section addresses, in greater detail, the specific countermeasures that can be used to deter the creation and use of covert channels in a secure system. Primary emphasis will be placed on certain types of covert channels that can be eliminated and associated elimination techniques. The following is a palette of countermeasures that may be used as the findings and requirements dictate. The determination and selection of a specific countermeasure to deter or prevent the use of a specific covert channel is application-dependent. Care should be taken not to assume that a particular countermeasure is sufficient for each and every application. On the contrary, careful scrutiny of the system in question, its use, the security policy, types of information processed, type of channel, open or closed environment, and many other factors must be considered before covert channel countermeasures can be implemented and supported.

9.10 ELIMINATION OF COVERT CHANNELS

Those new to computer security and particularly to covert channels often ask why all covert channels are not eliminated when they are discovered. As shown above, of the four channel/usage combinations, two don't require securing and one is easily secured. The fourth, in which system channels are used covertly, is not so tractable. Nevertheless, many of the techniques mentioned in this section can be applied with total (elimination) or partial (reduction) success. Considerable engineering effort is required to eliminate to the greatest extent such shared resources. Even after best efforts have been applied, there remains in most systems a need to retain the presence of certain shared resources that resist further reduction or elimination because these storage objects are intimately associated with the design of the operating system and are essential to its function. The guidelines section also recognizes and addresses this issue. Little theoretical work has been done to prove formally whether all such recalcitrant covert channels eventually can be eliminated through technological evolution while retaining a recognizable multilevel operating system, or whether a class of covert channels can be identified that is theoretically unsolvable.

With regard to covert protocols, what is needed is a universal covert protocol detection methodology regardless of the particular covert channel employed. As stated previously, covert protocols, usually manifested through Trojan horses, can operate within the architectural framework of the computer system. As such, any errors resulting from protocol violations should be investigated thoroughly. This could be an early clue that a covert protocol is being developed and is not quite debugged.

One of the best statements on covert channel elimination is found in Loepere,[21] which states that a standard way to eliminate covert channels is to remove the shareability of a resource, or at least its appearance of shareability. This drives the bandwidth to zero. Each security domain could be given a fixed share that is not varied by the resource demands of other processes, so that the fullness of that share is not detectable by other processes. System data and their associated variables can be virtualized so that a process cannot sense the actual value of internal data. Since the virtualization of time is not possible today, timing channels are far more intransigent to virtualization. It is practically axiomatic today that all covert channels in a system cannot be eliminated. As Loepere says, "You can always send a bit."[21]

Bandwidth Reduction Techniques

In many application-specific instances, several types of covert channels cannot be eliminated. This section will address and provide guidance on ways to limit the amount of data transmitted in a covert manner over known channels. Specific bandwidth reduction techniques will be examined and evaluated according to their technical feasibility and implementation characteristics. Which technique is used depends on initial bandwidth, number of channels,[22] and amount of time available for exploitation. Total bandwidth is also an aggregate of the bandwidth of the channel and the bandwidth of the Trojan horse driving it. This is the amount of data that can be transmitted in the time the Trojan horse can take from its normal functions without being noticed.[23]

Limited Access

One potential method to reduce covert channel bandwidth is through limiting access to the channel. Since a shared resource is required for a covert channel to exist, the reduction of access to that channel reduces the composite bandwidth potential. A complete investigation of the system architecture and processes is required. Information flow analysis would significantly aid in the process by determining the extent to which a channel is utilized. Once the channel utilization is known, a determination of the need for the channel can be made. It is possible that certain subjects (i.e., users) may not have access to system resources or specialty functions. If this is determined to be the case, the logical links to these channels can be removed, thus decreasing overall bandwidth of the channel.

Channel Sterilization

The access reduction countermeasure works hand in hand with the effectiveness of Trojan horse detection, reduction, and elimination. Ideally, a continuous protection environment could be set up, such as cited in section 4 of the Technical Rationale book,[24] one of the Yellow Books from the NCSC. If maintained properly, this environment could eliminate Trojan horses. Without Trojan horses, covert channels of any bandwidth would be rendered impotent, since they would lack the covert protocol to exploit them. This is analogous to taking away the cars instead of closing or restricting the road.

Noise Introduction

It is possible to introduce noise to limit covert channel bandwidth. The introduction of noise should not impede system performance or functionality but should rather increase the difficulty of using a known channel in a covert manner. The term "noise" is used to describe the insertion of random events. This can be accomplished through the modification of packet headers, a change in frequency utilization (RF communications), reallocation of resources, and many other techniques.

Since the use of covert channels is generally based on specific events, time, or conditions, it may prove beneficial to change those conditions randomly and without warning. Randomization of events whose average response time stays the same is a way to reduce covert timing channel bandwidths. The same randomization of storage allocations can reduce storage channel bandwidths. The theme here is to make ad hoc changes to the processing environment that do not hinder the current mission but which catch the perpetrator off guard.

Response time slowdowns and noise generation can be done statistically. When a monitoring routine notices that a process uses one or more resources more frequently than similar processes do, the monitoring routine throws obstacles like delays or noise into the use of these resources. The amount of delay or noise could be statistically and logarithmically increased to limit bandwidth to any degree desired. A process using, say, page faults, would see an ever-increasing penalty for setting or sensing page faults. If the resource is not used for some time, the delays or noise can be gradually lessened. The result should be that processes that use system resources normally would notice little if any inconvenience, whereas those that use system resources in a suspicious manner would incur time penalties in proportion to their irregular use of those resources.

Encryption

Encryption can provide a degree of assurance and bandwidth reduction against covert channels. If an object is being read by one process and signaled to another, the use of encryption may offer effective bandwidth reduction. If a process is expecting to see a certain character or bit and if that character or bit is encrypted, the process will still be able to signal the information but with little or no benefit. This countermeasure has limited application, since encryption of a shared resource would prevent its normal function. It is applicable to narrow portions of the problem where a class of processes can be identified which, for a period of time, need not have logical access to the resource but must maintain physical connectivity such that they can access the channel during legitimate periods.

9.11   DAMAGE CONFINEMENT

Monitoring Techniques for Remaining Covert Channels

Once a covert channel has been identified and limited in bandwidth, a procedure must be implemented that can monitor the bandwidth of the channel. Basically, the objective and control measures implemented must be able to be tested and monitored to provide assurance of their proper operation. In some instances, covert channels may exist without adequate means of limiting the bandwidth of the channel. For these cases it becomes imperative that monitoring techniques be implemented. Therefore, this section will describe techniques that can be used to monitor known covert channels.

Once a potential covert channel is identified a decision is required either to remove it or leave it intact. The decision may be to leave the channel unaltered, either because it cannot be removed for performance or functionality reasons or because the bandwidth is sufficiently low. If the channel is left intact, a second decision is required. This decision will be whether or not the channel requires monitoring. If the decision is to monitor the channel, a series of events should be orchestrated. First, a clear understanding of the channel and its usage is required. Second, the events and processes that have access to the channel should be identified. Third, the entities that could be altered and used to convey information should be analyzed. And finally, the point at which malicious logic would be required to use the channel successfully should be pinpointed. Once these activities are complete, the monitoring of anticipated actions can occur. To be effective, this technique requires that the user of the channel be identifiable and auditable. The way in which this is accomplished will vary between systems and the way in which audit records are generated and maintained.

A second, less desirable technique is to monitor the shared resource. The reason this method is less desirable is that it assumes that malicious logic has been introduced and reacts to uncommon use of a resource (channel) before counteraction can be initiated. If specific parameters of a channel can be quantified (i.e., use, characteristics, CPU utilization time, or other specific attribute), then a special monitoring method could be used. This monitoring method would keep a watchful eye over the continuous operation of the channel and would generate an alarm based on specified conditions.

Monitoring also has limitations. There is a relationship between the amount of monitoring performed and the digestibility of the data obtained. On one end of the spectrum, very little is monitored, but the monitored data are meticulously scrutinized by the system security officer staff. At the other end of the spectrum, every event related to a shared resource is monitored and an entry is generated in the monitoring log. This consumes not only some processing power and bandwidth, but generates huge amounts of audit trails, which must be analyzed to be effective. In the normal course of events, given fixed amounts of personnel available, the large volumes cannot be analyzed as meticulously for signs of program abnormalities as can small amounts of data. Data reduction techniques to deal effectively with the problem have not come forth. A more promising approach would be to generate a family of security software that can "psychoanalyze" processes on the fly and monitor only the activities of those that give signs of aberrant behavior. Also desirable would be software that could perform this function after the fact, from recorded audit trails, and thus preclude processing bandwidth consumption in the online system.

Configuration Management and Control

The identification, elimination, and monitoring of known covert channels must be an ongoing process. The security policy established for a secure network environment must identify known covert channels and system vulnerabilities. The security countermeasures implemented to satisfy the security policy (specifically covert channel bandwidth reduction techniques) must be managed and controlled. This section will provide guidance on how these issues can be controlled and managed to provide an additional level of assurance.

"Computer systems that process and store sensitive information depend on the hardware and software to protect that information. It follows that the hardware and software themselves must be protected against unauthorized changes that could cause a protection mechanism to malfunction or be bypassed completely. For this reason, changes to trusted computer systems, during their entire life cycle, must be carefully considered and controlled to ensure that the integrity of the protection mechanism is maintained. Only in this way can confidence be provided that the hardware and software interpretation of the security policy is maintained accurately and without distortion."[25]

The configuration management of a trusted system development effort and the subsequent managerial control of the developed system is a critical parameter associated with the avoidance and control of covert channels.

A comprehensive configuration management plan must be constructed and applied consistently and without error. This plan ensures that configuration management is performed in a specified manner. Configuration management is only effective if it is applied throughout the system's life cycle. Therefore, upon program initiation, configuration management must be established and applied. Once the system is implemented, configuration management remains intact and grows and matures in parallel with the system. Security mechanisms and the security policy itself must be examined and evaluated during each phase of system development and throughout the life cycle of the system. Modifications to the system architecture and to software should be thoroughly tested to ensure that they do not weaken or eliminate the intent of the established security policy. Only these measures will prevent security degradation through covert channels or Trojan horses introduced in "system upgrades" or newly added software or hardware.

Countermeasures used to monitor covert channels should be checked and validated in a consistent manner. Modifications to the system that increase the presence of communication channels should be examined, investigated, and logged. As was noted earlier, the ability to use a channel in a covert manner is predicated on the ability of a perpetrator to introduce malicious logic into the system. Therefore, the configuration management of a system should prevent or deter all vehicles that allow such an introduction.

9.12 SUMMARY

In this chapter, we've taken a detailed look at a serious threat to information network security: covert channels. We've also discussed various techniques by which potential problems may not only be uncovered but also reduced or eliminated.

In the next chapter, we'll continue with the prevention and cure theme, discussing practical approaches to network security measures.

END NOTES

1. Albert B. Jeng and Marshall D. Abrams, "On Network Covert Channel Analysis," unpublished paper, The MITRE Corporation, n.d.

2. National Computer Security Center, *Trusted Computer Systems Evaluation Criteria*, DoD 5200.28 STD, 1985.

3. Ibid.

4. K. Loepere, "Resolving Covert Channels within a B2 Class Secure System," *ACM Operating Systems Review*, volume 19, no. 3 (July 1985), 4-28.

5. National Computer Security Center, op. cit.

6. Ibid.

7. R. A. Kemmerer, "Shared Resource Matrix Methodology: An Approach to Identifying Storage and Timing Channels," *ACM Operating Systems Review* (August 1983).

8. Jeng and Abrams, op. cit.

9. Loepere, op. cit.

10. Kemmerer, op. cit.

11. E. D. Bell and L. D. LaPadula, "Secure Computer Systems," *Mitre Technical Report ESD-TR-73-278*, The MITRE Corporation, June 1974.

12. J. K. Millen, "Covert Channel Capacity," *Proceedings of the 1987 IEEE Symposium on Security and Privacy* (April 27-29 1987), 60-66.

13. Chii-ren Tsai and Virgil D. Gligor, "A Note on Information Flow and Covert Channel Analysis," *Proceedings of the 1987 IEEE Symposium on Security and Privacy* (April 27-29 1987), 91-95.

14. Chii-ren Tsai, Virgil D. Gligor, and C. Sekar Chandersekaran, "A Formal Method for the Indentification of Covert Storage Channels in Source Code," *Proceedings of the 1987 IEEE Symposium on Security and Privacy* (April 27-29 1987), 74-86.

15. Kemmerer, op. cit.

16. Millen, op. cit.

17. J. T. Haigh, R. A. Kemmerer, J. McHugh, and W. D. Young, "An Experience Using Two Covert Channel Analysis Techniques on a Real System Design," in *Proceedings of the 1986 Symposium on Security and Privacy* (New York: IEEE Computer Society), 1986, 14–24.

18. Shannon, "A Mathematical Theory of Communications," *Bell Systems Technical Journal* 27, no. 3 (July 1948), 16-23.

19. M. Pozzo, "Methods and Cost of Performing a Covert Channel Analysis," Honeywell Information Systems, 1984.

20. C. G. Girling, "Covert Channels in LANs," *IEEE Transactions on Software Engineering*, SE-13, no. 2 (February 1987), 292–296.

21. Loepere, op. cit.

22. Kemmerer, op. cit.

23. Loepere, op. cit.

24. National Computer Security Center, "Technical Rationale behind CSC-STD-004-85," *DoD Trusted Computer System Evaluation Criteria, Computer Security Requirements*, CSC-STD-004-85, 1985.

25. National Computer Security Center, op. cit.

10

Practical Approach to Network Security

10.1 INTRODUCTION

This chapter is a practical reflection of network security based on years of actual experience with real operational networks. The reader is encouraged to approach this chapter from a "lessons learned" point of view. Time and time again, experience has shown that the best laid plans for network security are plowed under by higher-priority projects and activities, budget cuts, and the inability to keep pace with continuously changing technology demands. Many managers and information system professionals buy network security through the acquisition of security countermeasures without first understanding the need for such countermeasures and their actual benefit to the network computing environment. As a result, dollars are spent without any tangible benefit in security protection. Finally, many security managers make the fatal mistake of attempting to implement a network security program without first gaining senior management commitment and support. These issues as well as a step-by-step approach to the network security life cycle is presented in this chapter.

10.2 PRACTICAL NETWORK SECURITY OBJECTIVES

For a network security program to be successful, there are certain objectives that should be continuously focused on. These include:

- Network security should be initiated at the beginning of a network design and development processes and be managed throughout the life cycle.

- The application of network security policies, procedures, and counter-measures should be driven by defined and quantifiable needs.

- The network security function must work hand in hand with other engineering/technical disciplines and all elements of the organization.

- High-level visibility and management support and commitment are absolutely essential for any network security program to be successful.

- The implementation of network security must not overburden the user or significantly impact network/system performance or mission objectives.

- Cost-effective solutions must be sought to ensure that the network security program is as efficient and cost effective as possible.

- Never assume that the previous solution used to solve a specific network security vulnerability will be sufficient or desirable for the same vulnerability next time. Technology moves too fast not to consider the market at the time the decision is made.

10.3 SENIOR MANAGEMENT COMMITMENT

A network security program can be effected only if there is recognized and obvious commitment from the highest levels of management within an organization. A recognized commitment to a network security program has a number of key attributes, including:

- Network security is defined as a high priority within the organization.

- The network security program is funded and recognized during the budgeting process.

- Specific levels of responsibility are defined and the necessary authority is granted to accomplish network security program goals and objectives.

- Network security is a fundamental part of the corporate/organizational planning process.

These four attributes are imperative before any hope in achieving an effective network security program can be realized. Selling such a program to senior management has always been tough due to the technical nature of the subject matter and the complexity associated with clearly defining a return on investment (ROI) commensurate with the required investment for the network security program. In numerous publications, writers have stated that it is not possible to define empirical bottom line loss in dollars for security penetrations, denial of service, malicious data modification, or other network security breaches. While this may be a difficult task, it is possible and is required to understand loss potential and damage and relate that understanding directly to bottom line ROI. It is not accurate to define security as simply an overhead expense, with no tangible benefits or cost savings resulting from its implementation and management. If network security is planned for, implemented, and managed properly, it can provide quantifiable benefits, both in productivity and in bottom line return. Examples can include an effective configuration management and backup procedures, which can be useful if the network is infected with a virus or if strict control is placed on the number of software copies allowed on the network. In addition, by focusing attention on a solid configuration management process, substantial gains in efficiency and productivity may be realized, directly supporting bottom line benefits. The practical approach to gaining senior management approval for a commitment to a network security program includes the following:

- Define value of information assets to the organization.
- Define specific types of sensitive information processed in the network (i.e., categorize information types such as research and development, sales forecasts, competition-sensitive).
- Define the threats against the network (and quantify the potential loss, damage, and monetary bottom line exposure if a threat is exercised).
- Based on the threat profile, define specific vulnerabilities of the network to the defined threats.
- Provide specific examples of how identified vulnerabilities could be exposed by the defined threat profile.
- Provide specific examples of similar companies/organizations in the same market that have experienced security breaches and what their actual projected loss for those breeches were.
- Select two companies that are considered to be competitors or that provide similar services/products and investigate their network security programs. Present the findings to senior management.

- Present a top 10 network security priority list and define the costs required for each activity. Provide a high-level plan for implementing these top 10 priorities to include support from all organizations affected by the activity.

The above information should be presented (in a formal presentation) to senior management and should be documented and presented in the form of a network security business plan. It is highly likely that the research to accomplish these activities can be funded; commitment to the suggested action plan is often the hard nut to crack. More often than not, people just assume that senior management understands the importance and need for network security. This is far from the truth and such an assumption will nearly always lead to limited or no commitment to any network security program. The bottom line, no pun intended, is that the cost of a network security program must be tied to the benefits it provides and the dollars it will save the organization. Subsequent sections in this chapter lay out the process for accomplishing the steps defined above.

10.4 NETWORK RISK ANALYSIS

Performing a comprehensive risk analysis with technically qualified security engineers is the most important network security activity. Risk analysis is logically subdivided into three activities, each providing additional insight into the security needs of a network. Figure 10.1 depicts the logical flow of events in a risk analysis. A sensitivity assessment is used to determine the actual value of the data and the criticality of the mission that is supported by the network and associated information processing assets. The risk assessment is the most significant activity of the overall risk analysis. It is used to define threats against a network, vulnerability of the network, and the risk levels that result from the postulated exploitation of network vulnerabilities by the defined threats against the network. The economic assessment is used to examine the potential loss expectancy, given various threat execution scenarios. The economic assessment attempts to quantify, to the greatest extent possible, loss expectancy in terms of real dollars.

A risk analysis is based on the premise that it is not possible to have a risk-free network. Risks, therefore, must be managed. Any risk can be defined as the resultant value derived from the mapping of perceived and known threats against perceived and known network vulnerabilities. The qualification of risks is one of the necessary activities in determining which threats should be controlled and managed. Therefore, a risk analysis is used primarily to identify those system risks that could potentially impact the

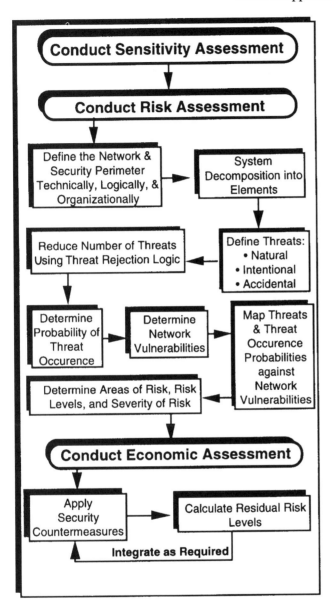

Figure 10.1 The Risk analysis process determines the need and functional application of network security.

secrecy, integrity, and/or operational continuity of the network being evaluated. Insights gained from the risk analysis process can then be used to support risk management and the cost-effective application of security countermeasures.

Benefits

A risk analysis defines the system being evaluated and sets the tone and direction for future security engineering activities. A risk analysis provides the ability to identify problems early in any network program and supports expeditious resolution, programmatic visibility, and technical cognizance. A risk analysis provides justification for the acquisition and use of security countermeasures. Blind application of security countermeasures without first understanding the inherent risks of a network is likely to be unproductive and costly.

Security Perimeter

The network, and thus the security perimeter, must be accurately defined and documented. Defining the security perimeter bounds the problem and allows the risk analysis effort to be focused on a quantifiable composite system. This may seem like a simple task and one that is intuitively obvious; however, this is very rarely the situation, especially for large multisite networks. Site surveys and comprehensive interaction with various individuals within an organization are normally required. Moreover, very few companies or organizations have a handle on what their network looks like or how many or what components and applications are used. It is beneficial during this process also to discuss future networking plans and requirements and factor those into the overall security perimeter definition and planning process.

System Decomposition

System decomposition involves the logical separation of the networking environment into elements. Elements may include people, facilities, hardware software assets, communications services, and actual information. This can also be a very time-consuming process. The elements defined for each system/network may be different on a case-by-case basis. The key is to ensure that the selection of elements defines clear attributes for an element, that the list is not too long, and that there is no possible redundancy in the list of elements.

The most obvious organizational asset, and the most commonly overlooked asset (during the risk analysis process), is people. The employees of the organization are its lifeblood. As more and more service-oriented markets arise, the value of people within the organization will continue to increase. As a result, any network security approach must ensure the protection of human life, and this value must be taken into consideration during the risk analysis process. Simply stated, it costs a lot of money to hire new people and train them.

Facilities can be treated as a risk analysis class or element. Facilities include such things as:

- Buildings
- Furniture
- Air conditioning and heating
- Electricity
- Water and plumbing facilities
- Fire control systems
- Backup power
- Supplies and materials

Facilities are quantifiable assets with clear value based on their acquisition cost or periodic cost. Many facility features and functions also help protect other facility assets and other information processing assets.

Hardware is an obvious information asset class and one that is most commonly thought of during a risk analysis. Hardware, however, is more than likely the area of least investment and total cost to the organization in relative comparison to the other classes being discussed here. Hardware may include such components as:

- Mainframe, mini- and microcomputers, and terminals
- Routers, bridges, concentrators, and cabling
- Front-end processors and gateways
- Printers, scanners, and plotters
- Modems, PBXs, and DSU/CSUs
- Tape drives and disk drives

In most cases, a wide variance will be seen in the software used in each network/system surveyed. This is especially true for application software. Each piece of software has an acquisition value and also an availability value. Software will normally include:

- Operating systems
- Network operating systems
- Network file systems
- Host applications (i.e., database, word processing, spreadsheet)

- Network applications (i.e., electronic mail, bulletin boards, calendar, file transfer)

- Office automation (i.e., IBM PROFS, DEC All-in-One, HP Deskmanager, Wang Office, and Unipex [UNIX])

- Communication protocols

- Specialized network components software (i.e., routing and bridging software)

Information or data will vary from site to site and network to network. Information and data are driven by the business, the personnel, and numerous other factors. Information has a value. For example, computer readable data has at least the value that it would take to reenter it into the system. Other data, if disclosed, could have an incredible value. The value of data, in the vast majority of cases, dwarfs the value of hardware and software. Typical examples of information include:

- Data contained on hard disks, diskettes, CD-ROM, and tape
- Online user files
- Operational databases
- Access control lists
- Audit information

From a practical perspective, it may not be possible to document every dimension or attribute of a network (i.e., connections to the network). In this example, what is important is that a class of connections be identified and defined. For example, it may not be possible to identify and specifically define every PC connected to the network; however, it may be possible to define a class of PC network connections as:

- PC-DOS device
- Ethernet 802.3
- TCP/IP
- Network File System (NFS)
- Microsoft applications (Word and Excel)

This way, a class of network connection can be evaluated and assessed in the context of the composite network security approach. This practical approach allows classes of systems to be evaluated versus each system, saving substantial time and money and making the process achievable over time.

Risk Analysis Team

Once the security perimeter is defined and the network decomposed into classes of information assets, it is then possible to understand the technical/management environment and select an appropriate risk analysis team. The risk analysis team is fundamental to success. Without the right set of individuals working on the activity, the risk analysis process will be doomed to failure. There is a broad set of activities throughout the risk analysis process, and it will be necessary to expand and contract the team as dictated by the requirements at hand.

The risk analysis team leader should be an individual from outside the organization. This may be a network security consultant or other professional, but it is important that the team leader be an unbiased participant. It is important that the team leader have experience in risk analyses for networked environments and in similar or exact business markets. The risk analysis team leader provides the know-how, experience, and processes to accomplish the task. What is then required is a thorough and comprehensive understanding of the business, the services provided by the networking information infrastructure, and the value and importance of the organization's information assets.

Therefore, senior management will need to be involved as well as the actual owners and users of networking services and information. Senior management will be able to shed light on the actual utilization of information, its need and importance in the organization, the services they employ, and the services they provide to the community. The owners and users of the network's information assets will have a very different (but equally important) view in the risk analysis process by providing their knowledge and expertise about how the network actually supports the business processes of the organization. They will also provide insight into what data is used and where, what network resources, applications, and services are used and where, and which users require access to which types of data to accomplish their daily job function.

Finally, it is essential to acquire the necessary technical expertise literally to dissect and understand internally the technical interworkings of the network and supported applications. This expertise may be acquired from within the organization or from an outside consultant. The key is to have the right expertise available when required to address specific technical requirements and to shed knowledge and expertise on assumptions and positions taken by the risk analysis team.

Sensitivity Assessment

The sensitivity assessment is used to define the value and criticality of all information types, hardware and software assets, and the overall mission of a network. This process must take into account the value of information secrecy and integrity, mission support and continuity, and the dollar value of the network resources.

From a networking perspective it is important that three types of information assets be known:

- Value of actual information
- Value of hardware and software components/elements in the network
- Value of the services provided by the network

These three types of information assets should be evaluated and assessed based on three criteria:

- Confidentiality
- Integrity
- Availability

It is important that the owner of the information asset be the one to assign the actual dollar value of the asset. The owner is the one closest to the asset and thus has the best understanding of its value to the company or organization. In every case, strive for a dollars and cents value for the information asset being valued.

Confidentiality refers to those services required to protect information from unauthorized disclosure. Personnel records, research and development reports, marketing strategies, advanced products, or highly classified intelligence information can all fall into the category of information that most likely would need to be protected from public access. To assess the value of the confidentiality of a specific information asset, attempt to assume what someone or an organization would pay for the information or the legal damage that the company may experience if the information found its way into the wrong hands.

Integrity refers to those services required to ensure that information is accurate, complete, and authentic when it is processed, transmitted, presented, and stored. The accuracy of information can be much more important and of more value than the confidentiality of the information. Posting the wrong price for merchandise is a good example of the value of accurate information and information processing.

Availability of networking resources, services, and information continues to increase in importance as the spread of network computing continues to grow. Availability can be valued by simply assessing the impact of having a service, resource, or data file cease to exist. Typically, it is important to define availability in two domains. The first domain provides a value based on the information asset being destroyed completely (i.e., never again available), and the second domain should provide a value over time (i.e., what is the value if an information asset is not available for 1 hour, 2 hours, 10 hours).

The availability over time domain is also an excellent way to determine thresholds of availability. For example, the cost resulting from a financial system being down from 2:00 A.M. to 4:00 A.M. may be $0.00, but what about the cost to the company if it is down on payday from 8:00 A.M. to 5:00 P.M.? It is also possible that a component being down for 20 minutes would not be a problem, but any time thereafter would cause tremendous problems. Understanding availability thresholds across the composite network is important in truly understanding the value of network information assets.

Technically, Logically, and Organizationally

The risk analysis team should spend the time necessary to understand technically the components and technical interactions that occur on the network. The team should also understand the mission that the network supports and how mission requirements are satisfied through network resources. Finally, the team needs to understand the organizations that utilize network resources, how they interact, and any unique requirements or needs they may have.

Valuation of Information Assets

Information assets should be valued from two perspectives. The first perspective is an information asset's intrinsic value. Intrinsic value is the actual physical value of the asset or the cost of what it would take to replace the asset. The second perspective is an information asset's acquired value. Acquired value is the value that an asset has acquired over time. A very simple example is a diskette. The intrinsic value of a diskette may be one dollar, but the acquired value of a diskette once user files are loaded may be thousands of dollars in value.

All values should be assigned in dollars. This way there is a consistent approach and metric for the entire valuation process. Never attempt to make this an exact science. The objective is to have a metric from which comparisons can be drawn and by which decisions concerning investment can be made. As mentioned earlier, the value of an information asset should take into consideration the value and need for the asset to have a high level of integrity, availability, and confidentiality. Asset values can be categorized into broad classes relative to dollars.

For example, to simplify the process, establish value threshold classes and categorize assets according to the class in which they fit (i.e., $100 or less, $100–$1,000, $1,000–$5,000, and so on). This approach works effectively simply because it is much easier to select a value, once a set of values are understood and established. Users and owners of data are much more apt to respond and support a question such as, "Would the loss cost the company more or less than $1,000?" versus "How much would the loss cost the company?"

The other approach that is effective is to do relative rankings in the valuation process. For example, people commonly compare events, attributes, capabilities, and functions to one another. This common trait in people can be used to extract useful user knowledge in the valuation process. For example, if the unavailability of resource A is considered to be $10,000 over a period of two hours, then ask the users and owners of data to compare the impact of other network resources and their availability against this known value. Users will commonly use relative comparisons such as, "The unavailability of resource B would be five times worse than the unavailability of resource A." As a result, the impact of having resource B available could be defined as having a value of $50,000.

Standard accounting practices can be used for hard tangible assets whose value is accounted for and being depreciated over time. The intrinsic value of such an information asset can be calculated by simply adding the book value (recorded value) and the accumulated depreciation. This approach is not recommended to determine replacement cost. With technology advancing at a very rapid pace, the book value plus the accumulated depreciation cannot be counted on as an accurate method for approximating the replacement value of an information asset. Rather, the best, most practical approach is to contact the vendor of the product and, if possible, other vendors of similar products to determine a replacement value. Depending on the size of the organization and the organization's dependence on information systems, the amount of data gathered during the valuation process can be quite large. As a result, it is absolutely essential that the data be gathered and documented in a consistent form. A common form to document the valuation process would include the following information:

1. Information asset
2. Description (i.e., serial number, license number, employee number, organizational element, database application, etc.)
3. Function/Purpose (i.e., financial, marketing, word processing)
4. Intrinsic value (in dollars)
5. Acquired value (in dollars considering confidentiality, integrity, and availability)
6. Total value (combine intrinsic and acquired values)
7. Date
8. Personnel involvement (identify the evaluator and all personnel involved in defining values for the various attributes of the information asset)

The information asset valuation provides three primary benefits:

1. A comprehensive configuration management record of all information assets (a true benefit and, very commonly, a unique benefit in itself)
2. A total company investment portfolio for all information assets
3. Input into the risk analysis process for ultimate decision making with regard to the network security program and overall investment plan for the program

In most cases, the valuation process, once the data is gathered, documented, and composed, represents a much larger value (often one to two orders of magnitude higher than original senior management estimates). In a few cases, the valuation of information assets is much lower than originally anticipated and the risk analysis process is expedited, simplified, focused, or completely stopped.

Identification of Threats

A threat can be defined as any accidental or intentional manmade or non-manmade event that could cause harm, damage, or loss. The important practical aspect of the threat identification process is to realize that there are literally thousands of potential threats; however, the vast majority of those threats may not be relevant to the particular network in question. For example, it is likely much more important to take into consideration protection against earthquake damage in the city of San Francisco, compared with protection against earthquake damage in Colorado Springs, Colorado.

Potential threats are defined for each system element or class of information asset. It is important that the threat definition process have specific focus and direction. For example, the threats identified during this process will be those that specifically target elements, systems, or information that is important to the operational availability and integrity or information confidentiality of the network being evaluated.

Threat Environment

There are four general types of threats to a network computing environment:

1. Natural threats
2. Accidental threats
3. Deliberate (manmade) active attacks
4. Deliberate (manmade) passive attacks

Any of these threats, or a combination of them, may impair a network through denial of service, unauthorized disclosure, or unauthorized modification.

Natural Threats

Natural threats occur independently of the purpose, function, or value of a given network computing environment. Networking components or information systems are not targeted by natural threats. The concern with natural threats involves the changes induced in the physical environment, the resultant vulnerabilities to subsequent collateral threats, and the possible interruption of network operations. The presence of highly sensitive networking equipment, fragile networking components, and regulated power systems increases susceptibility to natural threats. The uncertainty associated with the time and place of a natural threat occurrence compounds the complexity of assessing network vulnerabilities. If a network is weakened or disabled by natural threats, the network could be more susceptible to accidental or deliberate threats. The following chart provides a general list of natural threat types and their potential effects on networks.

Threat Types	Individual Threats	Collateral Threats	Effects
Geophysical disasters	Earthquakes, volcanic activities, induced floods	Fires, landslides, gas and chemical leaks, power outages	Equipment destruction or damage
Climate-dependent disasters	Hurricanes, typhoons, tornadoes	Floods, fires, accidents, gas and chemical leaks, power outages	Loss or degradation in network and communication, destruction of equipment and information
Meteorological disasters	Atmospheric weather, snow, wind, lightning, thunder, temperature extremes	Floods, accidents, power outages, electromagnetic pulse	Loss or degradation in network communication, destruction of equipment and information
Seasonal phenomena	Weather extremes, forest and brush fires	Floods, fires, accidents, power outages	Loss or degradation in network communication, destruction of equipment and information
Astrophysical phenomena	Solar phenomena (sun spots)		Satellite link loss or degradation
Biological phenomena	Disease and wildlife	Accidents	Damage to equipment and personnel

Accidental Threats

Accidental threats are the most significant threats to networks today. User, operator, and administrative errors account for the vast majority of network security problems and penetrations. Accidental threats are not premeditated or target-directed and may occur at any time and on any network. Accidents may vary in severity and impact. The main concern with accidental threats is the potential damage inflicted upon the network, which may cause disruption, degradation, or loss of communication services and operations. Accidental threats may also enable a would-be perpetrator to gain unauthorized access to a network. Accidental threats include:

- User errors
- Operator errors
- Administration error (especially component/software configuration and proper setup)
- Data preparation errors
- Output errors
- System errors
- Communication errors

Other accidental threats may include the following:

Threat Types	Individual Threats	Effects
Transportation	Aircraft, railroad, truck, automobile accidents	Equipment and information destruction
Industrial	Gas leaks, chemical spills, radioactive material leaks, fires, explosions, public utility interruptions	Network equipment and information damage and destruction, loss of capability and service
Environmental	Forest fires, floods, air pollution, epidemics	Degradation and destruction of network equipment services and information
Equipment	Network equipment failures, support equipment/software failure	Degradation and destruction of network equipment services and information.

Deliberate (Manmade) Active Attacks

Deliberate manmade active attacks pose a serious threat to any network. As we were finishing this manuscript, the New York World Trade Center bombing occurred: a high-profile case in point. These threats can disrupt communications operations to the extent that network services are denied to authorized users and organizations. Unauthorized access, unauthorized modifications, sabotage, or direct attack are examples of deliberate active attacks. A network hacker's attempts to penetrate a network, in an unauthorized way, would be considered a deliberate manmade active attack. Examples of deliberate man made active attacks and their potential effects are presented below.

Threat Types	*Individual Threats*	*Effects*
Civil disobedience	Protests, riots, union demonstrations	Personnel prevented from going to work, damage to equipment and personnel
Unauthorized access	Trusted personnel, unauthorized personnel, user spoofing	Loss, manipulation, damage, or compromise of data
Sabotage	Terrorism, bombings, computer software modifications, equipment vandalism	Destruction or damage of targeted equipment and personnel resulting in loss of service
Jamming	Spurious network traffic introduction, increased network frequency allocation, uplink and downlink jammers	Link/network loss or degradation and loss of service/data

Deliberate (Manmade) Passive Attacks

Deliberate manmade passive attacks include analysis of electromagnetic emanations, wiretapping, and exposure or release of sensitive information to unauthorized users. Each threat attempt will have an objective, and specific components will be targeted. Examples of deliberate manmade passive attacks are shown below.

Threat Types	*Individual Threats*	*Effects*
Electromagnetic emanations	Cables, land lines, microwave, computers, networking components	Unauthorized disclosure of information
Wiretapping or eavesdropping	Cables, land lines, microwave links	Unauthorized disclosure of information
Release of sensitive information	Loss by personnel, improper marking of information, improper handling of information, abuse of network resources	Unauthorized disclosure of information

Threat Categories

Natural threats, accidental threats, deliberate (manmade) active attacks, and deliberate (manmade) passive attacks may impair a network through denial of service to valid users and processes, the unauthorized disclosure of sensitive information, or the unauthorized modification to networking hardware, software, and data.

Denial of Service

Denial of service results when authorized users or processes are unable to perform networking functions/services within a required time frame. Denial of service may result from one or more of the following conditions:

- Physical destruction of networking segments or subnetworks
- Interoperability of networking segments or subnetworks due to equipment malfunction, software failures, or sabotage
- Degradation of performance from system saturation, link or bit error rates, or external factors (i.e., weather)
- Authorized users prevented physical access to networking equipment and services
- Any other condition that results in nonavailability of networking resources to valid users

Unauthorized Disclosure

Unauthorized disclosure of sensitive information results when information is provided to personnel who are not authorized to possess it. Unauthorized disclosure may occur in several ways, including:

- Accidental disclosure may be caused by users, operators, data preparation, output errors, system errors, or communications errors
- Violation of established access control procedures
- Malicious actions taken by personnel
- Active attempts by authorized personnel to gain access to sensitive information

Unauthorized Modification

Unauthorized modification of network resources and subnetworks can result in interruption or degradation of networking services. Unauthorized modifications can be made to network hardware, software, facilities, or information. Unauthorized modification may be performed by:

- Personnel actively working to sabotage or disrupt network operations/services

- Personnel who accidentally interfere with network operations/services
- External personnel

Threats—LAN Communications

LAN communications, including the physical distribution of the cable, should be protected at all times from threats of destruction (denial of service), eavesdropping, and passive and active wiretapping. These threats can be controlled through various security countermeasures.

Threats—Long-Haul Communications

Long-haul communications, unlike LAN communications, can be easily exploited and cannot be adequately protected with physical security countermeasures. Microwaves, long-lines, and satellites are all extremely vulnerable to electronic eavesdropping and a host of other threats. Long-haul data communications should be protected. It would not make sense to restrict access to information internally on a LAN and then broadcast the same sensitive information over public access airways. Therefore, in light of the potential vulnerabilities that accompany communications circuits, and since physical security cannot be adequately applied, it is recommended that encryption be used for long-haul communications used to transmit sensitive information.

It is further recommended that research be conducted to determine which network interfaces are used to transmit sensitive or proprietary information. It may be possible to apply cryptographic devices only on those communication circuits known to carry sensitive information. Cryptographic products are relatively inexpensive and can easily support both 56Kbps and T1 data rates.

Threat Logic Tree

Threats are illustrated in threat logic tree format. The logic tree enables a specific threat to be traced from a general description (e.g., denial of service) to finer granularity (e.g., resource exhaustion). Each threat is explained in detail (e.g., what does wiretapping mean and why is it a relevant threat to the network?).

It is important to note that approximately 85 percent of all reported computer and network security violations can be attributed to insiders. These insiders are individuals who have authorized and approved access to network resources, services, and information. When grouped by position, the greatest percentage can be attributed to functional network users. The four other positions that are commonly involved in insider security breaches are programmers, operators, analysts, and system monitors/administrators. To minimize this very substantial threat, it is important to observe the general behavior of employees, their level of work/compensation satisfaction, their level of participation in company activities, and their excitement/energy associated with their job. Other practical advice includes:

- Reassign employees with known personal problems to less critical/sensitive duties. Personal problems may include drug or alcohol abuse, marital problems, or psychological problems.

- Provide substantial management and direction for problem employees and always ensure that they are effectively supervised.

- If an employee is terminated, escort him or her to the door, remove all access authorizations, and notify appropriate personnel of the change.

Threat Rejection Logic

Threats to security exist; however, the likelihood of occurrence for some may be negligible. Threat rejection logic is an important aspect of the risk analysis process. For the purpose of performing tradeoff analyses, the number of initial threat models is normally large. Many, however, are subsequently discarded because they have ceased to be relevant. Only those threats determined to be relevant are investigated further. Once threats are identified, an analysis is used to show how those threats, through a logical threat manifestation process, could cause one of the following events to occur:

- Unauthorized disclosure of sensitive information (i.e., confidentiality)
- Unauthorized modification of sensitive information (i.e., integrity)
- Denial of service (i.e., availability)

Determining Vulnerability to Threats

Any given element's vulnerability to a specific threat is determined by combining the probability of threat occurrence and an element's weakness to the threat. The selection of the appropriate category or level (e.g., 3—high, 2—moderate, and 1—low) is a function of historical data, existing documents, practical experience, and a comprehensive analysis. This selection (i.e., high) defines an element's weakness to a threat. For example, if users of a network are encouraged to develop software, access bulletin boards, and bring any software from home into work with them, then the vulnerability of the networking components of the network to the introduction of malicious logic would be high (or level 3). On the other hand, if users are restricted from developing software and accessing external bulletin boards and specific policies and procedures exist for the introduction of new software, then the vulnerability to the introduction of malicious logic may be low (or level 1). This vulnerability level must then be coupled with a rating that defines the probability of threat occurrence. The probability of threat occurrence can be driven by historical data and other industry information (i.e., in 1992, 1 out of every 100 networked PCs was infected with a virus). The probability of threat occurrence can be rated in the same way as the vulnerability to specific threats as high (level 3), medium (level 2), or low (level 1). These two ratings are then mapped against one another in a matrix to determine the final vulnerability value. If necessary, the number of levels or ratings can be increased, such as high (level 5), moderately high (level 4), medium (level 3), moderately medium (level 2), and low (level 1). It is recommended that no more than five levels be used. Experience has shown that any more than five levels makes the judgment process between the levels very difficult and without justification in most cases. It is recommended that all ratings be rounded up. For example, if the probability of threat occurrence is considered to be high (3), and the element's weakness to the threat is estimated to be moderate (2), then the aggregate rating would be 2.5. This rating should be rounded up to a composite vulnerability rating of 3 (high). Figure 10.2 illustrates how to apply a matrix to define the vulnerability to a specific threat.

Degree of Risk

To determine any risk level, the severity of the threat and the element's level of vulnerability to that threat are combined. At this point, the severity of the threat must be determined. The most effective way to make this determination is to ascertain the monetary loss that could be incurred if the threat was exercised. Use of empirical industry data and historical information is the best means to determine the severity of any threat. If such information cannot be gathered, the determination must be made using common sense, comprehensive analysis based on the information obtained during the economic assessment, and personal experience. The degree of risk must be tied

Element's Weakness to Threat	Probability of Threat Occurence		
	High	Moderate	Low
High = 3	3	3	2
Moderate = 2	3	2	2
Low = 1	2	2	1

Figure 10.2 Matrix to define vulnerability to threat

back directly to a monetary loss before any actions can be taken to counter the risk. Figure 10.3 illustrates how to calculate the degree of risk for any threat/vulnerability pair. Note that ratings are also rounded to the next higher level.

Countermeasure Application

Countermeasure application is used to reduce risk. During this step, the value of applying a countermeasure must be quantified. In other words,

Severity of Threat	Level of Vulnerability		
	High	Moderate	Low
High = 3	3	3	2
Moderate = 2	3	2	2
Low = 1	2	2	1

Figure 10.3 Calculate degree of risk for threat

network security countermeasures should be selected and applied against specific and defined risks. This method provides systematic tractability for countermeasure application, as well as justification for the cost incurred for those countermeasures. Network security countermeasures are designed to support security objectives in three different capacities, which include:

1. Prevention mechanisms
2. Detection mechanisms
3. Correction mechanisms

There are situations where the application of a single countermeasure can be used to support risk reduction or elimination in several areas. For example, the use of encryption for data communications provides risk reduction against both information compromise and information modification. These multipurpose countermeasures may therefore be shown in several risk reduction scenarios.

Common network elements, threats, and associated countermeasures are shown in Figure 10.4.

Residual Risk

Residual risk is defined as the remaining risk value after countermeasures have been applied. Residual risk is determined by comparing the initial risk level against the utility of the selected countermeasure. Figure 10.5 illustrates how to compute residual risk. Note that the computation of residual risk assumes worst case. For example, if the degree of risk is moderate (level 2) and the countermeasure effectiveness is determined also to be moderate (level 2), the resulting value is not low (level 1); rather, it remains moderate (level 2).

Process Iteration

It may be necessary to iterate the two previous steps until residual risk is considered to be at an acceptable level. A residual risk of less than or equal to low, for all intents and purposes, is considered to be adequate. There are instances where a rating of low is necessary because of the sensitivity or criticality of a particular network service or the damage and financial exposure that could be caused by an information compromise. In these instances, residual risk may need to be decreased further through the application of additional countermeasures.

Network Element	Threat	Countermeasure
Network Operating Systems	• Unauthorized access • Unauthorized modification • Denial of service (i.e., introduction of malicious software)	• Trusted NOS • User identification & authentication services • Password management
Modems	• Theft of information • Access to network by hacker • Introduction of malicious software	• Prohibit access through the use of a centralized modem pool • Call-back modems • Identification & authentication services • Encryption
Workstations	• Network sniffing to compromise workstation passwords • Physical access to workstations without proper software protections	• Limit physical access • Alarm cable plant to recognize passive wiretapping • Use of fiber optic cable plant • Encryption & dynamic passwords
Removable Disks	• Theft of data (large quantities) • Theft of operating systems & applications	• Control physical access to network devices • Require that all removable disks be locked up each night
Nonremovable Disks	• Obvious theft of data	• Control physical access to network devices • User awareness • Schedule all defined maintenance activities & inform users
Diskettes	• Theft of data • Theft of operating systems & applications • Introduction of malicious SW	• Control physical access to network devices • User awareness • Schedule all defined maintenance activities & inform users
Network File Servers	• Theft or destruction • Unauthorized access & modification	• Control physical access • User identification & authentication services
Dial-in & Dial Out	• Unauthorized access by a hacker	• Call back modems • User identification & authentication services
Routers, Bridges, Brouters, & Concentrators	• Configuration modifications causing denial of service and / or access to additional resources	• Restrict access based on well-managed dynamic password scheme • Restrict access to network devices based on principle of least privilege.

Figure 10.4 Common network elements, threats, and countermeasures

The law of diminishing returns is applicable in the application of security countermeasures. At any given time, the utility of an additional countermeasure may not increase the security of a network but may actually be detrimental, causing significant performance impacts and increased system

Countermeasure Effectiveness	Degree of Risk		
	High	Moderate	Low
High = 3	2	1	1
Moderate = 2	3	2	1
Low = 1	3	2	1

Figure 10.5 Computing residual risk

maintenance costs. Risk reduction must strike a balance between the level of protection and performance impacts and cost.

Risk reduction is a function with multiple interwoven functions, facets, and parameters, all of which must be examined to strike a balance between the protection of operations, resources, information, performance, cost, and countermeasure benefit. The ultimate decision to apply additional counter-measures must be determined by the senior management and the management responsible for the operation of the network, in conjunction with the realities of budget and resources.

Certification Process

The certification process is a formal process designed to involve network and security engineering experts to assess the findings of the risk analysis and to determine their level of agreement or disagreement in the findings and comments on residual risk. Certification simply implies a second set of expert eyes to review the network, the risk analysis process, and the findings and to document agreement with the findings. More than anything else, the certification process serves as a final sanity check of the risk analysis findings and the application of network security countermeasures. This process has proven very successful based on actual risk analyses conducted on networks. The ability to step away from the process and allow a fresh and new view of the problem is absolutely worth the time and effort. Very rarely will the findings, process, or application of network security countermeasures remain the same after the review and certification process.

Network Accreditation

In the federal government, in order to process classified and/or sensitive but unclassified information, a network must be formally accredited by a designated approving authority (DAA). Accreditation is a formal process whereby a DAA authorizes a system or network to process classified or sensitive unclassified information. The DAA is normally a federal government employee with overall responsibility for the proper and secure operations of the system or network. The DAA is therefore very interested in the results and conclusions drawn from the risk analysis process as well as the assessments documented during the certification process. If a system or network is not granted accreditation by the DAA, the system or network is not permitted to go online and be operational until specific security problems, concerns, and defined vulnerabilities are addressed to a satisfactory level of detail and assurance. There are also specific requirements for communications security (COMSEC), computer security (COMPUSEC), information security (INFOSEC), TEMPEST, operations security (OPSEC), industrial security, and so on, that are levied by the federal government and cannot be deviated from. Therefore, when a network is used to process classified or sensitive but unclassified information, the decision to provide adequate security countermeasures is no longer an issue for debate but rather a directive that necessitates compliance.

Continuance

A complete, flawless, and totally accurate risk analysis is a theoretical impossibility. In addition, other vulnerabilities that may be latent at the time of the original risk analysis may appear later during the program. For this reason, and owing to the dynamic nature of networks, the risk analysis process must be an ongoing activity. When substantial network modifications occur or when a network security policy is modified, risk analysis documentation should be updated and the modifications and augmentations analyzed.

10.5   NETWORK SECURITY POLICY

Once the threats, vulnerabilities, and risks to the network are understood, a network security program must be implemented. The textbook first step to any network security program is to develop a network security policy. A network security policy is a statement that defines the objectives of the network security program and explains which information is to be protected and the rules that support and enforce these determinations. The policy also documents what data and network resources must be protected, why they must be protected, and how they will be protected. A network security policy also should be used to describe the system being protected, its physical and logical perimeters, and those individuals who have technical and managerial responsibility for the security of the network. It details the technical security countermeasures employed in the system and how those countermeasures are used. Examples can include access control devices, end-to-end encryption, and network audit trails. The security policy should specify the procedures to be implemented and managed. Examples may include the procedures to prevent the introduction of malicious logic (i.e., Trojan horses, viruses, worms) into the network. Discretionary access controls, mandatory access controls, accountability, assurance, physical security, and marking policies all should be defined in the network security policy.

The following information is provided as examples of statements that would commonly be found in a network security policy statement.

The security policy implemented by the network shall, at a minimum, incorporate the following characteristics and capabilities:

1. There shall be an explicit and well-defined security policy enforced by the network. The network shall be secured through an integrated security architecture that is articulated in the network security policy. This policy statement shall explain the objectives, goals, and explicit security requirements of the network.

2. Subjects (users and processes that act on behalf of users) and objects (passive entities that contain or receive information) must be identified to the network security system.

3. Given identified subjects and objects, there shall be a set of rules that are used by the network security system to determine whether a given subject can be permitted access to a specific object. The network security system shall mediate access to information as well as network resources based on a set of static (mandatory) and dynamic (discretionary) access control rules.

4. The network shall enforce a mandatory access control security policy. This policy shall be universally applied and nonmodifiable (except by authorized personnel or trusted subjects). This mandatory policy shall

be based on a defined information separation policy to support internal, external, and specific information processing requirements.

5. The network shall enforce a discretionary access control security policy. This policy shall provide a means for owners of data (users or processes) to allow other subjects to access their data. In addition, discretionary security controls are required to ensure that only selected users or groups of users may obtain access to information based on need-to-know limitations and the principle of least privilege.

6. The network shall provide the capability to mark accurately all output generated in the network. It shall be possible to associate a banner accurately and consistently (on the terminal or workstation screen) detailing the information category that the user is currently accessing (i.e., marketing-sensitive). In addition, all output from the network shall be marked on the front and back with the proper information category (i.e., competition-sensitive). Output markings and terminal/workstation banners shall be required only for data that has been designated as being protected under the network mandatory access control security policy. Information separated based on need-to-know and other discretionary controls is not required to be marked and/or bannered.

7. All users, prior to gaining access to the network, shall be briefed and trained on their responsibilities (with regard to security), the security mechanisms enforced by the network, and the penalties associated with tampering or otherwise purposely attempting to circumvent the security controls of the network.

8. All users who require access to the network shall be required to attend hands-on security training prior to being given a user account and access privileges.

Discretionary Access Controls

DAC is an important security consideration. Discretionary controls will allow specific data, files, and applications to be protected based on need-to-know restrictions. Within a network environment, users may wish to protect their own personal data, privacy data, or project-specific data. DAC provides this capability and can be enforced using identification and authentication mechanisms coupled with access control services.

User ID and Passwords

It is often recommended that user IDs and passwords be used as the primary identification and authentication mechanisms to enforce DAC. Host systems used to store information and files should be protected through the use of passwords. The granularity of protection can be determined after a security policy is developed and is ultimately determined by the owners of the data.

It is recommended that if passwords are used, they be (at a minimum) seven characters in length, be a mixture of alpha and numeric characters, be pronounceable but unrecognizable, and be changed, through forced automated processes, once every 30 days. It is further recommended that network passwords be automatically generated. Policies and procedures must be established and users must be trained on their responsibilities with regard to safeguarding passwords (i.e., don't write your password on a piece of paper and tape it to your workstation—this is a very common problem).

It is recommended that policies and procedures be developed and documented for the generation, dissemination, and protection of passwords. There should be set policies that describe who is responsible for the generation of passwords, how those passwords are disseminated to users at various sites, and how passwords are to be protected. There should also be procedures for adding users to the network and how those users are issued user IDs and passwords and how user accounts are taken off systems.

Host Discretionary Access Controls

Prior to additional host systems being interconnected into a network, their ability (if required) to protect data that they host should be examined and scrutinized. The MAC security policy enforcement described above should provide the necessary protections so that only authorized users can get to any network resource. Once the user has access to the resource and establishes a session, then the DAC security policy takes control of access mediation to specific data, files, and applications. It is recommended that products certified at the C2 level by NCSC be considered for DAC protections. The level of trust provided by an NCSC-certified product significantly increases the level of trust in the security services provided by the product.

Biometric—Discretionary Access Control

Normally, biometric identification and authentication devices work in conjunction with something that an authorized user of the network has knowledge of. Typically, biometric access control devices are used to restrict physical access to a facility or room, or possibly to limit access to workstations. A very common example would be the use of voice verification devices. When voice verification systems are used, they are typically used in conjunction with a personal identification number (PIN) or a password. The user initially enters the password or PIN and then is prompted or asked to state his or her name and some other supporting information. The voice verification, upon receiving a valid PIN or password, then checks the requesting user's voice patterns against stored authorized voice patterns. If these patterns match, the user is granted access to the network resource or facility. If the voice patterns do not match, then the user is normally given two additional chances to properly convey his or her voice pattern. If, after three attempts, the user is unable to properly provide an acceptable voice pattern, the voice verification system will generate an audit log as an indication of a security concern and terminate the session with the user. Other biometric access control systems include: fingerprint recognition systems, retina (human eye) scans, and the physical weight of an individual.

Mandatory Access Controls

If there are specific data types and network resources that require protection in a consistent and global manner, than a mandatory access control capability is required. For networks, this can be implemented in a number of ways. Recommended methods and countermeasures that can be used to enforce a security policy are discussed in the following sections.

MAC—Physical Separation

Any network zone, community of interest (COI), or group of users who does not require access to the system should not be connected. There is always a tendency within organizational networking to become overwhelmed with the network mating instinct and connect to as many possible networks and information resources as possible. There is nothing wrong with this approach if it is properly researched and does not become arbitrary.

Any zone not connected to the system is, by default, protected from external and many internal threats. If sections of the network can be logically and physically disconnected without severely impacting the user services and authorized access, this method should be considered because of its low-cost implementation. The recommendation is that each and every connection to the network be researched and justified prior to being interconnected.

MAC—Segmentation

To facilitate the logical and physical grouping of users into communities of interest, segmentation should be used wherever possible. The use of segmentation can support the implementation of a MAC network security policy. Zones should be allocated based on the users' communities of interest, their physical location, their work habits, the type of data they access, and their access authorizations.

MAC—Resource Isolation

Resource isolation, in the context of this discussion, is the process whereby resources are isolated from certain users, groups of users, or logical/physical network zones. Many networks offer a wealth of opportunity for this type of MAC policy implementation and enforcement. Network components that should be considered to enforce a MAC policy include:

- Gateways
- Local and remote bridges
- Routers

Marking Policy

For information that is specifically designated as requiring protection in accordance with the MAC security policy, a marking policy should be implemented and enforced. For example, corporate proprietary information protected in accordance with the established MAC security policy should be marked properly on output and also when presented to a user on a workstation screen.

Physical Security

The use of network filtering based on source and destination addresses to provide security for a network has one fundamental flaw. This flaw is the need for specific users to use the same workstations consistently, day in and day out. A user could possibly use a workstation on a network zone that he or she is not authorized to utilize. Since the access to network zones is based exclusively on source and destination addresses, the user theoretically would have the ability to access network resources that could not be accessed from the user's authorized workstation or network zone. This potential security vulnerability is offset by a second tier of security protection, since the user will still be prompted for a password prior to being granted access to specific data, files, or applications hosted on the penetrated system. Physical security is a very important attribute for networks. For this reason, security management must continue to focus on ensuring that physical security controls are in place and consistently applied.

Accountability

Accountability on a network can be accomplished through the use of security audit trails. Accountability provides the security management personnel with insight into the activities of users, information they access, and security-relevant events. Accountability is often an underutilized network security feature. In many instances, however, accountability has proven to be the most important tool for security managers. The reason that security auditing is an often unused tool is a direct result of the volume and complexity of the auditing reports generated by most systems today. In addition, in large networks there are very few tools that allow a security manager or systems administrator to gather audit/accountability information across the network. This is especially difficult, if not impossible, for those large networks that are composed of different types of devices employing different types of auditing tools and services. As a result, the ability to gather effectively, consolidate, correlate, and analyze intelligently the audit/accountability information from a networkwide perspective is incredibly difficult. Therefore, it is important that network security audit trails be as user friendly as possible. Audit reports should be condensed to the greatest extent possible to allow for ease of review. If additional detailed data is required for a specific security-relevant event, the security manager should have the capability to go back to the security audit application and extract the necessary additional data. For accountability to be a useful tool for security managers, it must be expeditious and simple to use.

Assurance

Assurance is critical to any security implementation. Assurance defines the level of trust and confidence that you have in the ability of the security system to enforce consistently the defined security policy. Assurance can be gained through two principal means. First, security mechanisms can be tested independently and given a rating relative to functionality, strength of mechanism, and level of trust. This type of evaluation is conducted at NSA's NCSC. The second technique is to conduct internal testing on the security mechanisms and attempt to circumvent or otherwise disable their ability to protect the system.

Because the products certified by the NCSC are evaluated in stand-alone operations and based on a very specific configuration, it is also recommended that formal in-house testing of the composite security network architecture be conducted to uncover any potential anomalies that result from the interconnection of the composite architecture.

The various security components on the network must, in their aggregate, provide a level of trust and assurance. The idea of a distributed Network Trusted Computing Base (NTCB) is discussed in the Trusted Network Interpretations (TNI). Given a typical network's operational environment, its distributed nature, and its intended mission, a distributed security policy and concept will be most appropriate.

10.6 SECURITY MANAGEMENT PERSONNEL

To ensure that the network is properly managed with regard to security, a security organization must be established. The selection of the right network security management personnel often can mean the success or failure of a network security program. Three functional areas of network security responsibility that should be considered in the selection of management personnel include: a network security manager, network security officer(s), and network security administrators. The time and effort required for network security management functions is directly related to the size, complexity, and relative value of information processed on a network. Often, through comprehensive training and awareness programs, existing network administration personnel can be very effective in implementing, enforcing, and managing a network security program. Network security management and administration functions can be added to the responsibilities of existing personnel with little or no impact. In many cases, much of the security management and administration functions is already being performed, but not in a consistent or efficient manner.

Network Security Manager

A network security manager should be appointed first. This individual will have overall responsibility for the network and will support and supervise the creation of security policy, procedures, and security technology implementation. This individual will be the principal point of contact for security issues, concerns, and problem resolution.

The successful implementation of a network security architecture will be a direct result of management involvement. High-level management must be kept aware of the security implications surrounding network design decisions that may preclude or complicate current or future security countermeasure or policy implementations. For this reason, it becomes necessary to appoint a security manager. This security manager provides the necessary progress, status, and technical support for all security engineering activities. It is also recommended that this individual be appointed by the director or vice president of the IS Department, since visibility and support from the highest levels will have a direct impact on the security manager's ability to succeed.

The security manager should orchestrate a plan of attack that details the overall security policy for the network, implementation schedules and follow-up operations and maintenance, and management support of these implementations. This schedule of events could be outlined and described in a network security plan and be used to guide and direct the personnel responsible for implementing the plan.

This security manager should attend network design reviews and engineering meetings and should review design correspondence and planning documentation to ensure consistency and compatibility with installed and forecasted security measures. The security manager should also establish relationships with key personnel outside the organization that directly or indirectly affect or support the security policy of the system.

Network Security Officer(s)

The second position to be considered is the network security officer. A network security officer is normally required for each physically distinct network site. Therefore, there may be multiple network security officers throughout an organization, depending on the size and location of the composite network.

Network Security Administrators

The third security management position is referred to as network security administrator. This position is typically a part-time responsibility that is delegated to an individual who already performs a full-time job. Network security administrators are normally assigned to subnetworks or communities of interest where their responsibilities include the configuration of servers, workstations, and subnetwork resources and services. Given their intimate knowledge of their working environment, their ability to implement network security provisions expeditiously and effectively is enhanced. The primary responsibility of a network security administrator is to enforce the established security policy of the network and to monitor personnel and their activities and report security incidents. The number of network security administrators required by the network will be driven strictly by the size, physical distribution, and layout of the network.

10.7 NETWORK SECURITY—POLICIES AND PROCEDURES

There are many support functions that are recommended in this section for the security management of a network. Security support functions fill a needed role within the security of any system. Security policies and procedures are recommended as they guide the day-to-day security activities. These policies and procedures should be developed by a knowledgeable person and be reviewed, documented, and formally published and given to management and staff personnel. The development of security policies and procedures will help support a consistent application of the security policy.

It is recommended that policies and procedures be developed for sensitive information storage, marking, dissemination, and destruction. Simply stated, sensitive information must be protected throughout its life cycle. Without guidance and direction, such information will never be successfully protected.

Training and Awareness

Security training instills awareness and enables users to understand the importance of security. In most organizations, security is viewed as something that is required, but not something that is truly vital. Most security training material distributed to users is either stuck in a drawer or immediately given away to someone else. The most effective way for security training to take root within an organization is for upper-level management to make security an important issue. Once this commitment is made at the higher levels, it will be passed on to lower-level management and their subordinates.

Security training is, in many instances, a commonly overlooked security countermeasure. Without security training, the most sophisticated and complex security countermeasures are useless. Security training must define to the user and management staff how security is enforced on a network, what each person's responsibilities are relative to security, and what the penalties are for deviation from the security policies and procedures established.

Security training should be given whenever a user is added to a network. Training should be performed on a timely basis and scheduled in advance, so that users may avail themselves of it without conflict. Security training must be presented in a serious manner. This is not typically the case and users may perceive that security training is only a formality required to check a box. For a network security program to be successful, security training must be interwoven into the operations of the system and be an integral part of each user's learning experience.

Probably the most important aspects of a successful migration to secure network computing operations are awareness and planning. By ensuring that the network design staff, developers, and management personnel are aware that to process sensitive information will require certain security features and characteristics, it is likely that decisions that would preclude or impede these future features and characteristics can be minimized. Awareness cannot be achieved through infrequent verbal discussions, but must be achieved through well-organized and documented thoughts, ideas, and recommendations. Awareness of key technologies and design drivers also must be conveyed to the engineering and management staffs to ensure that decisions are not made without considering the security ramifications.

Planning for future network security requirements and capabilities is also important. Planning and awareness must be worked simultaneously, as one is not effective without the other. Upper-level management must be told that by planning now we can better position ourselves for growth, business opportunities, and, above all, cost savings. The design staff must understand that installing a network at these physical locations will require them to completely retrofit the cable plant once the system is used to process classified data. Planning and training awareness must be at the level and understanding of the target audience. On numerous occasions, I have witnessed security purists speak at levels substantially over the target audience's heads. This is ineffective, costly, and unproductive. To be effective and useful, the discussion of security must be at a technical level that the audience can understand and utilize.

Software Development and Introduction

A major threat to a network is the introduction of malicious logic. Malicious logic can take the form of worms, viruses, trap doors, time bombs, or Trojan horses. It is important to establish policies and procedures regarding the introduction of software into a networked environment. Many networks are very vulnerable to Trojan horse attacks. This vulnerability results from the absence of software/hardware security countermeasures at the operating system level that can prevent these programs from operating. Many networks implement MAC protection only in the form of resource isolation; however, if a user has authorized access to a host and is able to utilize a Trojan horse, that malicious user can, without much difficulty, compromise any and all data on the host system. DAC security controls cannot prevent the use of Trojan horse programs.

For these reasons, the policies and procedures that define how, when, where, and by whom software may be developed on a network or introduced (via a disk or tape) must receive a high level of attention and visibility. Experience has shown that by effectively managing and controlling the software development process, systems are much less likely to be infected with malicious logic. It is important that all software development on networks be strictly monitored and controlled.

Require that all software, prior to being loaded onto a system attached to a network, be checked and tested. This technique is an excellent idea as long as it is viewed as a deterrent and not as a prevention. An average programmer could easily hide a Trojan horse within a source listing that would evade even the most experienced programmers. This assumes that the software source code, prior to being loaded onto a system, is desk checked. If the software is only tested prior to being loaded, the malicious executable could be tied to the system clock of the target host system and could be time delayed so that testing the software would not reveal any malicious activity. Perpetrators have implemented Trojan horses and virus attacks using this method in several documented instances. In summary, it is recommended that software development be limited to the greatest extent possible and that the loading of software on a system be restricted, unless previously approved.

System Backups

Policies and procedures should be established for system, application, and data backups for a network. These backups should be consistent, and the media used for the backups should be stored at an alternate location.

Reporting of Security Incidents

Security policies and procedures should be established for the reporting of security incidents. The procedures should define what constitutes a security incident and who should be alerted. Users should be made aware of their responsibilities with regard to reporting security incidents. The development and documentation of such a procedure will serve not only as guidance to the user community, but also as a deterrent to the would-be perpetrator.

10.8 MAXIMIZE INHERENT SECURITY CAPABILITIES IN DESIGN

One of the primary objectives of a successful network security program is to start early and begin security design activities in parallel with other initial design activities. This early involvement will allow security issues to be incorporated into the design of the network. If left until the end of a program, security is either ignored or implemented through painstaking retrofit and unnecessary financial strain. There are many network design attributes that can enhance the overall security of a network without incurring additional cost. For example, the physical layout of the network is important. To reduce physical security and other access control costs, users who require access to very similar types of data and services can be subnetworked into communities of interest. Bridging and routing technologies offer cost-free security through link layer filtering and source-explicit routing.

Security engineering involvement also may preclude serious design mistakes. All internal and external interfaces to the network should be examined to determine whether connectivity is actually required to perform a given function or task. If not required, then the system(s) or network should not be connected. Ensuring security consistency across network nodes is also important in the areas of user identification and authentication, encryption, password schemes, labeling, audit reporting, and the access control implementations. There are many network security features that are an inherent part of commercial networking product offerings today. Further, there are several installation and physical distribution techniques that can help support the creation of a secure network. Implementation of these techniques and strategies requires only common sense and little, if any, monetary or management investment. For these reasons, the security countermeasures discussed in this section should be strongly considered for existing networks.

Common Sense

The must underutilized inherent security countermeasure is common sense. Dramatically more security exposures, penetrations, and incidents of fraud could be stopped through the use of simple common-sense approaches to security than through the use of the most elaborate and expensive trusted operating systems, protocols, and applications. In most instances, security practitioners focus on the trees and totally miss the forest. Part of this results from the fact that most security practitioners tend to be perfectionists. As a result, the fact that doors are left open to a computer facility or that there is low employee morale may be overlooked because such problems are obvious and (believed to be) very easy to deal with and fix. On the other hand, the inherent security vulnerabilities of the MVS operating system provide the perfect opportunity for the security practitioners to spend an enormous amount of time fixing or filling the holes. This is obviously not a healthy approach or necessarily a good investment of time or energy. It is often useful to bring in an outside consultant to take a fresh and unbiased view of the network security environment within an organization. Many times, the most obvious things to an outsider will seem transparent to the personnel who work within the environment day after day. One very effective common-sense approach for network security is to get a group of technical and management personnel into a brainstorming session. The cooperative thoughts and interaction often prove to accomplish radically more than the same process conducted in a one-on-one session with each individual.

Principle of Least Privilege

Users and the processes that act on their behalf should be given access only to information that is required to perform their job. The enforcement of the principle of least privilege greatly decreases the possible exposure and vulnerability of a network. By enforcing the principle of least privilege, the threats of malicious insiders and accidental user errors are significantly decreased. Maximizing the inherent attributes of networking components, applications, and services, network security administrators should take into consideration the principle of least privilege.

Physical Separation

One of the most obvious ways to protect information is not to allow physical access to the information or the networking resources or services that store or manipulate the information. The security manager should review all interfaces to systems and other networks and determine if the need for such an interface is just assumed to be secure and/or nonthreatening. In today's networks, the notion of isolationism or physical separation may not seem like a palatable consideration however, in many instances, such an approach should be considered and reviewed.

Segmentation

Segmentation is the process of logically dividing a network into a series of communities of interest, or COIs. A COI is a logical grouping of individuals, services, and automated resources to support one or many organizational mission objectives. COIs have long been used to departmentalize networked automation resources within organizations. This departmentalization was typically done so that automated resources could be most cost effectively applied and be nearest to the individuals that needed them the most. Segmentation and departmentalization also provide an excellent way of separating users and data with minimal impact on acquisition costs, operations, or maintenance of the network.

When using segmentation as a security countermeasure, users are divided into groups with similar job functions and responsibilities. These groups often require the same information to do their day-to-day tasks and the same automated resources, applications, and services to support those tasks. In most instances, these groups of individuals also have similar access rights and privileges. Given these parameters, users can be logically grouped and isolated from other groups that do not require interdepartmental services. Through bridging, routing, or gateway technology, those users who require access to information or resources located on other zones of the network can gain access to required services. This access can be selective and filtered to ensure that only those users who have authorized access to extend beyond their local network zone are permitted to do so. The final benefit of segmentation is that all local information traffic on the zone is not seen on the main network backbone. Therefore, by localizing traffic through the use of COIs, benefits in both security and network performance can be realized.

Heterogeneous Implementations

The use of heterogeneous networking products and services (i.e., protocols, applications, operating systems, network operating systems, and file systems) can provide logical separation of data and users defined by the networking products and services that are accessible and their compatibility. Once again, in the current trends in open systems networking technologies, the notion of a network that won't talk and won't interoperate may seem far-fetched. Nevertheless, for those organizations interested in providing network security, the use of their existing computing resources in a well-thought-out and consistent manner may provide a cost-effective network security approach—at least as an interim solution.

Filtering Bridges and Routers

Filtering can be a very low cost network security countermeasure, if the bridges and routers used can be adequately protected from tampering and remote access. Bridges and routers can provide a security service by utilizing them as address filters. In fact, the use of a bridge for restricting access based on specific addresses can be used to enforce a MAC policy.

Most bridges and routers can be configured easily to restrict certain addresses from passing beyond certain domains or subnetworks. For example, user A is not permitted to access any information on network zone 2 but only information on his local network, zone 1. By simply specifying to the bridge the Ethernet address for that user, the bridge can be used to ensure that user A can never gain access to network zone 2. The same is true with a router by simply specifying IP addresses or even a specific type of protocol. For example, a router could be configured so that no Novell IPX traffic is allowed to be communicated between logical link (1) and logical link (2). Routers are also very effective at restricting information flow. The use of filtering has many advantages, including low-cost implementation, ease of reconfiguration, and flexibility. Most bridging and routing components require a valid user ID and password before any configuration parameters can be established or changed.

Dedicated Network Resources

In a distributed system, the use of dedicated network resources can provide increased levels of security. For example, information can be dedicated to a specific network server based on the type of information, applications provided, or physical location. If a network resource is dedicated to a single sensitivity, and only specific users are authorized to access that server, then minimal security risk is realized. Specific access controls and authorizations can be established for each network server and associated user community. This type of architecture allows for multiple server, groups of users, and network services to be provided across the network. In addition, it facilitates the logical separation of users, information, and services based on specific servers and which servers the users have authorization to access.

Selective Service/Access Menus

A selective service/access menu is a process whereby users are allowed to see only the network resources that they are permitted to access. For example, if user A was authorized to access hosts 1, 2, 4, 6, and 8, he or she would not even be aware that hosts 3, 5, and 7 existed. Selective service/access menus can be provided by a centralized network access center. The network access center requires that a user, prior to gaining access to any other network resource, first sign on to the centralized access center. The user then provides the access center with his or her identification and authentication information. Once the server identifies and authenticates the user, it downloads to a user-specific menu which defines to the user which network resources he or she is authorized to access.

The centralized access server can be used in conjunction with a name service so that the user is not able to access network resources through the use of hard or actual physical network addresses. Instead, the user is given a menu that specifies the network resources that he or she is authorized to access. For example, the menu may list the network resources as IBM 3090 (2nd Floor—Administration) or Laser Printer—4th Floor, etc. The user would then select one of these menu items and the centralized access server would, through the use of a name service, map a physical address against the selected menu item and thereby provide the intelligence necessary to establish an authorized connection.

Security Overhead and Transparency

To a large extent, network security causes unacceptable performance overhead and is time consuming and impeding to the network user. To the greatest extent possible, network security needs to be transparent to the user and have minimal performance overhead. If the implemented network security features are not easy to use, users will invariably find ways to work around them. Likewise, if security features cause substantial performance impacts, system/network administrators and operators will turn them off.

10.9   SUMMARY

In this chapter, we've looked at various measures you can use in organizing and executing your network security program. One of the most important steps is to analyze thoroughly the risk to your particular network and communications environment, and the material in this chapter can provide thorough guidance to this process.

11

Advanced Network Security Strategies

11.1 INTRODUCTION

Current network security technology deals almost exclusively with the protection of information for unauthorized disclosure. Data is protected through encryption, physical separation, and access control mechanisms. As a result of this fortress approach, network security can be very expensive and difficult to maintain. Many networks once thought to be highly secure have been penetrated through simple mechanisms or by inside personnel. In most cases, these malicious individuals have not been exposed or prosecuted. With a limited threat of being exposed, perpetrators are unhindered in their quest for information.

For future networks, a balanced approach is required, including protections against integrity attacks, denial of service, and the implementation and management of proven accountability technology. A useful analogy is the security of a house. Americans do not typically purchase a home and then spend thousands of dollars on security to install barbed wire, 30' cement walls, and 10' thick steel doors. Homeowners rely on a more balanced approach that includes simple preventions and the confidence that would-be criminals are deterred from breaking into their homes because they could be apprehended and punished.

11.2 INTEGRITY—THE NEW NETWORK SECURITY FRONTIER

Integrity continues to gain in importance as a security objective and, for many networks, a critical security requirement. The rationale behind this recent inclusion has not been defined or described clearly, but its impact has been noticed. Integrity now has increased its boundary of influence and is recognized as a more global security issue. In Part I of the Trusted Network Interpretations, the use of the term integrity is limited to the correct operation of the NTCB hardware and firmware and the protection against unauthorized modification of labels and data. In Part II of the TNI, the term integrity is expanded to include mechanisms for information transfer between distinct components. This communications integrity includes the issues of correctness of message transmission, authentication of source/destination, data/control/protocol correctness, and other related areas.

Since integrity is obviously critical in a truly distributed system, it can be postulated that integrity will continue to expand its security domain. The communications underlying the distributed processes within a system are addressed by the TNI, but guidance is currently required to address the cooperation and attributes that operate above the communications of a system. Distributed control, processing, and data will continue to become more cooperative, operating under the control of intelligent processes and applications and increasing the need for a high degree of integrity. The definition of these characteristics in an integrity policy will be difficult. Integrity disparity among various elements of a distributed system is also an area of concern. If, for example, a trusted distributed operating system provides a high degree of integrity, but the underlying communications upon which it depends does not provide as high a degree of integrity, there may be reason for concern, unless, of course, the level of integrity assurance is commensurate with that of the lowest integrity of any element of the composite system.

11.3 DENIAL OF SERVICE—DEPENDENCE ON RELIABILITY, MAINTAINABILITY, AND AVAILABILITY

Reliability, defined for this discussion as the ability to prevent denial of service, has a history similar to that of integrity. Both have been given new attention as a direct result of the overwhelming advancements in network computing. Networks already form the communications infrastructure of our country. Data integrity and service continuance are important and will become increasingly important as we become increasingly dependent on networks. Denial of service, for many years, has been categorized into other engineering disciplines, but has not been under the purview of security engineering. Until recently, denial of service concerns has been placed under engineering disciplines such as reliability, maintainability, and availability (RMA). Many RMA-type requirements have been satisfied through the use of fault-tolerant systems, sophisticated logistical support systems, and redundant/standby components.

Distributed technology increases the amount of interaction between components and the level of cooperation between them. Dependence on reliable interaction and communications between devices is dramatically increased, as systems become more distributed and cooperative. As the dependence on distributed technology increases, the need for reliability also increases. The prevention of denial of service is multifaceted and must not be isolated as only a security concern. Clearly, major technical and management challenges lie ahead in the area of highly reliable networking infrastructures.

11.4 ACCOUNTABILITY

For network security, highly intelligent and distributed automated accountability technology is the next frontier. The networks of the future will rely on the separation of users and data, but will also provide sophisticated accountability. Today's network security mechanisms are designed to keep users out. In the future, the focus will be on letting users in, but being able to monitor their activities proactively and kick them out if they do something inappropriate. Proactive accountability will provide the key and fundamental services to take network security to the next level. A paradigm shift is really what is required for network security to ever have a legitimate chance to stay in step with (or close behind) technology advancement.

The majority of today's auditing systems are totally ineffective. There are numerous examples and stories that depict this condition in today's networks and computer systems. Examples include large mainframe/terminal environments where the daily audit records (actually recorded and written to media and then printed) exceed 100 million bytes of information. Assuming 100 million bytes of information, a fast typist, typing at 60 words per minute, would be able to type approximately 180,000 characters in an eight-hour shift. At this rate, it would take in excess of 555 eight-hour days to type the audit trail from a single day of secure processing. The point is that no one is going to take the time to look through the audit trail information because there is too much information. Another example of the common problems with auditing in today's computer systems is that the processing of the audit information to filter and organize the information intelligently often takes longer than the useful life of the audit information. By the time the criminal act is found, it is too late to have any chance of doing anything about the perpetrator. There are also a large number of systems and networks where auditing is turned off or where no auditing capability exists. This contrast is consistent in the industry. There is either too much or too little auditing. The security purist community, who normally implement security mechanisms and security procedures for the sake of security, have a consistent track record of overauditing.

The next generation of accountability mechanisms must be capable of authenticating users and continuously tracking their activities through multithousand node networks. These systems will need to provide the capability to identify immediately security-relevant events and act on those events in real time to lessen the potential damage. These accountability systems will need to be fault tolerant, accurate, consistent, and provide a very high level of trust to ensure the authenticity of the data and events recorded. This information could then be used in the prosecution of malicious network perpetrators.

11.5 NETWORK SECURITY INTEGRATION

In a nutshell, the big question facing everyone now is trust integration. A variety of secure networking products are now available that possess a defined level of trust; however, the integration of these trusted elements to form integrated systems is not being addressed. Stand-alone UNIX systems, DBMSs, network products, and network protocols, all provide individual levels of protection, but the notion of an integrated security system is nonexistent. A defined set of network security standards, which is consistent with commonly used networking technologies, would be a major step in the right direction.

11.6 NETWORK SECURITY STANDARDS

There is an overwhelming need for security standardization in the networking industry. In Chapter 3, we discussed the problems with respect to slow standardization efforts; in the next chapter, we'll discuss some of the emerging standards efforts.

Before standards can be effective, it will be important to define clearly networks and distributed systems from a security perspective. A clearly discernible definition of distributed systems is needed. Without a common understanding of distributed systems, any attempt to provide security guidance on the subject will be difficult. What is really needed is a framework and structure to define where guidance is required. Due to the complexity of distributed technology, it will be useful to create a structure for which the elements of distributed systems and their relative dimensions can be organized and depicted. Once a structure is established, the characteristics of a system can be inserted into this structure and security issues can be drawn from its portfolio. This document can be used as a point of departure for a formal framework to accomplish this objective.

In most cases, it has been assumed by vendors of security mechanisms and products that they can rely on other parts of a network to provide certain levels of protection. This is fine if there is coordination and interaction, but, to date, this has been missing, producing unfounded assumptions and less than effective security countermeasures. Put simply into a hypothetical example: Vendor A develops a secure/trusted word processing product; however, this word processor can be used only on a host (platform) that implements a secure/trusted operating system with specific functionality. If the platform for which this word processor is implemented is not secure/trusted and does not provide the specific security functionality required, the word processor cannot be used for secure activities. This shortcoming is prevalent throughout the industry. Just as the TNI has dealt with communications, security guidance is needed for processing, control, and data, especially as these elements become increasingly distributed. In this structure, security is considered to be part of control and guidance is required to support the incorporation of security into interactive autonomous processes. What we have existing today is a small set of evaluated trusted operating systems and applications—primarily relational database management systems. It is likely that this list will grow substantially over the next 5 to 10 years. Running parallel with the development of trusted operating systems and applications are the developments of trusted interface units (trusted network components) and other trusted protocols. And finally, with the advent of distributed technology (that portion of the technology that has unique functionality and capability over those provided by networks), we have the third side to the security triangle. Researchers, developers, and implementors are all running down different paths and examining a single side of the triangle, but no integration of these efforts has been defined to examine the relation between the various aspects, interrelationships, and composite functions of the triangle. It would be useful to have a general description of where security functions provided by stand-alone operating systems, networks, and distributed entities have their place in the security triangle and how they can be used to complement one another.

If a group of secure components are interconnected through a secure network, there must be a clear delineation of responsibility and control. Therefore, the interface between the two becomes a mandatory requirement for operation. If we now add a distributed operating system or distributed application on top of these two, we create a second interface requirement. Much as the ISO layers are structured to facilitate modular construction and standardization, so have we created (possibly without intending to do so) layers for security implementation. The need for security standardization must include the definition of boundaries between trusted/secure entities, interfaces among them, and cooperation and interaction ensuring consistent support of the intended security policy.

11.7   SECURITY OVERHEAD AND TRANSPARENCY

To a large extent, network security causes unacceptable performance overhead and is time consuming and impeding to the network user. To the greatest extent possible, future network security will need to be transparent to the user and have minimal performance overhead.

11.8   HIGH-PERFORMANCE SYSTEMS

The entire area of high-performance systems must be researched to provide similar gains in network security technologies. As we achieve gigabit and terabit speeds, the protection of data transmission becomes a difficult problem. Major technical breakthroughs, possibly in the area of high-performance parallel encryption, are necessary to support the networks of the future.

11.9   PUBLIC DISCLOSURE OF SECURITY-RELEVANT INFORMATION

The vast majority of security holes, vulnerabilities, and incidents are not disclosed to the public. A major cultural change in the way in which network security-relevant issues, concerns, and vulnerabilities are handled needs to occur. Public disclosure of known security vulnerabilities in products, computers, and networking components (including operating systems and applications) would allow these problems to be fixed before they can be penetrated or abused. Public disclosure of security penetrations defining the vulnerability that was exploited and the means by which the penetration occurred would enable network security administrators to protect against specific attacks and develop operational procedures to combat defined methods. Major progress has been made in the area of viruses, and this approach can be emulated for other security-related issues. Use of bulletin boards and specialized tiger teams will continue to be an effective means of knowledge sharing.

11.10 INTRUSION DETECTION SYSTEMS (IDS)

IDS, as an applied security mechanism, appears to have made great strides in the past three years. There are several sites across the United States that have implemented intrusion detection systems with great success, namely, Los Alamos Labs, several U.S. Air Force bases, and multiple contractors, including the brainchild of the technology, Stanford Research Institute (SRI). Each of these sites has operational IDS systems. IDS has the potential to achieve the network security paradigm shift discussed earlier in that it provides the ability to implement a proactive and interactive network security policy versus a reactive and passive implementation. The implication is that should such technology become widely available, cost effective, and operationally feasible, the approach to computer security could change. Instead of using more locks, fewer locks could be used, but one's actions could be better scrutinized and responded to in real time.

IDS provides an excellent way to employ knowledge-based systems to model user and process patterns. Patterns can be used to define a common operational threat for a user or a process and if the user extends beyond this defined pattern, the IDS system can be used to recognize this anomaly and take appropriate action. Users are categorized by their activities, and if they extend beyond thresholds, alarms are triggered. Certain network patterns (i.e., external host connections, loading, time of access, and the number of accesses to a certain device) can also be monitored. Since most devices have auditing capabilities, a centralized device can be used to collect audited information across the network, correlate it, and identify any problems. Network sniffers that collect all network traffic can also be used to support the centralized auditing function.

There are some very obvious technical challenges that currently exist in the IDS environment. For example, by using a LAN sniffer on 802.3 broadcast networks, a sniffer is required on each bridged LAN segment, increasing cost, complexity, and administrative overhead. Complete network encryption prevents network monitoring. By using AI where user activities are monitored, it may be possible for a user to gradually increase or decrease activity so that the threshold mechanism gradually accepts variations in habit. In centralized auditing systems, if it is possible to penetrate the audit mechanism on a single network device, the credibility of the entire user audit record may be at question. It is also possible for a malicious user to masquerade or intentionally intercept and modify network traffic.

11.11   SECURITY MECHANISM COMMUNALITY

Security mechanism communality or uniformity is a large area of concern that will require additional guidance. The TNI very briefly discusses uniformity of labels; however, uniformity of labels is only a single technical issue and many other security mechanisms will require either uniformity or subjection to conversion algorithms to permit trusted interconnective, cooperative distributive processing to occur. Major security mechanisms (such as MAC, DAC, auditing, authentication/identification, encryption, key management, privilege passing, and many others) require additional guidance to support uniformity and communality.

11.12   UNIFORM USE OF ENCRYPTION MECHANISMS

Under the federal government's Commercial COMSEC Endorsement Program (CCEP), vendors have developed several network encryption products. These products, however, do not necessarily interoperate with one another. As systems become increasingly distributed and networks are interconnected, the encryption mechanisms used must be able to interact harmoniously and consistently.

Owing to the rapid potential outgrowth of network encryption, key management and distribution becomes an increasingly important issue. Without effective, high-performance key management and distribution, use of widespread encryption will be difficult. If encryption is used as a universal security countermeasure for many systems, the ability to generate and disseminate keying material securely becomes a critical issue. The dissemination of keying material can be an additional risk if current manual procedures remain in effect.

11.13   UNIFORM LABELING

As systems become increasingly distributed and cooperative (assuming labeling is used to enforce access controls), the need to support a universal labeling scheme is required. Furthermore, the reason and rationale behind the use and support of MACs is that they can be applied universally and consistently. In today's technology, MAC policies are typically enforced through labeling. The need for consistency and uniformity of labeling between cooperating processes is therefore a very important consideration. Label generation, label format, label content, consistent content meaning and value, and uniform label integrity are all areas requiring guidance.

11.14   COVERT CHANNELS

Covert channels (discussed at length in Chapter 9) have complicated and continue to complicate secure network development, verification, and certification. It is quite apparent that covert channels will continue to be viewed as a substantial threat to networked environments, especially in classified government networks. As a result of this perception, numerous networks have not been developed, owing to the massive threat posed by covert channels. In most cases, multiple networks are designed and implemented to separate information sensitivities into physically distinct systems. This approach obviously is inefficient and requires a substantially larger investment in components, facilities, and overall operations and management of the various systems.

In the simplest sense, covert channels are a direct result of communications. Distributed systems are designed to maximize communications, thereby facilitating cooperation. Since covert channels will abound and become more predominant as systems interact, cooperate, and communicate, it is important that the actual threat of covert channels be understood. If covert channels continue to be viewed as show-stoppers, then the ability to formally test, verify, and ultimately certify a trusted distributed system is not within the current state of the art. There is a very strong and persistent need within the security community to generate and disseminate guidance on the true threat of covert channels. For many individuals, the threat of Trojan horses, viruses, and trap doors was thought to be only in the minds of the believers and hopelessly remote from causing real harm to real computer systems and networks. With the latest headliners, much attention has been brought to bear on these threats and people are beginning to take heed, investigate system vulnerabilities, and take appropriate actions.

On the other hand, covert channels are a mystery to most and are assumed to be a formidable threat only because they are specifically cited in the Orange Book. This "threat by Orange Book reference" may not suffice much longer. People are beginning to ask questions and beginning to doubt. Trojan horses and viruses are intuitively much larger, broader, and threatening phenomena than covert channels. The public has been made aware of actual Trojan horse and virus attacks, and, because of this exposure, people believe and subsequently have adjusted their mind sets. On the other hand, when was the last time a covert channel was used to compromise information and was publicly discussed? If the argument for not disclosing information about covert channel utilization is because disclosure of such information could cause additional damage, then why is information about Trojan horses and viruses permitted to be discussed by our newspapers and distributed freely?

11.15 UPWARD COMPATIBILITY OF SECURITY SERVICES

Vertical as well as horizontal interoperability is important as systems become more distributed and cooperative. A potential example would be the need for interoperability between a secure operating system, a secure network interface unit, and a secure database management system.

11.16 COMPOSABILITY OF SECURITY PROPERTIES

Composability of security properties is an issue concerned with interoperability, consistency, and assurance. As systems and networks are interconnected, certain rules can be established with regard to composability. These same procedures must be examined relative to distributivity and cooperation among processing entities.

11.17 CAPABILITY-BASED PROTECTION

Due to the complexity involved in distributed technology, the ability to define capabilities for users and subjects within a composite system may prove beneficial in the long run. Since distributed processes, control, security, and other distributed entities may require full run of a system in order to accomplish a task successfully, the ability to restrict access based on certain allowable functions should be investigated and guidance generated based on the results.

11.18   MODELING DISTRIBUTED SYSTEMS

The degree of cooperation and intelligence needed to propagate a system will continue to make this job even more difficult. Techniques, concepts, and usable structures used to reduce the complexity of distributed systems would be very beneficial in this area. The ability to model cooperation among processing entities would also be a giant step forward.

11.19   SUMMARY

In this chapter, we've discussed various advanced strategies with respect to network security. In the next chapter, we'll take a closer look at various standardization efforts with respect to network security and how they fit into our discussions in this and the previous chapters.

12

Network Security Standards

12.1 INTRODUCTION

Several times in this book, we've mentioned the lack of standards to date—or at least the lack of widespread usage—with respect to network security. In this chapter, we'll briefly discuss two of the emerging standards efforts—the security component of the Simple Network Management Protocol (SNMP) and the IEEE 802.10 effort.

You will recall that in Chapter 6 we also briefly discussed the security components of the X.400 electronic mail standard (and, in passing, the X.509 Directory Services security component). Indeed, in that chapter, we focused on standard specifications—if not implementations—of services and the mechanisms to provide those services. Therefore, you could reasonably assume that the network security standards discipline is gaining momentum.

12.2 SNMP V2.0

The Simple Network Management Protocol (SNMP) is the network management component of the Internet protocol suite (which also includes TCP, IP, FTP, and Telnet). One of the major shortcomings of the original specification was the lack of security features. Version 2 of the standard—as specified in Request for Comments (RFC) 1352—includes security protocol enhancements.[1]

SNMP 2 specifies three security services:

- Data integrity
- Data origin authentication
- Data confidentiality

The goals of the SNMP security protocol include:

1. Verifying that a received SNMP message hasn't been modified during transmission and could therefore effect an unauthorized management operation

2. Verifying the identity of the originator of the message

3. Providing that the message is recent by virtue of the time it was generated

4. Ordering the time of that message in the context of other similar messages (that is, making sure that a message is time stamped after those already received)

5. Protecting message contents from accidental disclosure

The protocol includes a message digest algorithm—a 128-bit checksum that is calculated over the designated portion of an SNMP message—which is included as part of the message sent. A digest authentication protocol includes a secret value known only to the originator and recipient and which is prefixed to the message (which, in turn, implicitly verifies the message origin simply by verifying that the digest—the secret value—is correct). Additionally, a symmetric encryption algorithm—DES—is used to promote data confidentiality.

When an SNMP message is generated, the authInfo component "is constructed according to the authentication protocol identified for the SNMP party originating the message."[2] Using the digest authentication protocol, information is obtained from a local database (that information being the authentication clock, private authentication key, and other material), the authTimestamp component is set, and other values are set according the appropriate protocol.[3] Following some additional value setting, the authorization message value is then encapsulated according to the appropriate privacy protocol and transmitted to the recipient.

On the receiving end, the normal processing of SNMP messages is accompanied by security evaluation steps, including verifying the authInfo message component against correct authorized information. If this initial verification fails, the message is deemed to be unauthentic. Otherwise, various field components are extracted and compared against the recipient's local database for authorization clock and time stamp values to determine the authenticity.

The rest of the SNMP security protocol is defined in RFC 1352 and should be consulted as needed for network management security.[4]

12.3   IEEE 802.10

The Institute of Electrical and Electronics Engineers (IEEE) has long been a force within the networking and communications standards world. It is within this framework that the Ethernet (IEEE 802.3), Token Ring (IEEE 802.5), and other standards have been developed or adopted and achieved widespread implementation.

The IEEE 802.10 Standard for Interoperable LAN Security (SILS) effort was initially approved by the IEEE Standards Board in June 1988.[5] SILS is sponsored by both the IEEE LAN Standards Committee and the IEEE Technical Committee on Security and Privacy.

The objectives of 802.10 are:[6]

1. to specify security services available to IEEE 802 LANs,

2. to define logical and physical mechanisms for achieving security, along with the maximum interoperability of products within an OSI architecture (see Chapter 6), and

3. to produce a standard for services, protocols, data formats, and interfaces.

There are three areas covered by the standard:[7]

1. Secure data exchange at the data link layer
2. Management of cryptographic keys
3. Network management objectives

The services within the 802.10 framework will focus on data confidentiality and integrity and are intended to be independent of any particular cryptography algorithm.

802.10 Parts

The 802.10 standard is divided into four different parts:[8]

1. P802.10A—The Model
2. P802.10B—Secure Data Exchange (SDE)

3. P802.10C—Key Management
4. P802.10D—Security Management

Of these four parts, no drafts of the A and D parts were available as of mid-1992.

Secure Data Exchange (SDE)

The SDE resides at layer 2 of the OSI Reference Model.[9] SDE provides a connectionless service as part of the Logical Link Control (LLC) sublayer, which is immediately above the MAC sublayer. Figure 12.1 shows how the SDE-802.10B exists in conjunction with the other members of the 802.xx family.[10]

The SDE security services, and the threats against which they are intended to protect, are listed below (consult Chapters 4 and 6 for complete details):

Services

Data confidentiality
Connectionless integrity
Data origin authentication
Access control

Threats

Unauthorized disclosure
Masquerade
Unauthorized data modification
Unauthorized resource use

Note that not all stations in a LAN or MAN need to employ the SDE protocol; appropriate network design should be employed to determine which stations need to employ those facilities.

SDE is required to be transparent to existing implementations, meaning that existing IEEE 802 entities should be able to recover if they receive an SDE protected packet. Likewise, SDE entities need to be able to accept non-SDE protected packets without impairing their own operations. Finally, the addition of SDE security shouldn't cause any modifications of either the upper or lower layers at which the security is applied.

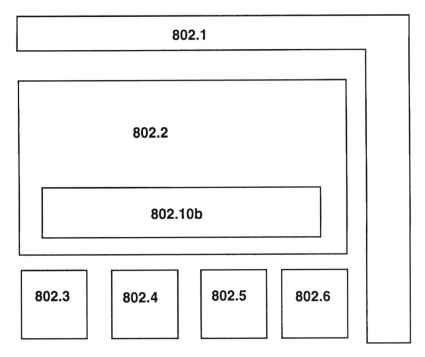

Figure 12.1 IEEE 802 components

The SDE Protocol Data Unit (PDU) contains the following elements:[11]

- The clear header, which identifies the SDE PDUs and aids in information processing. This is an optional element and, when it is included, has a variable length (from 7 to 27 octets, inclusive).

- SDE designator, which is mandatory when the clear header is present. This is used to ensure that a non-SDE entity that contains an LLC-entity won't process the SDE PDU.

- Security association identifier (SAID), which identifies the security association of the destination SDE entity. The destination may be a group address (if applicable) and is also mandatory when the clear header is used.

- The management-defined field (MDF), used to transfer information that facilitates—but isn't required for—PDU processing.

- Protected header, which contains a station ID (optional) that is used to identify the message originator.

- The data, which contains padding, integrity check values (ICVs), and other components.

Layer 2 Security Services versus those of OSI

In Chapter 6, we discussed the OSI Reference Model security architecture as defined in ISO 7498-2. In that chapter, we mentioned that the OSI security architecture specified only one security service—data confidentiality—for the link layer of the protocol. Under the 802.10 architecture—which might be viewed as ISO 7498-2 plus LAN services—the link layer adds the security services of authentication, access control, and data integrity to that of data confidentiality. It is important to note that this distinction is "based on changes in networking practices since ISO 7498-2 was completed, not on deficiencies intrinsic to ISO 7498-2 as it was originally conceived . . . Because of changes in LAN technology, the risks to LANs have become more critical than first considered. High-speed, long distance LANs . . . filtering LAN bridges, and LAN server facilities have increased the range of resources which are vulnerable to abuse."[12]

Key Management

802.10C—key management—is another component of SILS. Key management is considered to be an OSI architecture layer 7 function (along with security management and association control).[13] Within the layer 7 overall functions are the following entities:[14]

- Key management application process (KMAP)
- Key management application service object (KMASO)
- Control function (CF)
- Key management application service entity (KMASE)
- Association control service element (ACSE)

KMAP is not specified by 802.10C, but rather uses OSI communication services in accordance with locally defined security policy. KMAP provides the top-level interface to users, with users defined as people or application processes.

KMAP is composed of one or more entities of the other types listed above. KMASE is used to define peer-to-peer key management, while ACSE is the standard ISO OSI (as defined by International Standard 8650) application service element used to establish and terminate all application layer associations. CF defines KMASE and ACSE interactions.

All of the 802.10C algorithms are registered in a security register,[15] with each register node given an object identifier—a qualified name dependent on the node's parent. The register functions as a tree structure and is based on the X.500 directory information base structure.

The 802.10C component of SILS contains examples and algorithms for a variety of key management paradigms, including centralized key management, distributed key management, and related topics.

12.4 SUMMARY

Both of the standards efforts discussed in this chapter—V2.0 of SNMP and IEEE 802.10 SILS—can be classified as emerging standards. Both support the overall spirit of network security in terms of defined and layered services, specified threats against which those services protect, and various mechanisms by which those services may be provided. It is highly advisable that as part of the network security implementation process we propose and discuss in this book that these and similar standards be carefully examined with respect to any given organization's security program. The respective standards documents, or at least the current versions, discuss message protocols, message formats, and related characteristics and components in detail and should be consulted.

END NOTES

1. J. Galvin, K. McCloghrie, and J. Davin, *Request for Comments 1352: SNMP Security Protocols,* July 1992.

2. Ibid., section 4.1.

3. Ibid.

4. Ibid.

5. IEEE Computer Society, *Cipher: Newsletter of the Technical Committee on Security and Privacy* (January 1989): 5.

6. Ibid.

7. Ibid.

8. Wen-Pai Lu, IEEE 802.10 cover letter, June 17, 1992.

9. *IEEE 802.10 Standard, Part B—Secure Data Exchange* (November 9, 1991): 9.

10. Ibid., 10.

11. Ibid., 24–28. Consult the standard for bit and octet positions.

12. Ibid., Appendix A—Service Rationale, 2.

13. *IEEE 802.10 Standard, Part C—Key Management* (April 10, 1992): 8.

14. Ibid.

15. Ibid., 15.

Appendix

Representative Network Security Programs

A.1   INTRODUCTION

In this appendix, we'll take a look at a variety of network security programs, discussing the various security modes, policies, and ratings mentioned in earlier chapters.

A.2   GOVERNMENT AND DoD POLICY, GUIDANCE, AND REGULATIONS: SECURITY MODES

The leader in initial experimentation, and later wide deployment, of network security resources was the government, specifically the DoD. The most significant impact that results from the processing of classified information, as the DoD must do, is a wide array of government and DoD security policies, guidance, and regulations, many of which have to do with the security of communications. U.S. Air Force Regulation (AFR) 205-16, for example, requires an exhaustive set of documentation to be prepared and accepted prior to a system being given the authorization to go into operation. Documentation includes:

- Security policy
- Security plans and procedures
- Risk analysis (sensitivity and criticality assessment, risk assessment, and economic assessment)

- Security management plan
- System accreditation plan
- Security test and valuation (ST&E)
- Security test reports
- Final accreditation package

As a result of the multiple government and DoD regulations, securing the system when it is used to process classified information becomes a more formal process. Let's look more closely at some of the different security modes used by the U.S. Air Force, as we continue our background discussion in security technology. These different security modes form the basis for establishing security *requirements*, an important step in determining what network security technology to deploy.

Operational Mode

Prior to processing information that is sensitive (but unclassified) or classified, the Air Force must prescribe an approved DoD mode of *operation*. The selection of the UNIS operational security mode will heavily influence the security features that the system must provide and enforce. The operational security modes are:

- Dedicated
- System high
- Controlled mode
- Compartmented/multilevel

Dedicated Security Mode

In the dedicated security mode, all users are cleared to the highest level of information processed by the system and also have a need-to-know for all information processed by the system. All users are trusted. The dedicated security mode requires little, if any, automated security controls, and the majority of security is provided through physical security countermeasures and manual security management practices, policies, and procedures.

System High Security Mode

In the system high security mode, all users are cleared to the highest level of information processed by the system but do not necessarily have a need-to-know for all information processed by the system. User identification and authentication as well as discretionary (software-based) security countermeasures are required when operating in the system high security mode. In addition, the ability to audit security-relevant events must be provided.

Controlled Security Mode

In the controlled security mode, there may be users who are neither cleared for nor have a need-to-know for all information processed by the system. The controlled security mode is commonly used for those systems that process two different sensitivities of data (i.e., secret and top secret) simultaneously. The controlled security mode, however, is limited by regulation to two adjacent security levels. In other words, the controlled security mode would be appropriate for a system used to process confidential and secret, but would not be appropriate for a system used to process unclassified and secret information. The controlled security mode is typically enforced through both automated and manual methods and countermeasures.

Multilevel Security Mode

The multilevel security mode is characterized by an environment where there may be users who are neither cleared for nor have a need-to-know for all information processed by the system. In addition, a multilevel system must support the simultaneous processing of two nonadjacent information sensitivities and up to three adjacent sensitivities (i.e., unclassified, confidential, and secret). It is quite possible that a multilevel system could support the simultaneous processing of more than three information sensitivities; however, current technology and DoD direction typically restricts implementation to three adjacent information sensitivities. The multilevel security mode is provided almost exclusively by internal security controls and mechanisms that have been thoroughly tested and scrutinized.

System Accreditation

Systems used to process sensitive (but unclassified) or classified information are required to be formally accredited prior to operational status. The system, therefore, will require a designated approving authority (DAA) to accredit the system formally prior to classified operations. Accreditation is a formal written statement by the DAA that explains that the system has been evaluated and found to provide the necessary and adequate level of security based on the sensitivity of the information processed and the criticality of the mission supported by the system.

A.3 TRUSTED DISTRIBUTED SYSTEM EFFORTS AND PROGRAMS

Let's examine some of the secure distributed systems that have been or are currently being fielded. For the most part, these systems are used to support the DoD and its DoD secure communication needs. Each system is explained at a high, general level. Next, the distributable elements (users, communications, processing, data, and control) of each system are examined and rated by their degree of distributivity. Rating are divided into three broad categories, which are low, medium, and high. For example, the users serviced by the Defense Data Network (DDN) have a rating of moderate distributivity since there are many users who are separated by many miles and have a low degree of cooperation among them. Once each element is assigned a distributivity rating, security issues resulting from these ratings are examined and discussed. For convenience and tractability, the issues are listed under the three major security control objectives (policy, accountability, and assurance). It is important to note that the issues, in many cases, may intuitively overlap control objective boundaries; however, it is the intent to place security issues under the security control objective that is most influenced or impacted.

Several vendors currently develop technology to support secure distributed systems. These vendors and their products are discussed in the same format. This is not to be construed as a comprehensive, all-encompassing list. The issues identified for a particular system or vendor offering will more than likely reflect issues that other systems, programs, and products will also be required to deal with in the future.

BLACKER

The BLACKER program has been ongoing since the early 1970s when concepts and ideas concerning the program were first formulated. The purpose of the BLACKER program is to facilitate the transmission of unclassified, classified, and highly classified information in support of the intelligence community specifically and other communities within the DoD. The network for which BLACKER was first designed is the DoD Intelligence Information System, or DODIIS. The DDN, the most recent DoD packet-switching network, will utilize BLACKER to protect sensitive information. BLACKER's role in this network is to provide a means for separating various sensitivities of information and also to protect the information while en route (i.e., encryption).

The use of BLACKER allows users, processing, communications, data, and control elements to be distributed into a secure architecture. BLACKER is composed of three primary entities: the BLACKER Front End (BFE), the access control center (ACC), and the key distribution center (KDC). A fourth element, basic to BLACKER operation, is the BLACKER Variable Carrier (BVC). The BVC is inserted within the BFE and provides the BFE with host-specific characteristics. The BVC is basically the communication interface intelligent processor for the BFE.

The BLACKER program is unique in that it attempts to deal with and satisfy requirements of both COMSEC and COMPUSEC. These two areas are often used to complement one another, but, as witnessed by BLACKER, harmonious operation has become mandatory. COMSEC, via encryption, provides many services including authentication, separation of sensitivity levels, and the protection of sensitive information over unsecured media. The COMPUSEC side of BLACKER implements a MAC policy and provides accountability and additional assurance. The combination of multiple security mechanisms (to include distributed TCBs) has been applied to this complex network and may prove to be the general security methodology for future WANs.

As stated earlier, one of the basic security control mechanisms used in BLACKER is encryption. When a user on the network requests a connection to a remote host, the BFE requests the connection (on behalf of the user) to the ACC. The ACC performs necessary authentication and access control validation for host-to-host connections on the network. Therefore, the user's request is seen as a host-to-host request by the ACC and is permitted or denied based on a preestablished privileges database maintained on the ACC. If the ACC authorizes the connection, it then makes a request to the KDC to distribute keys to the authorized hosts. A unique key is generated for each authorized host-to-host session by the KDC. This unique key is used for the duration of the session and then disposed of once the session is terminated. Encryption could be used to separate the various compartments of information on the network. BLACKER BFEs are also used to check each IP datagram received over the network to ensure that the label carried by a datagram is within the acceptable range of the receiving host. Each BFE on a network is responsible for gathering information on connections granted or denied and forwarding this audit information periodically to the ACC for processing and review.

BLACKER hardware and software products are developed by the System Development Corporation (SDC). The use of BLACKER technology has not progressed as rapidly as desired. The BLACKER products (in composite) form a system that will be evaluated against A1 criteria. The BLACKER TCB is distributed, and each element (BFE, ACC, KDC, and BVC) is considered to contain a subset of TCB functionality, trust, and assurance.

BLACKER facilitates certain distributed characteristics. These include the distribution of users, processing, data, and communications. Control of the network is somewhat centralized; however, security control can be considered distributed since multiple distributed BFEs support a networkwide security policy. The TCB implementation is distributed among numerous BFEs and is physically remote from one another, denoting a certain level of distributivity. On the other hand, the cooperation, interaction, and knowledge between BFEs is highly restrictive or nonexistent. No single BFE has cognizance from a security standpoint about any other BFE on a network and hence a high degree of cooperation and knowledge is unachievable. The lack of cooperation does not currently present an implementation or security problem to the DDN since the network is divided into subnetworks, each used to support a single sensitivity level of information.

BLACKER Elements and Levels of Distributivity

The BLACKER program has characteristics relative to distributed elements and the dimensions of those elements, as discussed in the following subsections.

Users   The users who are provided access to BLACKER have a moderate degree of distributivity. Many users in the continental United States and overseas countries will be provided secure and protected services through the incorporation of BLACKER technology. Users serviced by BLACKER will also have a moderate degree of cooperation. A moderate level of cooperation is based on the estimated interaction between users as part of their defined job function for the coordination and execution of specific missions.

Communications   The communications associated with and supporting BLACKER implementation have a medium degree of distributivity. Even though the communications used in conjunction with BLACKER will be diverse and in composite large, they are not highly cooperative.

Processing Processing provided by the BLACKER program is limited to that associated with security. Since this processing is somewhat centralized, the rating given for the distributivity of processing is low. Very limited cooperation between processes is currently envisioned for the composite network.

Data The distributivity of data is given a rating of medium. With the advent of BLACKER technology, data can now be separated and protected in transit, therefore allowing the data to be shared, accessed, and manipulated from heterogeneous locations, users, and processes. A medium instead of high rating is levied, since there is not a high degree of knowledge at each node of data residency, consistency, and structure at other nodes.

Control Control is given a rating of medium. BLACKER will interconnect many heterogeneous control entities and the interaction and support of security control is distributed on multiple devices throughout the network. Control was not considered to be highly distributed since the bulk of security control is performed at a series of centralized locations or devices. Also, there is not a high degree of cooperation between the control processes of the interconnected hosts on the network.

Therefore, the composite rating given for the distributivity of BLACKER is as follows:

Users	Medium
Communications	Medium
Processing	Low
Data	Medium
Control	Medium

BLACKER Security Issues by Control Objective

Policy The security policy issues arising from this configuration of distributiveness for the BLACKER program include the fact that the security policy supported through the use of BLACKER must clearly support a mandatory access control policy. The BLACKER ACC is the centralized point of mediation for either authorizing or denying access to network components. The BFE requests connections on behalf of users and therefore must be trusted to properly represent the true identity of the user requesting a connection. The KDC must also be trusted to distribute keys to the appropriate, authorized BFEs for any connection over the network. Therefore, due to the distributed nature of the network utilizing the BLACKER components, the security policy must be enforced through the use of three distinct identities (i.e., BFE, ACC, KDC). In essence, the three components, or portions of those components, make up the TCB for the network. Modeling of this distributed TCB implementation has been very difficult to achieve.

Accountability   The accountability issues arising from this configuration of distributiveness for the BLACKER program include:

1. Identification—Since the potential user population is very large and diverse, the potential for undetected, unauthorized penetration becomes a greater threat to the overall security of the system. For this reason, it becomes imperative that each user/subject have a defined set of access control permissions so that identification and authentication can be accurately ensured. The ability to support a trusted path between the user and the identification and authentication mechanism may be difficult to ensure. Further, the ability to propagate a trusted path, so that users can access multiple devices on the network, is also a difficult problem.

2. Accountability—Since accountability information is gathered throughout the network, there is no way of discerning on a real-time basis who has access to what information. BLACKER only monitors and provides audit information on connection information. Once the user has been permitted access to a host, that user may then access data without the permission of the BLACKER ACC. BLACKER assumes that the host provides the required mediation of data within its perimeter of control and audits access to that data. It becomes very difficult to conceive a concept of operation whereby each host on the network submits audit data in various formats (i.e., from different device types with various auditing routines) to a centralized location for review. A malicious user may attempt an unauthorized access to every host on the network. While a single access attempt on one host may be ignored as a mishap, the composite attempts may constitute a serious security condition. Due to the high distribution of users and the medium distribution of communications and control, it becomes difficult to manage strong accountability of the system and the users of that system. Even if audit data could be consolidated for review, the review of that data would be difficult for the reasons mentioned above (various formats, understanding, presentation, representation).

3. Data Residency—The distribution of data on the network could cause potential security vulnerabilities. For example, if data is distributed

among a series of different devices, it may be difficult for the owner of the data to know at any certain time where the data (in composite) is located and how many copies of the data actually exist (or have ever existed). If the data is not centrally controlled and managed, it may be maliciously modified without notice. Unsuspecting users may then use the modified data and jeopardize a particular mission owing to the inaccuracy of the data used to compile plans and operations. The creator or owner of the data cannot be assured of the accuracy of the data, since it cannot be reviewed from a consistent location. Moreover, if it is determined that the data has been corrupted, where would the administrator(s) look for the data? If data can be moved from one location to another, it must have traceability that can be audited. Data residency creates many potential problems that require increased attention.

4. Data Consistency—Within the network secured through the use of BLACKER, data may be shared by several subjects. If the data is static, it can be protected from modification and therefore maintain its consistency by being write-protected or read-only. If the data changes dynamically over time, other considerations must be addressed. If various parts of a file are accessed by subjects at different sensitivity levels, it may become difficult to determine under what conditions the data may be accessed. If several copies of a data file exist in a system, have the same directory name, the same access privileges, etc., and one file is updated with information classified at a level higher than that of the original file, it may prove difficult to update other copies of the file since by upgrading the file it may restrict authorized users from accessing it. The real issue becomes: Can more than one copy of a potentially dynamic file (relative to sensitivity level) exist at the same time within the same network?

Assurance   The assurance issues arising from this configuration of distributiveness for the BLACKER program include:

1. Independent monitoring and analysis tools must be available for each of the three BLACKER components to validate the proper operation of security mechanisms. In the event of a failure, it may be difficult to disseminate this failure-status information to the remainder of the network nodes.

2. BLACKER must ensure integrity of labels over the network. The use of standard protocols and communications media between devices po-

tentially deteriorates the integrity of the labels. It may become difficult to draw a box around the elements within the network that are required to be trusted and therefore provide a degree of assurance.

DODIIS Network Security for Information Exchange (DNSIX)

DNSIX is used to support the DODIIS network and intelligence community. DNSIX is a software module that is installed in a network front-end processor and, in some instances, partially on host processors. DNSIX enforces security through the use of labels. For remote host-to-host connections, BLACKER encryption could be layered on top of DNSIX labeling to protect the data en route and to add an additional layer of security. DNSIX is trusted to ensure that all outgoing data packets are properly labeled and that all incoming packets are within the accreditation range of the host.

As with the BLACKER program, there has not been a wide acceptance of DNSIX within the intelligence community. DNSIX or a similar concept provides a degree of security and assurance for the distribution of users, communications, processing, data, and, to some degree, control.

DNSIX Elements and Levels of Distributivity

DNSIX has the following characteristics relative to distributed elements and the dimensions of those elements.

Users   The users supported through the use of DNSIX have a moderate degree of cooperation and interaction and can be distributed physically over many miles. For these reasons the distributivity of users is rated as moderate.

Communications   DNSIX provides standardized security and communication interfaces for all hosts with DNSIX implementations. Because DNSIX allows heterogeneous hosts to be interconnected and support standardized interfaces, communications has been given a medium rating.

Processing   Processing provided by the DNSIX implementation is limited to that associated with security. The cooperation among processing entities supported by DNSIX is minimal and therefore the rating for processing is considered to be low.

Data   The distributivity of data is given a rating of medium. With the advent of DNSIX, data can now be labeled, thereby allowing the data to be shared, accessed, and manipulated from heterogeneous locations, users, and processes on a common network.

Control   Control is given a rating of medium because DNSIX will interconnect many heterogeneous control entities and because the interaction and support of security controls is distributed. Control was not considered to be highly distributed, since there is not a high degree of cooperation between DNSIX security modules.

Therefore, the composite rating given for the distributivity of DNSIX is as follows:

Users	Medium
Communications	Medium
Processing	Low
Data	Medium
Control	Medium

DNSIX Security Issues by Control Objective

Policy   The security policy issues arising from this configuration of distributiveness for the DNSIX program include:

1. The security policy supported through the use of DNSIX clearly supports a MAC policy. The DNSIX trusted software provides mediation for incoming packets and properly labels outgoing packets. DNSIX implementation clearly demonstrates a distributed TCB concept. Modeling of this distributed TCB implementation has been very difficult to achieve.

2. It is difficult for DNSIX to front-end a multilevel host processor and be capable of generating labels for various levels or compartments for outgoing classified information. Generally, DNSIX is configured to support only a single outgoing and incoming classification level or compartment and therefore a multilevel host interface may present additional configuration problems. This issue may limit the type of host devices that can be attacked to the network through DNSIX.

3. The use of DNSIX to achieve a specified security policy requires all components with access to the network to be front-ended or augmented with DNSIX. Therefore, a homogeneous security architecture is mandated, which could potentially restrict certain types of interfaces.

Accountability   The accountability issues arising from this configuration of distributiveness for DNSIX include indentification and accountability.

Since users are distributed, the potential for undetected, unauthorized penetration becomes a greater threat to the overall security of the system. It is imperative that each user/subject have a defined set of access control permissions so that identification and authentication can be accurately ensured. DNSIX relies on the hosts on the network to properly identify and authenticate each user/subject. This could cause problems if each host does not provide the same degree of mediation and discretionary access controls. Risk propagation may arise. Furthermore, if the procedures and policies implemented by the host vary, the identification and authentication of users may prove to be inconsistent.

Since accountability information (audit trail) is gathered throughout the network by each DNSIX module and host processor, there is no way of discerning (on a real-time basis) who has access to what information. DNSIX only monitors and provides audit information on connection information; however, once the user has been permitted access to a host, that user may then access data without mediation from DNSIX, since DNSIX assumes that the host provides the required mediation of data within its perimeter of control and audits access to that data. It becomes very difficult to conceive a concept of operation whereby each host on the network submits audit data, in various formats (i.e., from different device types with various auditing routines) to a centralized location for review. This presents a problem because a malicious user may attempt an unauthorized access to every host on the network. While a single access attempt on one host may be ignored as a mishap, the composite attempts may constitute a serious security condition. Due to the high distribution of users and the medium distribution of communications and control, it becomes difficult to manage a strong accountability of the system and the users of that system. Even if audit data could be consolidated for review, the review of that data would be difficult for the reasons mentioned above (various formats, understanding, presentation, representation).

Assurance   The assurance issues arising from this configuration of distributiveness for DNSIX include:

1. Independent monitoring and analysis tools must be available for each DNSIX module to validate the proper operation of security mechanisms. In the event of a failure, it may be difficult to disseminate this failure-status information to other DNSIX modules on the network. Therefore, the consistency of network security assurance may be jeopardized.

2. DNSIX must ensure integrity of labels transmitted over the network. The use of standard protocols and communications media potentially hinders the integrity of the labels. It becomes difficult to draw a box around the elements of the network that require degrees of assurance. DNSIX must ensure integrity for label generation, but then it must trust the transmission of those labels and the protection of them en route to other entities (i.e., protocols, encryption, communications media, etc.).

3. Since DNSIX, for certain host interfaces and implementations, is required to be installed in separate devices (i.e., partially on the host and partially on a front-end processor), the interworkings, interactions, and levels of assurance become questionable. If this is the case, DNSIX's ability to provide the same degree of protection and assurance may be lessened. Instead of the security for the host being provided on the outbound side and in a single device, the protection has now been split between the two devices. The composite operation of the DNSIX software must act as if it were on a single device with the same degree of assurance. An attack on the security software can now be mounted against two devices instead of only one. Many other security issues arise from this fragmentation issue including secure communications between the two devices, increased physical security boundary, and many others.

4. Since DNSIX relies exclusively on labels for data/user mediation, MAC implementation, and communication session authorization, it also relies on a secure medium for communications. If the transmission medium is not secure, some form of encryption (or protected distribution system in local applications) must be used to protect the data and its integrity en route. This issue may seem simple to solve; however, most local area encryption systems being designed today provide a security connection management system to authorize and deny connections across a network. If this is the case, then DNSIX and network encryption would provide essentially redundant services for connection authorization, whereby one method would rely on keys for authorized connections and the other would rely on labels as the basis for accepting or denying access to network resources.

Defense Data Network

The DDN is a common-user, wide area packet-switching data internet (a network consisting of networks) for the DoD. It is a robust, survivable network that utilizes proven technology. The DDN supports multiple distributed connections and networks for both CONUS and non-CONUS locations. DDN uses separate backbones to support different classification levels of information. The four major networks are:

MILNET—Unclassified, Global Segment
DSNET 1 (DISNET)—Secret, Global Segment
DSNET 2 (WINCS)—Top Secret, Global Segment
DSNET 3 (SCINET)—TS/SCI Segment for DIA

The security features of the DDN include the use of separate physical segments per security level and TEMPEST-protected nodes at physically guarded locations. End-to-end encryption is used so that the use of multilevel components can be avoided. Link encryption is also used for traffic flow security and to counter active wiretapping. Terminal user authentication, as well as various integrity measures at all protocol levels, is available. Current planning includes the ultimate combination of the various segments into a single network. This will be accomplished using BLACKER technology and components at each node location.

The DDN supports the distribution of users, communications, and data and will evolve to support the distribution of processing and control.

DDN Elements and Levels of Distributivity

The DDN program has the following characteristics relative to distributed elements and the dimensions of those elements.

Users   The users supported through the use of DDN will have little cooperation but will be physically distributed over thousands of miles. Many users with various clearance levels will use the DDN to communicate data ranging in sensitivity level from unclassified to top secret sensitive compartmented information. The distributivity for users is therefore rated as moderate.

Communications   The communication entities of DDN may be thousands of miles apart, and the number of communication entities is very large. Communication devices have a relatively low degree of cooperation and do not currently support standardization for connection management, interaction of processes, process-to-process communications, session initiation and termination, status control, and other issues. Based on these dimensions, the communications element of DDN is given a moderate distributivity rating.

Processing Processing provided by DDN is limited to communications. The cooperation among processing entities supported by DDN is minimal and therefore the rating for processing is considered to be low.

Data The distributivity of data is given a rating of moderate. Generally, one node on DDN is unaware of the data structure, schema, residency, and other characteristics of data at other nodes; therefore, cooperation is low. There are many data processing nodes and the volume and distribution of data is very high.

Control Control is given a rating of medium. DDN will interconnect many heterogeneous control entities, and these control entities are physically distributed. Control was not considered to be highly distributed, since there is not a high degree of cooperation between DDN control entities.

The composite rating given for the distributivity of DDN is as follows:

Users	Medium
Communications	Medium
Processing	Low
Data	Medium
Control	Medium

DDN Security Issues by Control Objective

Policy The security policy issues arising from this configuration of DDN include:

1. Very large and distributed user community—The security risks to a system can increase in proportion to the number of users with physical or logical access. The larger the population of users, the larger the span of control, security perimeter, and the threat of a malicious user. The more types (i.e., different clearance levels and authorizations) of users with access to a system, the greater the chance for a compromise, the introduction of malicious logic (i.e., Trojan horse, virus), and the greater the opportunity for malicious modification of data and destruction of resources. Because of the large user population and its physical distribution, data, and communications within the DDN, many of the above-mentioned threats and associated vulnerabilities become potential outgrowths.

2. Mandatory and discretionary access controls—MAC and DAC associated with DDN are required, and as such they constitute a potentially

insurmountable configuration management problem. As the number of users, the distance between those users, and the amount of data (at different sensitivity levels) shared among those users all increase, the complexity associated with establishing and enforcing security access controls becomes more difficult, probably in an increasingly non-linear manner. User accounts, adding and deleting users, and access control lists all contribute to the complexity of security management. Security complexity will increase, including managerial responsibilities, configuration management, and security officer responsibilities.

3. Multiple security officers are required to enforce the established security policy at various sites and therefore coordination among the officers is required and a clear delineation of their responsibilities and authorities must be specified. This creates additional security management overhead, as managers must coordinate among themselves.

4. Because of the diverse user population supported by DDN and the various types of users with access to the network, a global policy for users of the composite system may be very difficult to establish, maintain, and enforce. This is particularly true when DDN eventually evolves and interconnects all of the currently separate DDN networks into one very large multilevel composite network.

5. Policy and procedure modifications may be difficult to implement. Each site may be required to implement and enforce the security policy, modify user accounts, and perform other security-related tasks. If these activities become commonplace and dynamic, the ability to transfer these updates and modifications to other DDN sites and nodes could become a formidable task. If modifications cannot be managed properly and disseminated efficiently, the burden on the users of the network and the threat of inaccurate policy enforcement could become high.

6. DDN currently uses a central organization to permit and certify access to the network. A DDN-certified protocol suite is required and other constraints and criteria are levied against applicants for access to DDN. The security requirements (which are logically on top of the ground rule requirements) are an additional constraint. A valid need must be demonstrated, encryption must be available and properly implemented (if required), and a site security plan of operation is required. This central organization must also interpret policy and decide which sites, locations, and users can have access to DDN, under what conditions, and for what type of activity. These requirements,

coupled with the anticipated demand for DDN, could cause this central organization to be overloaded and cause new—potentially critical—network connections to be delayed. Therefore, for a distributed network such as DDN with the characteristics of distributivity of DDN, the security administration and enforcement of a specified security policy could have negative effects on the intended availability of DDN.

7. As the data contained, processed, and accessed through the DDN becomes more distributed, the ability to enforce access controls accurately becomes more difficult. Should a subject's authentication data be forwarded to each device or process involved in a data access request? Since data may be received from a number of devices, which device is responsible for authenticating the subject prior to the release of the data? These questions impact the cooperation among security elements of the DDN. If data is distributed among a series of physically distinct entities, then a user may be forced to manually sign on, identify himself or herself, be authenticated, audited, and so on by each device storing data requested by the user. This process could become a burden to the user community. The ability for a user to be identified and authenticated once by the DDN network and then have the device, component, partitioned TCB, or other security-related function act vicariously for the duration of the session, seems very desirable, but may not be possible in the present scheme.

8. The DDN includes diverse distributed communication resources. As the distance between communication nodes increases, the range of exploitable points in the communications system increases and encryption is required to protect communication links. Therefore, key distribution and key updates must be handled effectively. If globally applied to protect DDN communications, the overhead associated with encryption may become managerially and financially impractical.

9. The number and type of controllers in a system may preclude connectivity with other systems or components if an established security policy cannot be maintained. This may be the case if dissimilar security policies, endorsed by separate systems, are interconnected. In addition, the same constraint can occur if an interface or connection to a particular device or system raises the accreditation range of the newly formed composite system. This is referred to as the cascading problem. If diverse communication resources are accredited for different sensitivity ranges and then connected, a cascading problem may result. How can the cascading problem be dealt with? What policies

should be established for communications between systems that create an increased accreditation range because of connectivity? The cascading problem is a phenomenon that results from the interconnection of systems with different accreditation ranges. Specifically, "the cascading problem exists when a penetrator can take advantage of network connections to compromise information across a range of security levels that is greater than the accreditation range of any of the component systems that must be defeated to do so."[1] A simple example can be used to define the issue. System A is a multilevel system which has been accredited to process confidential and secret information simultaneously. System B is also a multilevel system and has been accredited to simultaneously process top secret and secret information categories simultaneously. The systems were accredited as stand-alone devices and now mission requirements dictate that these two devices must be interconnected so that secret information can be shared between them. Since both systems are multilevel secure and have been tested as such, the risk does not seem (at first glance) to be significantly increased. If, on the other hand, the two devices are seen as a composite system, there is a significant change to the risk factor. While the risk of compromise in each of them is small enough to justify their use with two levels of information, the composite system as a whole now has three levels of information. This fact increases the potential harm that could be caused by a compromise. When the two systems are connected so that secret information can be passed between them, a perpetrator able to defeat the protection mechanisms in these systems can make top secret information available at the confidential level.

Consider the following example: A perpetrator overcomes the protection mechanisms in System B and downgrades top secret information to secret. Next the perpetrator passes this information over the network to System A. The perpetrator then defeats the protection mechanism in System A and downgrades the same information to confidential. This particular issue can be a result of the increase in the distribution of users, data, and communications. As these distributed elements increase, the likelihood that a cascading problem could arise also increases. If any facet of this issue requires additional thought and guidance, it is in the area of defining the problem. Cascading can be increased dramatically in a system where processing and control elements have a high degree of cooperation.

Accountability The accountability issues arising from this configuration of distributiveness for DDN include:

1. Identification—Since users are physically distributed, the potential for undetected, unauthorized penetration becomes a threat to the overall security of the system. DDN, as the backbone communications media, relies on hosts within the network and other security mechanisms to properly identify and authenticate each user/subject. This could cause problems if each host does not provide the same level of assurance and discretionary access controls. Furthermore, if the procedures and policies implemented by the host vary, the identification and authentication of users may prove to be inconsistent and hence vulnerable.

2. Accountability—Since accountability information (audit trail) is gathered throughout the network by various DDN nodes and host processors, there is no way of discerning, on a real-time basis, who has access to what information. DDN assumes that hosts and other security mechanisms provide the required mediation of data within their perimeter of control. Owing to the distribution of users and communications, it becomes difficult to manage a strong accountability of the system and the users of that system. Even if audit data could be consolidated for review, the review of that data would be difficult, since the data may be presented in various formats.

3. As users become more cooperative and interactive with one another (as is currently envisioned for DDN), they can learn more about one another (i.e., type of work, department, sensitivity of work, etc.). This allows a malicious user to target information of value for compromise, malicious modification, or destruction. As the user community of DDN becomes increasingly cooperative and interactive, the risk of a malicious user acquiring sensitive knowledge about the operations of other users becomes more likely. This creates additional avenues to the malicious user and puts additional stress on the security of the DDN. Inference abilities are also magnified as cooperation among entities increases.

4. Since data may be distributed and stored on different physical devices (even for a single file), how can the sensitivity level of the data be determined once it is broken up and separated? Which portion of the data file is sensitive?

5. When data is updated, and multiple updates are required as part of the update process, how are process-to-process and device-to-device access controls and privileges enforced? If the update to a specific file increases the sensitivity of that file, a user can change the sensitivity manually . However, how can a sensitivity update be handled if multiple copies require updates, and the process, not the human user, has the responsibility? Past solutions to this problem include "strong tranquility," whereby an object's sensitivity level cannot be changed, or trusted subjects,[2] whereby an object's sensitivity level cannot be changed unless the change is being activated by a trusted subject (generally a human being such as a system security officer). The ability for an object's sensitivity level to be changed by a trusted subject is also referred to as weak tranquility. These solutions have been applied to solve immediate security problems but may not be applicable for complex, distributed systems of today or tomorrow. As systems become more complex and larger, the ability for human intervention in the process of downgrading or upgrading information may become impractical.

Assurance   Independent monitoring and analysis tools must be available for each DDN security element to validate the proper operation of security mechanisms. In the event of a failure, it may be difficult to disseminate this failure-status information to other DDN nodes on the network.

DDN will be responsible for handling very sensitive data and security information associated with that data. Therefore, the reliability of the DDN becomes an issue of concern. Should the reliability of communications be considered a security requirement? Many experts in the field of trusted distributed systems submit that reliability and security are inseparable concepts. In addition, for a system to provide reliable service, one assumes that the integrity of the service is high. If a service does not provide a high degree of integrity, the reliability of that service becomes questionable. It is this marriage between reliability and security that causes additional system vulnerabilities to become visible in a distributed system. In a network environment, reliability is ensured through a number of mechanisms.

To keep this discussion simple and tractable, the following scenario is used: Systems A and B are hosts on a network. Both systems are accredited to handle classified information. System A processes up to secret while System B processes up to top secret information. These two systems are attached to a LAN. System A is required to send periodic secret information to System B, so that System B can include this information in top secret reports. System B does not send top secret information to System A. This scenario seems very simple and very secure at first glance, but when reliability becomes a requirement, the complexity of the situation increases. When System A sends System B a message, how does System A know that the message has been received, unaltered, by System B?

The answer is quite simple. Upon receiving the message, System B calculates a CRC value and compares this value against the one sent in the packet of information. If the values compute correctly, System B assumes the information has a high level of integrity and accepts the data. System A, however, is still wondering whether or not the information was properly received. System B then sends an acknowledgment to System A explaining that the packet has been received, unaltered. A reliable, high-integrity communications channel now exists between host A and host B. The problem, however, is what has happened to the security of the network?

As stated earlier, System B processes top secret information and System A processes up to secret. There is now a two way information flow between a secret and a top secret processor. Using a very standard modeling concept like the Bell and LaPadula Model,[3] this type of information transfer would not be possible. Even if processor A was certified at the A1 level, it would still not be able to accept information from a top secret entity. In reality, it would be trusted not to. Since the vast majority of standardized protocols for networks today ensure reliable information transfer based on two-way information flow, this issue commands attention.

DDN will support a physically distributed user community, heterogeneous host processors, and various sensitivity levels of data through distributed communications. With these distributivity parameters, DDN raises additional security issues associated with assurance. For example, since DDN will support various security policy implementations (for various classification levels of data), it must ensure a high degree of assurance across a spectrum of missions, operations, trusted software implementations, and device types. In aggregate, this issue could create an intractable problem. Ensuring on a continuous basis that all security-relevant devices and implementations are operating properly, that any additional interface is secured, and that any modifications to network user permissions can be effectively managed with a high degree of assurance may be very difficult to achieve. There are plans for DDN to migrate to a fully multilevel network in the future, whereby all users, devices, and data types share the same network backbone.

The ultimate intent or objective of communications is to enable cooperation between peer entities. To take this concept a step further, the cooperation between communications resources could also include intelligent decision making. For example, *if* DDN's communication resources become distributed to the point that they include highly cooperative interaction, those resources could decide which communication paths are most appropriate, create dynamic routing based on failed links or components, determine statistically which communication paths provide the most effective throughput, and even which communication paths must be supported based on specific mission criteria. This cooperation has potential impacts and raises additional issues on the security of DDN. It seems possible that a trusted path may be required between communicating entities. If this becomes the case, it may be difficult to support such a requirement with current state-of-the-art communication protocols. If DDN communications becomes highly cooperative, the cooperation mechanisms (protocols, software, etc.) within the communication devices, where intelligent decision processes take place, may require formal testing and certification. This could be necessitated since the decisions made and executed by these intelligent elements of DDN could potentially adversely affect the security of the overall DDN network.

Covert timing and storage channels facilitated by the distributed nature of DDN raise many potential issues. The variance between covert channels in monolithic computer systems and those in distributed systems is large. This variance is caused by the two-way information flow and distributed control prevalent in communication systems. Embedded within almost any definition of a covert channel are the words "shared resource." This is a major reason why covert storage and timing channels become more prevalent as systems are distributed. One of the fundamental reasons for distributing resources is so that they can be shared by a larger community. This sharing of resources paves the way for the potential use of many covert channels. It becomes intuitively obvious that distributed processing and the sharing of resources is in direct contradiction with the prevention of covert channels. On one hand, we want to increase cooperation and communication, and, on the other, we want to restrict information flow and resource sharing. The issue is not an easy one to solve, since it hits at the philosophical pinnacle of security versus technology advancement. It may be that covert channels, which may be mere nuisances in monolithic systems, will become the ultimate Achilles' heel of secure distributed processing.

Protocols, the fundamental communication tool for systems today create a major threat to covert channels. In the simplest sense, a system at a high level may desire to transmit high-level information (contrary to the security policy of the system) to a low-level user. The high system could accomplish this by simply modulating information carried in the protocol headers. The information could be conveyed by the high-level system (requesting) reads to the low-level system. The possibilities for covert channels through the use of protocol headers are endless and will continue to be a major security issue for distributed systems.

If one assumes two-way information flow between processing entities at different sensitivity levels, one or more exploitable covert channels exists. Based on current technology, the existence of exploitable channels in a distributed system is inescapable. The important issue, however, is how to deal with their existence and to determine how much emphasis to direct toward their resolution. This becomes a cost/benefit analysis based on perceived and known threats and the system's vulnerability to the introduction of malicious instructions which could be used to modulate information to a process or person contrary to the security policy of the system.

As the number of processors increases, the ability for a perpetrator to circumvent the security controls of a single element within a composite system increases. If the perpetrator is able to penetrate the security controls of one system, he may then be able to access many devices, resources, and types of information now available to him. The ability to maintain security cognizance over the entire system becomes more difficult. It becomes more difficult to ensure security implementation consistency and assurance among multiple processes.

The primary problem with distributed data is that the degree of cooperation is almost proportional to the unavoidability of covert channels. Two processes at dissimilar levels locking the same file/ record/field is a common example.

Dissimilar controllers (operating systems and security controls) may impede the ability to interconnect heterogeneous devices and systems due to the inability to successfully maintain security control consistency and the required level of assurance.

As the degree of cooperation between controllers increases, the security complexity increases. The ability to provide assurance in a composite system with heterogeneous, cooperative, distributed security control becomes more difficult to achieve.

Commercial COMSEC Endorsement Program (CCEP)

Several vendors have developed LAN and WAN encryption products under the guidance of the CCEP. The CCEP also supports the development of link encryption devices like the KG-84A, radio encryption devices, and satellite and microwave encryption devices. In this discussion, only encryption products being developed for LAN and WANs are considered. At the present time, the PE-Systems GILLAROO has achieved endorsement from NSA as a Type I device that can be used to support secure communications in a LAN environment processing classified data. The Xerox XEU, Wang TIU, and several LAN/WAN encryption products from Motorola have all been endorsed by NSA as meeting Type I criteria. The GILLAROO device does not provide the performance, operational flexibility, or transparency characteristic of other LAN encryption products currently being developed under the CCEP. Specifically, the GILLAROO device provides link encryption whereby the entire data stream is encrypted. This type of encryption is not efficient for packet networks. Stand-alone products, like the Xerox XEU, support data rates up to 10Mbps. Embedded units support a variety of data rates and be placed either on boards or within interface units. Products developed under the CCEP program, once endorsed by NSA as Type I products, are permitted to protect classified information. This is predicated on the assumption that the target system is accredited by a cognizant DAA prior to classified operations. NSA has also recently formed a class of encryption product criteria that can be used to protect sensitive (but unclassified) information. This class of encryption products is referred to as Type II, whereas the CCEP criteria applied to encryption devices used to protect classified information is referred to as Type I.

The keys for these devices are distributed and managed using one of two methods. The first method is manual keying, whereby keys are developed prior to a device's operation and are manually loaded using approved techniques. The second method is automated, whereby the keys can be randomly generated and exchanged by authorized devices on the network. This key management technique is referred to as "fire-fly."

The use of network encryption serves three general purposes:

1. It protects data on the media from tampering and compromise caused by wiretapping, electromagnetic emanations, or other malicious methods.

2. It separates data from users and devices into categories, levels, or compartments. Media protection afforded by encryption is a function of nondeducibility. Data separation is provided through the use of different encryption keys. Therefore, the LAN encryption products developed under the CCEP will promote secure distributed systems. The use of fire-fly keying is a distributed control/security process, which can be used to recognize the movement of users to various devices and authorize connections and permissions based on who the

user is, what his or her privileges are, and not where the user resides (i.e., physical address where the user signs on).

3. It provides integrity protection, since tampered data will not decode properly. If some kind of error detection such as checksum or CRC is included prior to encryption, an integrity error will be noted.

CCEP Elements and Levels of Distributivity

The CCEP is a program that sponsors and certifies encryption components in accordance with specified criteria. Since encryption products are only supportive components of a system, the distributivity of elements is not addressed here. Therefore, only the security issues associated with the CCEP are addressed.

CCEP Security Issues by Control Objective

Policy The CCEP, specifically those devices developed to support networking technology (end-to-end encryption E3), provides certain security features. Encryption is only a partial solution to security for distributed systems. A general misconception about encryption for LANs is that once a network implements NSA-endorsed encryption, the network is now capable of multi-level processing, independent of any other security measures in the system. This belief is obviously false and must be corrected through guidance and examples of applications where encryption supports the security of the system. In certain instances, encryption can be used to provide information separation over common media. For example, if unclassified, secret, and top secret users share the same satellite bandwidth, encryption may be used to separate and protect the information. This type of situation also assumes that the users do not cooperate and do not share or disseminate data between or among the various classification levels.

Encryption can be used to enforce a portion of a security policy, but generally is not used to label information or support DAC policies. In fact, it is commonly assumed that the host processors on a particular network will be allocated the responsibility for the data they store and process. This responsibility includes access control to the data (specifically DAC) and auditing event and other miscellaneous security control measures. In many cases, this assumption is made without any regard for what the host really can provide or whether all hosts on the network provide the same or similar functionality.

Key generation and dissemination appears to be a very large shortcoming in the CCEP program. Since the CCEP program was initiated to encourage the development, advancement, and commercial cost-effective availability of encryption products, one assumes that other processes that support encryption would also mature. This does not seem to be the case in several areas. The most blatant area of concern has to do with the creation and dissemination of keying material (RED/classified keys). NSA will generate all RED/classified keys used to support CCEP encryption products and programs. Since NSA has always generated keying material to support secure (classified) communications security, it is believed that these same processes can be effectively used to support network encryption. It is not the same, however, when one considers the potential implementation base that is possible for this new LAN encryption technology.

It may become impossible for NSA to effectively support the generation and dissemination of keying material, especially if manual keying practices continue. Networks are built to be dynamic and flexible. Users can be added and deleted from the network easily, components can be swapped in and out, and so on. This flexibility becomes highly impacted if a site cannot be responsible for the generation, dissemination, control, and protection of encryption keys for their operation. What happens if a site is using a number of Xerox XEU devices which require manual keying and the site has the need to add another user to the network? First, we must generate a request for another hot key from NSA, NSA must generate the key, send the key via a courier or other secure means, and then it can be loaded, tested, and used. What if the key on the diskette is bad? We go through the process once again. The courier process also jeopardizes the secure dissemination of keying material. It only adds another element of risk into the equation. The issue or concern is that key management is the most burdening issue associated with encryption today, and it does not appear that this will change based on current plans and operations.

Accountability   Encryption mechanisms are generally not used to audit connection information, information access, or other security-relevant events. Therefore, in a multilevel LAN application, many additional security mechanisms are required before the system can be used to process and protect sensitive information. Encryption can be used to support a trusted path between communicating entities.

Identification and authentication can be supported by the use of encryption. An example of authentication may be through the use of a public key, and, hence, user identification could also be achieved through the recognition of a specific encryption key, assuming the key cannot be compromised.

Assurance   Certified encryption is considered to have a high degree of assurance that the information content, once encrypted, cannot be deduced. Encryption has been used for many years to protect sensitive information over insecure media. Encryption will continue to be used in years to come and will contribute to the overall security assurance of distributed systems. Encryption may provide unfounded overconfidence. Since encryption has been used for years, it is assumed to be secure and to have a high degree of assurance. Certain adversaries also believe this, but their assumptions may not be totally accurate. Since encryption is so widely used and is something that we use as a building block for satisfying so many security issues, it becomes important that the technology be examined and scrutinized so that we can continue to have a high degree of assurance. The general security concern or issue here is that encryption may not receive enough scrutiny or evaluation and may be taken for granted. This "taken for granted" feeling may place secure communications in a vulnerable position.

The assurance associated with the protection of data using encryption is predicated entirely on the fact that the key is continuously protected from compromise. Therefore, network encryption devices must be tamperproof and continuously protected.

Data Encryption Standard

The major difference between DES encryption products and those developed under the CCEP is that DES products cannot be used to protect classified information. Generally, DES-based products are used to protect sensitive but unclassified information or company proprietary data. There are products currently available for LANs that provide DES encryption, thereby promoting a secure distributed systems environment.

DES Elements and Level of Distributivity

Since encryption products are only supportive components of a system, the distributivity of elements is not addressed here. Therefore, only the security issues associated with DES encryption are addressed here.

DES Security Issues by Control Objective

There are a few differences between DES encryption and the encryption products being developed under the CCEP. The major difference is that DES is not approved for the protection of classified information. The other major difference is that unlike NSA-endorsed CCEP E3 products, DES encryption is widely available and is effectively applied for the protection of sensitive but unclassified information. Both local and wide area network DES technology is available today to support the protection of information over insecure media. Only issues that vary from those stated in the previous section will be mentioned and discussed below. Generally, the issues are the same in both cases.

Policy   DES is an element, or contributing factor, to the overall security of a system. It is not, however, the complete solution for securing distributed systems. This is a security issue since many acquiring agencies and their associated personnel (both government and commercial) believe that encryption provides the total solution to security in distributed systems. In some cases it may, but in most it will not.

Accountability   Even though the key management techniques are more advanced in DES than what is available currently for CCEP products, DES key management can still be greatly improved. To be accepted and used properly, encryption systems must support a very simple and nonmanpower-intensive key management system.

Assurance   The major assurance issue for DES encryption is that in the minds of many, it is a vulnerable solution. This stems particularly from the nonendorsement of DES for classified communications. Additional research is required to determine the usefulness of DES and to instill a feeling of security and trust in DES products. If DES is found to be nonsecure for whatever reason, then the deficiencies must be investigated. In any case, there is a divergence of opinion surrounding the level of assurance from compromise provided by DES encryption, and this divergence must be dealt with.

A.4   VENDORS INVOLVED IN THE DEVELOPMENT OF PRODUCTS

In this section we use that same format whereby a system is described, the distributable elements of that system are given a rating of high, medium, or low, and issues are raised based on the distributivity of these elements and the system itself. Once issues are identified, they are grouped under one of the three major security control objectives (policy, accountability, and assurance).

This section differs from the previous section because actual products (versus programs) are examined. The products described below are being developed by commercial vendors in an attempt to further advance the state of the art in secure distributed systems. In section A.1, most if not all of the programs discussed were supported in one way or another by the DoD. In this section, the products described are being developed independent of government funding or support. Additional products (generally sponsored by research grants) are also discussed in this section.

SYBASE

The SYBASE Secure DataServer (SYSDS) was developed in a joint venture between SYBASE and TRW. The secure data server is being designed to meet the requirements of the B2 evaluation class.[4] Future plans may include meeting A1 requirements. The development effort has two significant attributes: 1) the secure data server will remain a high-performance database (even with the added security features), and 2) the secure data server will be a trusted distributed application and, further, a trusted distributed database.

The SYSDS design will use a reference monitor approach to system security to achieve a multilevel secure DBMS without sacrificing performance. It will utilize rows (records) of the database as the mandatory controlled security objects and databases and tables as the discretionary controlled security objects. This will enable the system design to take advantage of existing SYBASE DataServer software while introducing new security mechanisms.[5] The SYSDS will also be designed to support integrity, auditing, and other trusted operations.

More important to the focus of this report is that SYBASE intends to develop a truly distributed database management system. Major strides have already been made in this area, including a two-phase commit feature which is currently available with the product. Current objectives include the migration to distributed processing, which will include (at some undetermined date) multilevel security. Specific technical data, plans, and schedules are not currently available for the distributed version of the SYSDS.

SYBASE Elements and Level of Distributivity

The following ratings are based on the SYBASE product SYSDS, as it is planned to operate, and the underlying principles that are envisioned for its use. The product is nowhere near completion; however, to review the issues that result from a truly distributed application, the following descriptions and ratings were postulated.

Users   Users with access to the SYBASE DBMS application could have a high degree of cooperation, be large in number, and be separated by many miles. For these reasons, users are rated as having a high degree of distributivity.

Communications   The communications supporting a SYBASE application would be required to be highly cooperative. Application-to-application (ISO layer 7) peer protocols will facilitate this high degree of cooperative communications. The number of communication resources may be large and the distance between them may also be large. Communications is rated as having a high degree of distributivity.

Processing   Processing, the heart of the SYBASE DBMS application, will have a high degree of distributivity based on the extensive amount of cooperative processing between distributed entities. There may be many processes accessible to users, and they may be separated by large distances. Processing is given a rating of high distributivity.

Data   The data elements maintained by the application would be highly cooperative (supported by SYBASE application), and there may be a very large volume of data in composite. Data could be stored on many different devices, depending on where the data is required and based on the movement of data closer to the area of most demand. Data is rated as having a high degree of distributivity.

Control   Control would maintain and support a multilevel security policy for data accessed, processed, and organized by the database. In addition, each controlling portion of the database (potentially hosted on numerous devices) would be responsible for controlling certain criteria associated with the application and also with security. To accomplish these objectives, the distributed control entities would be required to have a high degree of cooperation. Control is rated as having a high level of distributivity.

Therefore, the composite rating given for the distributivity of the SYBASE SYSDS is as follows:

Users	High
Communications	High
Processing	High
Data	High
Control	High

SYBASE Security Issues by Control Objective

Policy The degree of cooperation between processors and applications may have the single greatest impact on the distribution of a composite system. This is caused by the need for the other element within a system also to become highly cooperative to support highly cooperative processing and applications. Control and security fall into this domino effect. If processing is highly cooperative, the security policy of the system must reflect the various conditions which result from this cooperation.

On the other hand, the use of distributed applications like databases may provide, in the future, its own unique TCB implementation, allowing a multilevel application to be used on a nonmultilevel system (i.e., nontrusted operating system). Therefore, the processing that takes place in a given distributed system can be widespread and could include applications that traverse multiple physical devices. The ability to use a trusted process or application as a single multilevel entity within the confines of a nontrusted composite system requires additional research.

Can the processing element (i.e., database application) be used to perform trusted functions? For example, can a process, while executing, be trusted to extract only authorized data from a database, or should a trusted operating system or partitioned TCB control all access to all data? This issue arises when a trusted application initiates a request for access to the operating system to, say, I/O to disk. If the operating system is not trusted, the fact that the application is trusted may not hold water, since an intermediary, untrusted process is directly in the middle of secure information flow. The issue also arises when the system's operating system is trusted (potentially to a level higher than that of the application). If this is the case, it becomes difficult to determine who's in charge or who can trust whom?

How would a TCB or partitioned TCB interface with trusted processes? Would the trusted processes be viewed as separate, independent, trusted mechanisms, or would they be considered subordinate to the operating system TCB or network front-end partitioned TCB? This particular issue commands attention, since vendors who develop trusted operating systems assume that they must interface with untrusted applications, and the same is true for trusted network product developers and trusted application developers. There is no clear delineation of lines of responsibility, span of control, or levels of authority within a trusted distributed system that utilizes multiple trusted elements.

Process-to-process communications and transfer of control are very difficult issues to deal with in a secure distributed environment. Is a trusted path between processes required? Which process decides if it can take a transfer of control or data from another process? Distributed systems and network technology are specifically designed to support transfer of control processes. A simple example is the use of higher-level protocols to call on the services of lower-level protocols to enable communications across the network. A second example is when a user spools a print job to a print queue that resides on a print server, which in turn calls upon the services of a third part (the printer). A single user keystroke may kick off many, many sequential or simultaneous processes across a distributed system. This issue is a formidable one.

Does a process maintain a static or dynamic sensitivity level? Is the process's sensitivity level dependent on the highest sensitivity level of any data that has ever been touched by the process, or can it purge itself of residual data and then dynamically change its sensitivity level based on the current sensitivity of the data being processed? If a process can dynamically support various sensitivity levels and processing by changing its own sensitivity level, how can this random modification be tracked and audited? If there is more than one copy of the same process or application operating on any number of different physical devices, how can uniqueness and identity between the applications be maintained? These series of issues arise because of distributed technology and are examples of where network security issues differ from distributed ones. With the high degree of cooperation and intelligence associated with processing, these types of issues surface and must be dealt with. In order to avoid a tremendous amount of redundancy in a distributed system, it may become desirable for a process to be able to service multiple users/subjects which maintain different security clearance levels. In other words, the distributed process, intermediary, or driver could dynamically reduce or upgrade its level of sensitivity in a secure manner based on the requesting party.

A second issue, very similar to that described above is how multiple requests to use a process can be handled. Specifically, the security concern arises when a process is supporting secret processing, and during execution it is requested to handle unclassified processing. This issue provides insight into another potential solution to the multilevel processing problem: that of creating multiple versions of the process to handle various requests from low- to high-level subjects.

It is possible to postulate a distributed system where processes could be distributed among various machines and share common memory, storage, and peripheral devices. These same processes could operate on different sensitivity levels and be dynamically relocated to a different machine under the same conditions. This may be an ultimate objective of a distributed application where the application or driver colocates itself with the data and the requesting party, performs its function, and then relocates itself to where the demand is high. It is difficult to believe that this type of situation could occur in a multilevel environment; however, it is very likely that this situation can occur. Under what conditions would a trusted distributed application be able to perform as described above, and, just as important, what constraints, criteria, and security requirements would be imposed on the system to support an application like this one?

Accountability Since users are physically distributed, the potential for undetected, unauthorized penetration becomes a threat to the overall security of the system. For identification and authentication purposes, SYBASE SYSDS either would need to perform this function itself or rely on the security policy of other devices. If identification and authentication are performed by an entity other than the SYSDS, it could cause problems if each host did not provide the same level of assurance and discretionary access controls. Furthermore, if the procedures and policies implemented by the host vary, the identification and authentication of users may prove to be inconsistent and, hence, vulnerable. An interface between SYSDS and the secure entity would also be required so that the users' permissions could be securely transferred.

Accountability information (audit trail) is gathered throughout the network by various database segments, so there is no way of discerning, on a real-time basis, who has access to what information. Owing to the distribution of users and processing, it becomes difficult to manage a strong accountability of the system and the users of that system.

As the user community becomes increasingly cooperative and interactive, the risk of a malicious user acquiring sensitive knowledge about the operations of other users becomes more likely. This creates additional avenues for the malicious user. Inference abilities are also magnified as cooperation among processes increases. Inference is a major problem for distributed processing and may impact distributed databases like SYBASE more than other distributed applications.

Since data may be distributed and stored on different physical devices (even for a single file), how can the sensitivity level of the data be determined once it is broken up and separated? Which portion of the data file is sensitive?

When data is updated, and multiple updates are required as part of the update process (two-phase commit for example), how are process-to-process and device-to-device access controls and privileges enforced? If the update to a specific file increases the sensitivity of that file, a user can change the sensitivity manually. However, how can a sensitivity update be handled if multiple copies require updates and the process, not the human user, has the responsibility?

For distributed, highly cooperative applications, data residency becomes a security issue. What criteria or security constraints should be levied on the processing, storage, and movement of data? Is it important to have a continuous idea of where data is in a system? Which device, which subject, is currently utilizing the data? Should an authorized user be able to specify a specific device for data storage (i.e., override distributed data processing)?

The issue of data aggregation is also a concern for the SYBASE SYSDS, particularly since it is a database application. In distributed systems, where data is shared and used by various processing entities, the potential for data aggregation and overclassification becomes prevalent. The movement of data, processes affecting data, and communications of data are all aspects of distributed systems. If an object's or subject's sensitivity level is based on the objects or subjects with which it comes into contact, a trusted distributed system would soon assume a single classification level (the highest maintained on the network). The phenomenon is referred to as aggregation. For example, if System B communicates an acknowledgment to System A, System A later is forced to upgrade a portion or all of its processing to top secret. If a database application receives a byte of secret information that is incorporated into an unclassified report, what is the classification level of the report? Secret. Furthermore, when the report is sent across a network to another device, what is the classification level of the report? Secret. If any other process, user, or device requires access to the report, what is the clearance level required to access the report? Secret. More importantly, if only a portion of the report is required by a user, without the secret information, the user must still have an active secret clearance to review the unclassified portion of the report.

It can be seen that by using this type of classification methodology, information can very quickly become overclassified. In a distributed environment, automated processes and data should be able to move freely through a network, ultimately to where they are most desired. This ability, however, could cause aggregation. It becomes apparent that the granularity of information separation based on sensitivity will be important in a trusted distributed system. For example, if a single record within a database file is classified secret, but the remainder of the file is unclassified, an unclassified user should be able to access (with appropriate discretionary authorization) the unclassified portion of the file. This obviously imposes a security requirement on the database to ensure that the database can accurately maintain and enforce mandatory controls to a certain granularity.

The second issue that is raised by aggregation is intelligent review and downgrading capabilities. This would be performed by a trusted process, more than likely utilizing artificial intelligence to review information and extract the appropriate data and classify the results appropriately. This is well beyond the state of the art or current security accreditation criteria; however, it is an area of study that will greatly facilitate true trusted distributed systems.

Assurance   The security assurance issues arising from this configuration of distributiveness for the SYBASE SYSDS include:

1. Independent monitoring and analysis tools must be available for each SYSDS security element to validate the proper operation of its security mechanisms. In the event of a failure, it may be difficult to disseminate this failure-status information to other SYSDS elements on a network.

2. Integrity is a critical requirement for database applications. Since SYSDS will be a multilevel distributed application, the need for integrity is even greater. The ability to support security levels and integrity levels in the same multilevel application may significantly impede performance, configuration management, and application flexibility.

3. A trusted path may be required between SYSDS entities. If this becomes the case, it may be difficult to support such a requirement with current state-of-the-art communication protocols. SYSDS would be required to rely on lower-level (potentially untrusted) protocols to provide connectivity and to allow for the transfer of information to other SYSDS entities.

4. Many covert timing and storage channels result from the use and application of highly cooperative distributed processing. The primary problem with distributed data is that the degree of cooperation is almost proportional to the unavoidability of covert channels. Two processes at dissimilar levels locking the same file/record/field is a common example.

5. As the number of processors increases, the ability for a perpetrator to circumvent the security controls of a single element within a composite system increases. If the perpetrator is able to penetrate the security controls of one system, he or she may then be able to access many devices, resources, and types of information now available. The ability to maintain security cognizance over the entire system becomes more

difficult. It becomes more difficult to ensure security implementation consistency and assurance among multiple processes. This issue is directly impacted by the heterogeneous nature of the processors and their associated security policies. If a user is able to beat the security mechanisms, on a host and this host passes the unauthorized user to SYSDS as an authorized user, SYSDS may perform securely, while allowing the unauthorized user to compromise information.

Multilevel Secure LANs

The Boeing MLS LAN and the E-Systems MLS LAN are very similar, at least in their attempt to develop a multilevel secure LAN. The implementation of these LANs will undoubtedly be different; however, they are combined here for convenience of discussion.

The Boeing Multilevel network has been developed through internal research and development activities and has been certified by NCSC at the A1 level. The network is designed to support multilevel network applications required to process data, voice, and video. The network supports and implements the DoD protocol suite.

E-Systems is involved in research and development activities to develop a multilevel secure LAN. The network will be designed to support data, voice, and video communications over either broadband or fiber media. Data rates in excess of 100Mbps are anticipated. The network will be designed to be electromagnetic pulse (EMP) protected, as well as TEMPEST certified. The LAN will provide separation of data necessary in an MLS environment through the use of embedded NSA-endorsed encryption modules in the Bus Interface Units (BIUs), which interface to the network media. Network management and control, auditing, user authentication and identification, and both discretionary and mandatory access controls are planned to be supported by the network. Other information concerning the product is either proprietary or not available at this time.

Boeing and E-Systems MLS LAN Elements and Levels of Distributivity

These products are used to support secure local area networking programs. The programs supported through the use of these products have many application-dependent aspects associated with them. A series of ratings have been assigned based on generally known requirements for LANs.

Users   Users with access to a secure LAN will generally have a low degree of cooperation with other users outside their community of interest and will not be many in number. Since these products are designed to support multiple classification levels over a single medium, they can be used to allow various classes of users to access a network in a secure manner. The network becomes a series of separate logical networks, since different encryption keys and/or trusted labels are used to separate subjects and objects based on clearance level. Users will also generally not be separated by significant physical distance. Based on these dimensions, the users for this system are rated as having a low level of distributivity.

Communications   Due to the high-performance characteristics of LANS, communications generally must have a high degree of cooperation. The proximity between communications resources will be very limited, as will the number of communication resources. Communications, therefore, have a medium level of distributivity.

Processing   A multilevel network used to communicate and process various classification levels of information may have a large number of heterogeneous processes, applications, operating systems, and hardware entities. Each group of components and processes within a certain community of interest will (more than likely) operate at the same security level. These processes within this confined group will generally have a high degree of cooperation; however, they will have little if any cooperation with other processes on the network. The number of processes will usually be small, and the proximity between processing entities will be relatively limited. Processing is rated as having a low level of distributivity. The security provided through the use of multilevel networking components does not rely on the processing characteristics of the host that is being attached to the network; rather, the network provides the bulk of the required security mechanisms and assurance to allow heterogeneous entities to communicate in a secure fashion.

Data   The distributivity of data is given a rating of medium. With the advent of multilevel LAN technology, data could be separated and protected in transit and labeled correctly; thereby allowing data to be shared, accessed, and manipulated by multiple users and processes in a secure way. A medium instead of high rating is levied since the data is not highly cooperative and storage locations are generally static.

Control   Distributed security control is required to maintain and support a multilevel security policy for data accessed and processed by a network. In addition, each controlling portion of the network is distributed on multiple devices (distributed TCBs), and each is responsible for controlling certain criteria associated with the security policy. Even though the control is highly distributed, it will be configured in a manual way and will not have cooperation with other control mechanisms in the network. Each control mechanism will act basically autonomously. Control is rated as having a medium level of distributivity.

The composite rating given for the distributivity of these MLS LANs is as follows:

Users	Low
Communications	Medium
Processing	Low
Data	Medium
Control	Medium

Boeing and E-Systems MLS LAN Security Issues by Control Objective

Policy   The security policy issues arising from this configuration of distributiveness for these MLS LANs include:

1. If the degree of dissimilar controllers and security components is such that secure interoperability is not possible, interconnection may be facilitated by a front-end distributed, partitioned TCB. Therefore, the network could be used to enforce a specified security policy without major security contributions required from the interconnected processors and hosts. This is the methodology behind the Boeing and E-Systems MLS LANs.

2. Should a hierarchy of authority be established for systems that implement distributed control? These MLS network components allow heterogeneous hosts and other devices to be interconnected to form a network and also to provide security for these components. In the event of a certified multilevel host that is attached to a secure multilevel network, there must be some division of authority established. The host will output packets that are properly labeled and the front-end network security device will have to trust the host (the host is in charge) or strip the label and put on its own, based on what it knows about the host (network in charge). Independent of who's in charge, the issue of multiple layers of security causes many problems. In one

sense it is a blessing, because there are multiple levels of protection. In another sense it is a curse, because even though various levels of security exist, they can not work together and therefore the system becomes useless.

3. How can resource contention problems be resolved? What can be done to prevent conflicting security operations from occurring, and, if they do, how can they be resolved? The example would be a security control mechanism on device A that allows a connection to device B. Device B does not allow the connection, but device A continues to authorize the access. Which device is in control? What mediation between conflicting devices is required, if any? Once again, the issue is caused by potentially heterogeneous security policies and redundant security mechanisms.

Accountability Many secure network features are provided through the recognition of pairwise relationships (i.e., Ethernet-to-Ethernet addresses). In many cases, connections are permitted or denied based on the requesting address when compared against the address requested for a connection. This, in essence, is the way the network identifies and authenticates users, since a user is considered to be directly associated with a logical or physical address. E-Systems MLS LAN will provide much of the pairwise connection services and will enforce these services through the use of separate encryption keys. The issue that results from a pairwise connection scheme is that users may decide to circumvent the security policy by using the workstation down the hall instead of their own. If a user is able to determine the physical location of a terminal or workstation that is used by a person with a higher clearance level, or one that is associated with a sensitive project, the malicious user, if physical access was availed, could circumvent the security of the system. This issue is one that will be prevalent in years to come since many of the network encryption products being developed support pairwise security management. Another issue raised through the use of pairwise connections is their inability to be flexible to change.

Since accountability information (audit trail) is gathered throughout the network by various MLS network nodes and host processors, there is no way of discerning, on a real-time basis, who has access to what information. Owing to the distribution of users and communications, it becomes difficult to manage a strong accountability of the system and the users of that system. Even if audit data could be consolidated for review, the review of that data would be difficult, since the data may be presented in various formats.

Assurance The Boeing MLS LAN utilizes partitioned TCBs within multiple network components to achieve a composite multilevel security policy. Independent monitoring and analysis tools must be available for each partitioned TCB segment to validate the proper operation of its security mechanisms. In the event of a failure, it may be difficult to disseminate this failure-status information to other TCB partitions in the network.

This ensures on a continuous basis that all security-relevant devices and implementations are operating properly, that all interfaces are continuously secure, and that any modifications to network user permissions can be effectively managed with a high degree of assurance.

To allow for continuous assurance in a secure multilevel network, a trusted path may be required between all partitioned TCB elements. If this becomes the case, it may be difficult to support such a requirement with present-day communication protocols. In addition, through the creation of a networkwide trusted path, covert channels may also be created.

For missions that are of a critical nature (i.e., missile warning or electronic funds transfer), the need for continuous operation is imperative and may escalate during crisis periods. It may be necessary, in many scenarios, that security not be a limiting factor to the performance of the mission. In other words, the potential for unauthorized access becomes a very low priority when compared to the ability to access the required information in an uninhibited manner. Users with secret level clearances may require access to top secret information to do their jobs. Manpower may dictate as much, and the user must be given freedom to access all necessary data to ensure the success of the mission. In such a scenario, the system security officer or cognizant security representative may be given the authority to redefine the security policy of the system. It may include turning off security.

This is not a fictitious "what if" situation, but rather a potentially real one. The specific security issue that accompanies this situation and that deals specifically with assurance is the process of returning to reality. Once the crisis is over, and things can return to normal, how much assurance can be placed in the security system as it *now* exists? It is possible that every device on the network during the crisis period acted in ways contrary to the security policy of the system. This issue is not discussed much and in our opinion requires additional thought.

As the number of processors increases, the likelihood that a perpetrator could circumvent the security controls of a single element within a composite system increases. If the perpetrator is able to penetrate the security controls of one system, he or she may then be able to access many devices, resources, and types of information now available. The ability to maintain security cognizance over the entire system becomes more difficult. It becomes more difficult to ensure security implementation consistency and assurance among multiple processes.

VERDIX

The VERDIX Secure Local Area Network (VSLAN) has been certified by the National Computer Security Center (NCSC) at the B2 level in accordance with the Trusted Network Interpretations of the Trusted Computer System Evaluation Criteria. VSLAN enables simultaneous processing of information at several levels of classification or sensitivities. VERDIX uses labeling, versus encryption, to ensure effective access control. VSLAN uses a Datakey to identify and authenticate individual operating nodes on the network. VSLAN audits all attempted security violations and also enables auditing of security administrator activities. A security adminstrator can exercise centralized control over the operation of a LAN from the VERDIX Network Security Center. Backup and recovery capabilities can also be provided. The VSLAN architecture does not require major modifications to an existing network, rather, the VSLAN devices can easily be "added on" to provide additional levels of security protection.

END NOTES

1. National Computer Security Center, *Trusted Network Interpretations,* NCSC-TG-005 Version 1, July 1987.

2. D. E. Bell and L. J. LaPadula, "Secure Computer System: Unified Exposition and Multics Interpretation," Technical Report ESD-TR-75-306 (Bedford, MA: Electronic Systems Division, AFSC, Hanscom Air Force Base), January 1976.

3. Ibid.

4. National Computer Security Center, as defined in *DoD Trusted Computer System Evaluation Criteria,* DoD 5200.28 STD, 1985.

5. P. A. Rougeau and E. D. Sturms, *The SYBASE Secure DataServer: A Solution to the Multi-Level Secure DBMS Problem,* TRW Federal Systems Group.

Bibliography

Anderson, D. P., and P. V. Rangan. "A Basis for Secure Communications in Large Distributed Systems," 167–172. In *IEEE Symposium on Security and Privacy, April 27–29, 1987*. New York: IEEE Press, 1987.

Bell, D. E. "Security Policy Modeling for the Next-Generation Packet Switch," 212–216. In *IEEE Symposium on Security and Privacy, April 18–21, 1988*. New York: IEEE Press, 1988.

Bell, D. E., and L. J. LaPadula. "Secure Computer System: Unified Exposition and Multics Interpretation." Technical Report ESD-TR-75-306. Bedford, MA: Electronic Systems Division, AFSC, Hanscom Air Force Base, January 1976.

Biba, K. J. "Integrity Considerations for Secure Computer Systems." Technical Report MTR-3153. The MITRE Corporation, April 1977.

Boebert, W. E., and R. Y. Kain. "Secure Computing: The Secure Ada Target Approach." *The Scientific Honeyweller* 6, no. 2, (July 1985): 1–17.

Casey, T., D. Weber, and S. Vinter. "Multi-Level Security Features in SDOS." In *IEEE Symposium on Security and Privacy, April 18–21, 1988*. New York: IEEE Press, 1988.

Casey, T. A., S. T. Vinter, D. G. Weber, V. Varadarajan, and D. Rosenthal, "A Secure Distributed Operating System," 27–38. In *IEEE Symposium on Security and Privacy, April 18–21, 1988*. New York: IEEE Press, 1988.

Congress of the United States, Office of Technology Assessments. *Defending Secrets, Sharing Data: New Locks and Keys for Electronic Information*, 1987.

DataPro "Network Services," (New York: McGraw-Hill): 1992.

Denning, D. E., T. F. Lunt, R. R. Schell, W. R. Shockley, and M. Heckman. "The SeaView Security Model," 218–233. In *IEEE Symposium on Security and Privacy, April 18–21, 1988*. New York: IEEE Press, 1988.

Denning, D. E., S. G. Akl, M. Heckman, T. F. Lunt, M. Morgenstern, P. G. Neumann, and R.R. Schell. "Views for Multilevel Database Security." *IEEE Transactions on Software Engineering*, SE-13, no. 2 (February 1987): 129–140.

Denning, D. E., T. F. Lunt, P. G. Neumann, R. R. Schell, M. Heckman, and W. R. Shockley. "Security Policy and Interpretation for a Class A1 Multilevel Secure Relational Database System," *Proceedings from the 1986 IEEE Symposium on Security and Privacy* (May 7-9 1986), 147-169.

Denning, D. E., "A Lattice Model of Secure Information Flow." *Communications of the ACM* 19, no. 5 (May 1976): 236–243.

Department of Defense. Computer Security Center. *Proceedings of the Department of Defense Computer Security Center Invitational Workshop on Network Security, New Orleans, LA, March 1985.*

Diffie, W., and M. Hellman, "New Directions in Cryptography." *IEEE Transactions on Information Theory* IT-22(6) (November 1976): 644–654.

Dinolt, D. E. "Security Policies and Models for Computer Networks," 2-39–2-48. In *DoDCSC Invitational Workshop on Network Security, March 1985.*

Estrin, D., and G. Tsudik. "Visa Scheme for Inter-Organization Network Security," 174–183. In *IEEE Symposium on Security and Privacy, April 27–29, 1987.* New York: IEEE Press, 1987.

Federal Information Processing Standards Publication 46 (FIPS 1977), January 15, 1977.

Girling, C. G. "Covert Channels in LANs." *IEEE Transactions on Software Engineering* SE-13, no. 2 (February 1987): 292–296.

Glasgow, J. I., and G. H. MacEwen. "A Computational Model for Distributed Systems Using Operator Nets." In *Proceedings of the European Conference on Parallel Architectures and Languages,* June 1987.

Glasgow, J. I., and G. H. MacEwen. "The Development and Proof of a Formal Specification for a Multi-Level Secure System." *ACM Transactions on Computing Systems* 5, no. 2 (May 1987): 151–184.

Glasgow, J. I., and G. H. MacEwen. "Reasoning about Knowledge in Multi-Level Secure Distributed Systems," 122–128. In *IEEE Symposium on Security and Privacy, April 18–21, 1988.* New York: IEEE Press, 1988.

Glasgow, J. I., and G. H. MacEwen. "A Two-Level Security Model for a Secure Network," 56–63. In *8th Proceedings of the National Computer Conference, NBS/DoD, 1985.*

Glasgow, J. I., G. H. MacEwen, F. Ouabdesselam, and T. Mercouris. "Specifying Multi-Level Security in a Distributed System," 56–63. In *7th DoD/NBS Computer Security Conference,* 1984.

Goguen, J. A., and J. Meseguer. "Unwinding and Inference Control." In *Proceedings of the 1984 Symposium on Security and Privacy, April 1984.*

Haigh, J. T., R. A. Kemmerer, J. McHugh, and W. D. Young. "An Experience Using Two Covert Channel Analysis Techniques on a Real System Design," 14–24. In *Proceedings of the 1986 Symposium on Security and Privacy, IEEE Computer Society.* New York: IEEE Press, 1986.

Halpern, J., and Y. O. Moses. "Knowledge and Common Knowledge in a Distributed Environment," 50–61. In *Proceedings of the 3rd ACM Conference on Principles of Distributed Computing, 1984.* New York: ACM Press, 1984.

Heitmeyer, C. L., C. E. Landwehr, and J. McLean. "A Security Model for Military Message Systems." *ACM Transactions on Computer Systems* (August 1984).

Hinke, T. H. "Inference Aggregation Detection in Database Management Systems," 96–106. In *IEEE Symposium on Security and Privacy, April 18–21, 1988.* New York: IEEE Press, 1988.

International Standards Organization. *Information Processing Systems—Open Systems Interconnection—Basic Reference Model, Part 2: Security Architecture* (ISO/IEC 7498-2), February 15, 1989.

Karger, P. A. "Authentication and Discretionary Access Controls in Computer Networks." *Computer Networks and ISDN Systems* 10, no. 1 (January 1986): 27–37.

Landwehr, C. E. "A Security Model for Military Message Systems." *NRL Report 8806.* Washington, DC: Naval Research Laboratory, May 1984.

Lane, J. "Report of the Policy and Models Group," 2-3–2-37. In *DoDCSC Invitational Workshop on Network Security, March 1985.*

MacEwen, G. H. "A Model for Multilevel Security Based on Operator Nets," 150–160. In *IEEE Symposium on Security and Privacy, April 27–29, 1987.* New York: IEEE Press, 1987.

MacEwen, G. H. "Secure Information Flow in Distributed Systems." In *Biennial Symposium on Communications,* Queens University, May 1982.

McCauley, E. J., and P. J. Drongowski. "KSOS: The Design of a Secure Operating System," 345–353. In *AFIPS Conference Proceedings 48, 1979* NCC. Arlington, VA: AFIPS Press, 1979.

McCullough, D. "Noninterference and the Composability of Security Properties," 177–186. In *IEEE Symposium on Security and Privacy, April 18–21, 1988.* New York: IEEE Press, 1988.

McCullough, D. "Specifications for Multi-Level Security and a Hook-Up Property," 161–166. In *IEEE Symposium on Security and Privacy, April 27–29, 1987.* New York: IEEE Press, 1987.

McCullough, D., and S. Perlo. "A Hook-Up Theorem for Multi-Level Secure Processes." Technical report to be published. Ithaca, NY: Odyssey Research Associates.

McHugh, J., and A. P. Moore. "A Security Policy and Formal Top Level Specification for a Multi-Level Secure Local Area Network," 34–39. In *IEEE Symposium on Security and Privacy, April 1986*. New York: IEEE Press, 1986.

Morgenstern, M. "Controlling Logical Inference in Multilevel Database Systems," 243–255. In *IEEE Symposium on Security and Privacy, April 18–21, 1988*. New York: IEEE Press, 1988.

Mullender, S. J., and A. S. Tanenbaum. "Protection and Resource Control in Distributed Operating Systems." *Computer Networks* 8 (1984): 421–432.

National Computer Security Center. *DoD Trusted Computer System Evaluation Criteria*. DoD 5200.28 STD. December 1985.

National Computer Security Center. *Trusted Network Interpretations. NCSC-TG-005 Version 1, July 1987*.

Needham, R. M., and M. D. Schroeder. "Using Encryption for Authentication in Large Networks of Computers." *Communications of the ACM* 21, no. 12 (December 1978): 993–999.

Rangan, P. V. "An Axiomatic Basis of Trust in Distributed Systems," 204–210. In *IEEE Symposium on Security and Privacy, April 18–21, 1988*. New York: IEEE Press, 1988.

Rivest, R., A. Shamir, and L. Aldeman, "A Method for Obtaining Digital Signatures and Public-key Crytosystems." *Communications of the ACM* (February 1978): 120–126.

Rougeau, P. A., and E. D. Sturms. *The SYBASE Secure DataServer: A Solution to the Multi-Level Secure DBMS Problem*. TRW Federal Systems Group.

Rushby, J. M., and B. Randell. "A Distributed Secure System." *IEEE Computer* 16, no. 7 (July 1983): 55–67.

Schaefer, M., and D. E. Bell. "Network Security Assurance," 64–69. In *8th National Computer Security Conference, September 30–October 3, 1985*.

Schell, R. R., and T. F. Tao. "Microcomputer-Based Trusted Systems for Communications and Workstation Applications," 277–290. In *Proceedings of the 7th Annual DoD/NBS Computer Security Conference, September 1984*.

Sollins, K. R. "Cascaded Authentication," 156–163. *IEEE Symposium on Security and Privacy, April 18–21, 1988*. New York: IEEE Press, 1988.

Spafford, Eugene H. "The Internet Worm Program: An Analysis." *Purdue Technical Report, CSD-TR-823, November 29, 1988*.

Sutherland, D. "A Model of Information." In *Proceedings of the 9th National Computer Security Conference, September 1986*.

Tsai, Chii-ren, and Virgil D. Gligor, "A Note on Information Flow and Covert Channel Analysis," *IEEE*, May 1986.

Tsai, Chii-ren, Virgil D. Gligor, and C. Sekar Chandersekaran, "A Formal Method for the Indentification of Covert Storage Channels in Source Code," *IEEE*, 1987.

Vinter, S. T. "Extended Discretionary Access Controls," 39–49. In *IEEE Symposium on Security and Privacy, April 18–21, 1988*. New York: IEEE Press, 1988.

Williams, J., and G. Dinolt. "A Graph-Theoretic Formulation of Multi-Level Secure Distributed Systems: An Overview," 97–103. In *IEEE Symposium on Security and Privacy, 1987*. New York: IEEE Press, 1987.

Wilson, J. "Views as the Security Objects in a Multilevel Secure Relational Database Management System," 70–84. In *IEEE Symposium on Security and Privacy, April 18–21, 1988*. New York: IEEE Press, 1988.

Wiseman, S., P. Terry, A. Wood, and C. Harrold. "The Trusted Path between SMITE and the User," 147–155. In *IEEE Symposium on Security and Privacy, April 18–21, 1988*. New York: IEEE Press, 1988.

Woodward, J. P. L. "Exploiting the Dual Nature of Sensitivity Labels," 23–30. In *IEEE Symposium on Security and Privacy, April 27–29, 1987*. New York: IEEE Press, 1987.

Index